AGADIR
BUILDING THE MODERN AFROPOLIS

AGADIR
BUILDING THE MODERN
AFROPOLIS

Tom Avermaete
Maxime Zaugg

PARK BOOKS

TABLE OF CONTENTS

INTRODUCTION

Tom Avermaete, Cathelijne Nuijsink

THE MODERN AFROPOLIS

Our understanding of how urban designers and architects can design cities is still largely affected by Western urban conditions and perspectives. The European city in particular, with its steady and controlled growth, has served for a long time as the background against which new urban design methods and instruments were developed. Recently, scholars have begun to heavily criticise this conception of Western countries and cities as pinnacles of architectural progress, ignoring key developments in other regions and territories.[1] Geographer Jennifer Robinson, for example, claims that the geographies of urban design history are characterised by an enduring divide between 'First World' cities and regions that are seen as models, generating theory and policy, and 'Third World' towns and territories that are seen as problems, requiring diagnosis and reform. Moreover, she holds that these First World biases do not remain without impact and that much of twentieth-century historiography, with its roots lying overwhelmingly in the Global North-West, suffers from intellectual parochialism.[2]

Our reason for looking at Agadir is the fact that urbanisation and urban design are not prerogatives of the Western world. Quite the contrary: we argue that rapid urban development is undoubtedly as much a phenomenon of other geographies, such as those of the African continent. Sparked by colonisation in the nineteenth century, and propelled by industrialisation and modernisation into the twenty-first century, large urban nuclei have emerged in Africa. These cities have a different genetic code from those of Western cities: they develop according to other logics and generate different urban experiences. The rapidly grown African city has urban realities in its own right and is, nowadays, described as the 'booming city', 'mega-city' or 'Afropolis'.[3] The specific nature of the Afropolis has challenged architects and urban designers to develop alternative approaches for the design of the city. In other words, the Afropolis has often been a laboratory for new methods and tools of urban design.

This book wishes to contribute to the broader scholarly field that aims to explore these 'other' design approaches of the city and to attempt to open up a better understanding of the logics developed in the non-West. Parallel to Western methods – and in close relation to the Afropolis – foreign and local architects and urban designers have devised alternative ways in which to analyse, conceive and project urban development. Often out of sheer necessity, architects like Jane Drew, Éliane Castelnau, Hassan Fathy, Michel Écochard and Georges Candilis have focused on different aspects and elements of urbanisation and subsequently developed other conceptual lenses, design concepts and instruments. Though very different in character, these other approaches seem to have in common the way in which they no longer focus on idealised, final images of the modern city or on the complete control of the life of its inhabitants, but rather try to engage with its everyday dynamics. Unfortunately, however, very often these alternative approaches to the modern city have not been given a full-fledged place in our historiographies of architecture and urbanism.

UNEXPLORED AGADIR

The urban design for the reconstruction of Agadir is a case in point. Despite its innovative strategies and tools, the project for this city at the foot of the Moroccan Atlas Mountains has remained largely in the shadow of the canonical histories of twentieth-century urban design. The urban design narrative of this Afropolis remains – unjustly so – largely untold to the present day.[4] The saga of the urban project for Agadir starts quite dramatically. On 29 February 1960, shortly before midnight, an earthquake measuring 5.7 on the Richter scale struck the city. There were 15,000 deaths out of the 45,000 inhabitants of Agadir at the time, 12,000 wounded and hundreds of homeless. Although it was qualified as being of so-called 'moderate intensity', the 1960 Agadir earthquake was nevertheless one of the deadliest of the twentieth century because of the poor quality of the buildings. The damage was enormous. Some parts of the city (Founti, Yachech, Kasbah and Talborjt) were 90 per cent or even 95 per cent demolished, and infrastructure and roads generally were completely destroyed.

As a result, people were without housing and deprived of collective urban spaces such as schools, hospitals and meeting places. Moroccan King Mohammed V made it a national priority to rebuild the city of Agadir soon after the quake, and launched an international rebuilding programme for a 'Modern Islamic City'.[5] Planning and reconstruction began quickly, and within six months most of the rebuilding was well under way. The programme envisaged a new city composed of industry, commerce, housing, green space and tourist areas linked by pedestrian paths and gardens.

To achieve this international reconstruction programme, a unique urban design approach was developed. This approach consisted of installing the Haut Commissariat à la Reconstruction d'Agadir (High Committee for the Reconstruction of Agadir, HCRA): a state organisation that played the role of curator of the new urban development.[6] Jean Challet and Pierre Mas – two former colleagues of Michel Écochard, at the Service de l'Urbanisme, a national urban planning administration – as well as Moroccan architect Mourad Ben Embarek, would become

9

leading figures within the reconstruction. Unprecedented in the postwar period, but echoing other reconstruction projects like those for the cities of Saint-Malo by Raymond Cornon or Le Havre by Auguste Perret – both destroyed in the war – the Haut Commissariat à la Reconstruction d'Agadir defined the reconstruction of the city not through a well-conceived plan but rather as a matter of a particular set of codes and conventions.[7] These so-called Normes Agadir 1960, a written document of building codes to be respected for all construction in the city, outlined an architectural idiom of *béton brut* (raw concrete) frames combined with infills of white-rendered masonry and natural stone as a common language in which to rebuild the various public, private and collective components of the city.

This idiom functioned as a common infrastructure for the numerous architects working on the reconstruction of the centre of Agadir – including such names as French architects Émile-Jean Duhon, Éliane Castelnau and Henri Tastemain; Moroccan architects Élie Azagury and Mourad Ben Embarek; and the Moroccan-born French architect Jean-François Zevaco – and, more importantly, it installed a binding logic between the many diverse projects that composed the city. Thus, the Normes Agadir 1960 acted simultaneously as a formal toolbox for creating specific buildings and as a common denominator of the various components of the city. Lacking any specific typological or formal articulation, the material idiom that was specified in the Normes Agadir 1960 fulfils the role of an infrastructure that can be, time and time again, discovered, appropriated and even amended by the architects and citizens of Agadir while, at the same time, functioning as a continuous material decorum that maintains an important coherence in the city.

A COMMON RESEARCH PROJECT

This book project came about as a collaborative effort of the members of the Chair of the History and Theory of Urban Design at ETH Zurich. It takes the character of an *inventaire raisonné* that records the various components of the large-scale urban design project for the reconstruction of Agadir. We worked with local collaborators to compose this inventory; wrote chapters in different formations;

and combined multiple sources collected from various archives, study visits, private collections and libraries. Our research brought us to municipal archives in Agadir in order to trace the original drawings and documentation of the building processes but also profited from access to the private collections of local historians Lahsen Roussafi, Omar Ech-Chafadi, Hassan Bouziane, Marie-France Dartois, Régine Caïs-Terrier, scholar Lahbib El Moumni and Moroccan-based French architect Laure Augereau. During our research visits, sometimes together with students, we exchanged information with the local architects Yasser Hachim, Oudad Abdeslam and Bougarba Azzouz, and with inhabitants who work and live on an everyday basis in the city of Agadir. The different components of this book – divided into the sections Foundations, Translations and Transformations and four visual essays – reflect the ambitions of this *inventaire raisonné*.

In Foundations, we question the driving forces behind the reconstruction and focus on the basic principles upon which it relied – such as its codes, the method of commissioning and the financing behind the buildings. The section opens with an interview with the historian Lahsen Roussafi, an eyewitness to the 1960 earthquake, which provides a resident's account of the conditions met immediately after the earthquake. Next, Tom Avermaete's *Urbanisme Solidaire* discusses how the reconstruction of Agadir can be regarded as an alternative way to design a city. In this 'other' urban design approach, the city is not regarded as a condition that can be controlled by a single urban planner or urban plan. Instead, the design of the city is considered as collective labour that needs to be accommodated. Cathelijne Nuijsink, in The Contact Zone of Agadir's Emergency Aid Operations, looks at the emergency aid operations in the wake of the 1960 Agadir earthquake as a 'contact zone' between local and international rescuers, experts, citizens, organisations and governments. Through an analysis of the modus operandi of the emergency aid programme, her chapter reveals how the international development aid was not unconditionally accepted but underwent a typical process of transculturation that also transpired in the architecture of rebuilt Agadir. Finally, Lahbib El Moumni, Imad Dahmani and Laure Augereau, in Brutalism: The Gem of Morocco's Contribution to World Culture, review the birth, evolution and transformation of the Brutalism movement in Morocco to conclude that, in the 1960s, the country's architects saw in Brutalist architecture a link between Moroccan and international architectural production.

In Translations, we capture the ways in which the concepts and approaches to the modern Afropolis of Agadir were translated into built form – ranging from single public buildings to collective infrastructures and entire housing estates. A second interview with Roussafi discusses the reconstruction procedures, from the temporary barracks and initial emergency settlements to the forced relocations and the start of the rebuilding process. The interview highlights the influential role of the High Commission as coordinator of the reconstruction, mediating between citizens, architects, planners, French construction companies, local builders and financial sponsors like Banque Populaire. In On Squares, Stairs, Paths, Plinths, Trees and Shade in Agadir's Reconstructed Centre, Hans Teerds examines the public spaces of the reconstruction plan. He tries to elucidate the tension between the modernist ideals of large, public, Western-style civic spaces and specific Moroccan approaches such as alleyways, covered streets, souk-like struc-tures and unprecedented elements. Janina Gosseye explores, in Reorganising Agadir, Reconstructing the Neighbourhood, how the modern Afropolis of Agadir was in need of new centres that could become the focal points of public life in the large, modern city. Gosseye reveals how a broad spectrum of public facilities – some very large and aiming to serve all the citizens, and others more limited in size and oriented towards local citizenry – were carefully planned in the city. Schools, markets and commercial centres were combined with strong public spaces and were dispersed throughout the urban fabric of the new city with the aim of creating a new social cohesion, which was only partially achieved. In Housing Figures: Social and Spatial A-Synchronicities, Irina Davidovici explores the relationship between housing typologies and social structures in the architec-ture and urban planning of Agadir. She argues that the housing norms that governed the design of the various typologies illustrate a social and spatial misalignment between the aspirations of the progressive architects and the capacity of the population to absorb the necessary changes to traditional ways of life.

In Transformations, we explore how the modern Afropolis of Agadir has performed over time and, in several chapters, interrogate the ways in which the constructions have functioned in the last six decades of their existence. A third interview with Roussafi talks about the longer-term development of the city of Agadir and the evolution of its modernist principles and ideals after the explosive demographic growth of the mid-1970s. He argues that the new lifestyles of a younger generation – focusing on car mobility, shopping malls and suburban living – render the walkable city centre a museum. Architecture of Resilience: Privacy and Privatisation in Agadir Housing, by Tom Avermaete and Irina Davidovici, analyses the multi scalar transformations of the residential fabric, identifying a double / mutual resilience of architecture (through its capacity to absorb change) and of its users (through their willingness to render the formal, material and spatial structures suitable to their own needs). In Agadir's Shifted Centralities, Janina Gosseye and Hans Teerds analyse a decline of public life in Agadir's city centre that was not foreseen in the reconstruction plan. This plan mentions the development of the city towards the mountains, whereas today it is clear that the southwest axis proved stronger. Finally, a Coda by Cathelijne Nuijsink and Maxime Zaugg again emphasises the book project's collaborative character, the variety of sources addressed and the multiple viewpoints on the reconstruction of Agadir resulting from it. Besides pointing out the lessons learnt from this research project, it also offers scholars new lines of research along which to extend it.

Interspersed throughout the book are three visual essays by Maxime Zaugg that set the stage for the essays in the following sections. Mapping Agadir is a collection of historical and newly produced open-source digital maps that situates the growth of the city in a historical context while simultaneously sketching the condition of Agadir today. Building Agadir presents unpublished plan documentation retrieved from the 'hidden archives' of the Hôtel de Ville (Town Hall) in Agadir together with historical photographs. Each project illustrated in this chapter is labelled with some essential facts about the architecture of the reconstruction of Agadir. Inhabiting Agadir features five axonometric drawings produced in the context of a seminar week with students from ETH Zurich. The detailed drawings illustrate the transformation and appropriation of Agadir's public space and architecture. The book concludes with a fourth visual essay Regarding Agadir by London-based architecture photographer David Grandorge with an introduction written by Irina Davidovici. This photo essay frames a vision of present-day Agadir that contrasts the despondency of abandoned or decaying structures with the optimistic modernism that shaped them in the first place.

1
For scholarship that includes architectural innovations outside the West, see, for example, Ching, Francis D. K., Mark Jarzombek and Vikramaditya Prakash, *A Global History of Architecture*, Hoboken, NJ: John Wiley & Sons, 2007; Cohen, Jean-Louis, *The Future of Architecture Since 1889*, London: Phaidon, 2012; Ingersoll, Richard, *World Architecture: A Cross-Cultural History*, Oxford: Oxford University Press, 2019; and Fletcher, Banister, Murray Fraser and Catherine Gregg, *Sir Banister Fletcher's Global History of Architecture*, 21st edn, London: Bloomsbury Visual Arts, 2020. For scholarship that explicitly starts from non-Western developments, see, for example, Lu, Duanfang, *Third World Modernism: Architecture, Development and Identity*, Abingdon: Routledge, 2011; Lim, William Siew Wai and Jiat-Hwee Chang, *Non-West Modernist Past: On Architecture & Modernities*, Singapore: World Scientific Publishing, 2012; and Stanek, Łukasz, *Architecture in Global Socialism: Eastern Europe, West Africa, and the Middle East in the Cold War*, Princeton, NJ and Oxford: Princeton University Press, 2020.

2
Robinson, Jennifer, *Ordinary Cities: Between Modernity and Development*, London: Routledge, 2006.

3
See, for instance, Singh, R. B., *Urban Development Challenges, Risks and Resilience in Asian Mega Cities*, Tokyo: Springer, 2015; and Nuttall, Sarah and Achille Mbembe, *Johannesburg: The Elusive Metropolis*, Johannesburg: Wits University Press, 2008.

4
Scholarship on the reconstruction of Agadir remains limited even today. From the perspective of architectural history, smaller studies have been made, amongst others by Thierry Nadeau in the context of the book Culot, Maurice and Jean-Marie Thiveaud (eds), *Architectures Françaises D'outre-Mer*, Liège: Mardaga, 1992. Alongside these contributions from architectural historiography, local historians have gathered a large amount of data on the reconstruction, as can be seen at the websites www.agadir1960.com and mfd.agadir.free.fr (both accessed 7 July 2021). Finally, an important study from the realm of social and political history is Segalla, Spencer D., *Empire and Catastrophe: Decolonization and Environmental Disaster in North Africa and Mediterranean France since 1954*, Lincoln, NE: University of Nebraska Press, 2020 / JSTOR, www.jstor.org/stable/j.ctv10crdt6 (accessed 7 July 2021). This last-named book, however, lays the foundations of a new research angle and takes an integrated look at the reconstruction of Agadir at large. Based on fundamental research, it relies heavily on original documents retrieved from hidden archives, never-published photography and a close look at actors in the reconstruction process who have hitherto been ignored.

5
King Mohammed V announced his plans for a new Agadir and proposed his son as a coordinator in a speech delivered on 1 March 1960; extracts were republished in multiple newspapers, such as *Al Aman*.

6
Key actors include High Commissioners Mohamed Imani, Mohamed Bel Hadj Soulami, Bel Larbi and M. A. Ben Hammou; architects Abdeslam Faraoui and Mourad Ben Embarek; leaders of the Service de l'Urbanisme; and Pierre Mas (urban planner), Claude Beurret (architect), Jean Challet (landscape architect) and J.-L. Lamarque Caupenne (administrator) of the Bureau Central des Études team. Other collaborators with the Haut Commissariat à la Reconstruction include engineer Michel Pariat, in charge of the technical aspects of earthquake reconstruction; administrators Janin and Mr. Marty, responsible for accounting; architects Philippon, Berthelet, Sylvie, Torres and Reis; and building engineers Bombezy, Wuillaume, Etienne, Hedde, Lucas, Coupois, Lary and Donguy.

7
See, for instance, Voldman, Danièle, *Images, discours et enjeux de la reconstruction des villes Françaises après 1945*, Paris: Institut d'histoire du temps présent, 1987 and Clout, Hugh, 'Place Annihilation and Urban Reconstruction: The Experience of Four Towns in Brittany, 1940 to 1960', Geografiska Annaler. Series B, *Human Geography*, vol. 82, no. 3 (2000), pp. 165–80, http://www.jstor.org/stable/491095 (accessed 8 July 2021).

Agadir after the earthquake of 29 February 1960

MAPPING AGADIR

Maxime Zaugg

Practised by European and Arab map-makers, the discipline of cartography flourished around the Mediterranean and Atlantic coast from the late Middle Ages onwards. Important trade routes along the West African coasts meant that the region around today's Agadir was crucial for commerce and is, therefore, well documented. The practice of cartography in the region during the following centuries was multifaceted. It ranged from recording trade routes along the coast, including trading posts for navigation and orientation at sea, to surveying territories by means of topographic, climatic, geological or military maps. This geographical and military mapping was an essential part of the country's pre-colonisation and control by the French. It was crucial for the comprehension and imagination of Agadir in its regional and national context. The diaries *Reconnaissance du Maroc* (Reconnaissance of Morocco), written at the end of the nineteenth century by French explorer Charles de Foucauld, who was awarded the gold medal by the Societé Géographique de Paris (Geographical Society of Paris), contained ethnological, linguistic, geographical and historical information on the country of Morocco and would become an important source for the establishment of the future French Protectorate. These diaries also contained detailed knowledge of Moroccan territory and served as the groundwork to support the increasing practice of French military cartography in the country during this period. As a tool for controlling the Moroccan territory, mapping responded to French economic and colonial interests.[1] The act of cartography was used to understand and control the Moroccan territory and was, therefore, an act not only of exercising military power but also of governmental power. Moreover, the maps produced were important artefacts of the colonial authorities, and were used for tactical and geopolitical purposes. This chapter seeks to explore the structure of the city of Agadir and the Moroccan territory in two ways. First, a selection of the numerous historical maps of Agadir and its surroundings produced by the Service Géographique du Maroc (Geographical Service of Morocco) shows the transformation of Agadir from a small village on the coast of the Atlantic Ocean to a lively city. Second, digitally created contemporary maps show the city of Agadir as we know it today.

The first part of this chapter looks closely at the cartography of the Moroccan territory and the ways in which the city of Agadir and its surroundings were represented on maps. Many military maps of the Agadir region are at our disposal today and have been crucial for our explorations. Furthermore, this chapter will examine maps of Agadir from different periods and at different scales – namely, the pre-protectorate period, the period of the French Protectorate and the postcolonial era before and after the earthquake of 1960. The wide range of maps shows how Agadir has been shaped and redeveloped time and time again during these periods, but also how it has been imagined by various actors. The second part of the chapter maps the city of Agadir in its territorial context at different scales. Using open-source geo data from Open Street Map and the digital-drawing software Mathematica, our colleague Luca Can created new, contemporary maps of Agadir and its surroundings, providing fresh knowledge about the city. The first map at the territorial scale locates Agadir in its national context as a 'gateway' between southern and northern Morocco, as well as its multifaceted relationship with Marrakesh and Casablanca. The map at the scale of the province situates Agadir in its economic context and the landscape of the four provinces forming the Souss-Massa region. Finally, the urban and city scales represent the urban condition of the city of Agadir and its relationship with its urban and agricultural surroundings by showing land use and infrastructure today.

1
Martonne, Edouard-Guillaume de, 'Développement de la cartographie militaire au Maroc', in *Annales de Géographie*, vol. 30, no. 166 (1921), pp. 304–7.

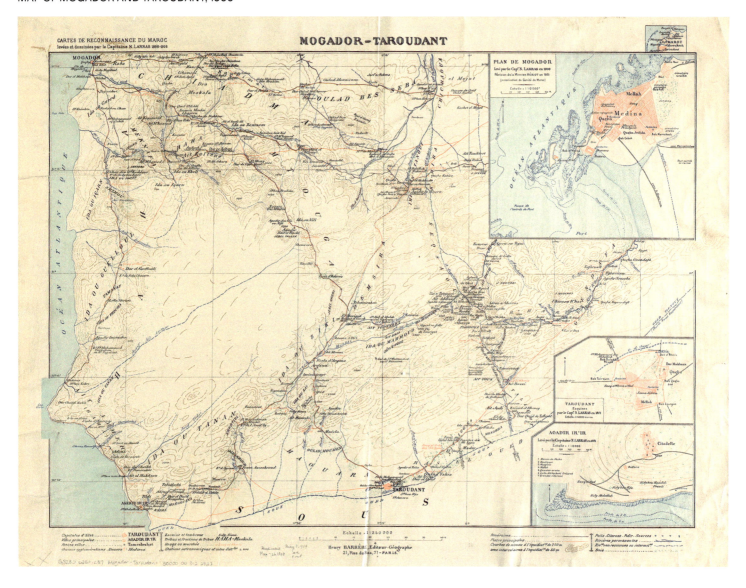

The topographical map *Carte de Reconnaissance du Maroc* (Exploration Map of Morocco) was drawn by French military captain N. Larras between 1898 and 1906, and published by the editor-geographer Henry Barrère in Paris. Showing the Moroccan region of Mogador-Taroudant, it was an integral part of the French national mapping campaign during the pre-protectorate period in the nineteenth century. Situated on the Atlantic Ocean, the city of Agadir is shown within its triangular relationship with the towns of Mogador (today's Essaouira) and Taroudant – cities situated, at the time, within a day's travel from each other. Agadir's location is closely linked to domestic trade routes to the south of the country and defined by the topography of the Atlas Mountains and the ocean. Its harbour, however, was never really used for commercial purposes due to the importance of Mogador's significantly larger port. Therefore, important trade routes developed to Mogador but also to Agadir's hinterland. Until the end of the nineteenth century, around the time when this map was drawn, Agadir was considered a small town that served as a supply destination for travels to the south.

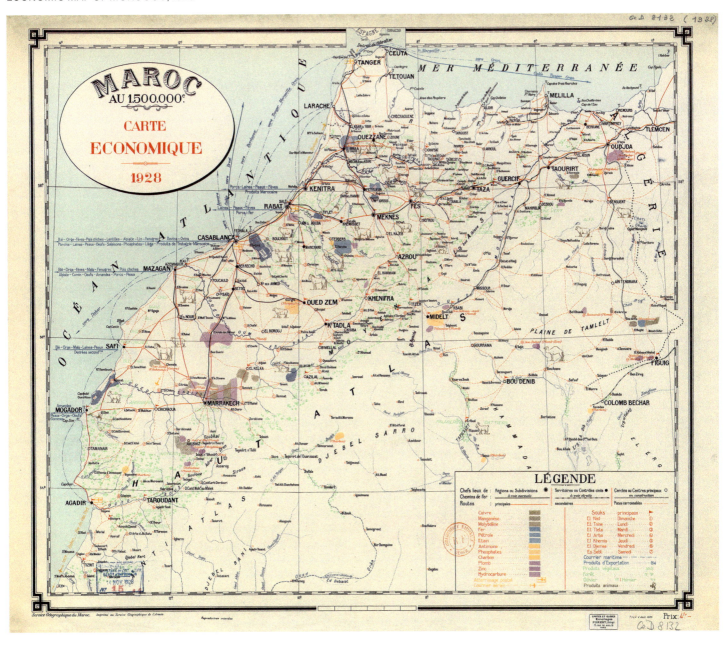

The *Carte Économique* (Economic Map) – produced by the Service Géographique du Maroc (Geographical Service of Morocco), printed by the Service Géographique de l'Armée (Geographical Service of the Army) and published by Cartes et Globes, Entoilages Forest in Paris in 1928 – illustrates the French Protectorate's economic interests by colour-coding the mineral resources of the country and marking the main transport routes by land, water and air. The imprinted indication 'reproduction interdite' emphasises the geopolitical importance and sensitivity of colonial regimes' military maps at this time. This map shows that the city of Agadir, with its airport, became a stop on the international route of the French Compagnie Générale Aéropostale (General Air Postal Company) that connected Paris, the French capital, with South America via the West African coast. It also shows that the city was surrounded by a forested area and had no significant mineral resources except for some phosphates, indicated with the orange coding. Naturally isolated from the country's north by the Atlas Mountains, Agadir was connected by one crucial main road to Casablanca via Mogador. This economic map reveals the lasting role of Agadir in its national context as an important city for Morocco's entire south.

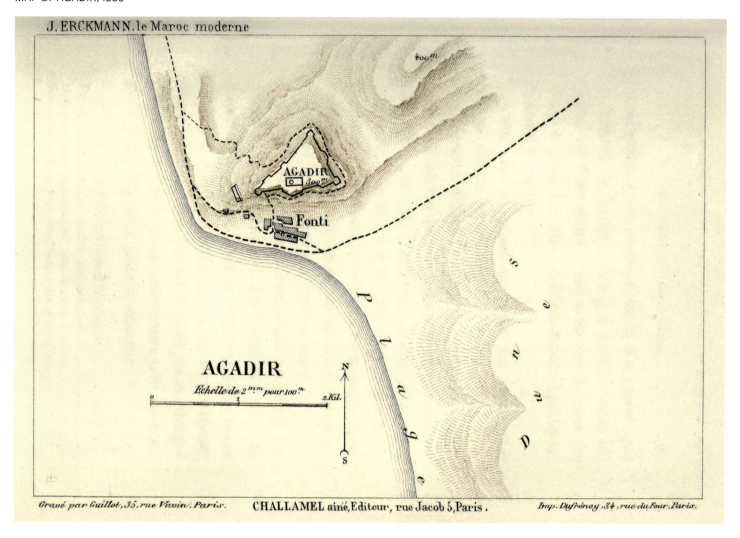

From the *Dictionnaire des Racines Berbères* (Dictionary of Berber Word Stems), one can see that the name Agadir translates as 'collective fortified granary' – which refers to its kasbah, built in 1572 and located on the top of the hill by the ocean. Agadir and the small fishing village of Founti (or Fonti), built at the foot of the hill on which the kasbah is situated, can be found on maps of the African west coast as far back as the fifteenth century. The site of Founti was used as a natural harbour in which ships could take shelter and unload or load goods. It maintained its role over the centuries, its use intensifying with the arrival of the Portuguese at the beginning of the sixteenth century. In 1731, the small town of Agadir and its surroundings were destroyed by an earthquake and rebuilt in 1746 at the foot of the kasbah. Around the kasbah, during the coming centuries, smaller settlements like Anza evolved, forming part of the city known today as Agadir. The riverbeds to the east of Founti can already be seen; they would play a decisive role in the later development of the city of Agadir.

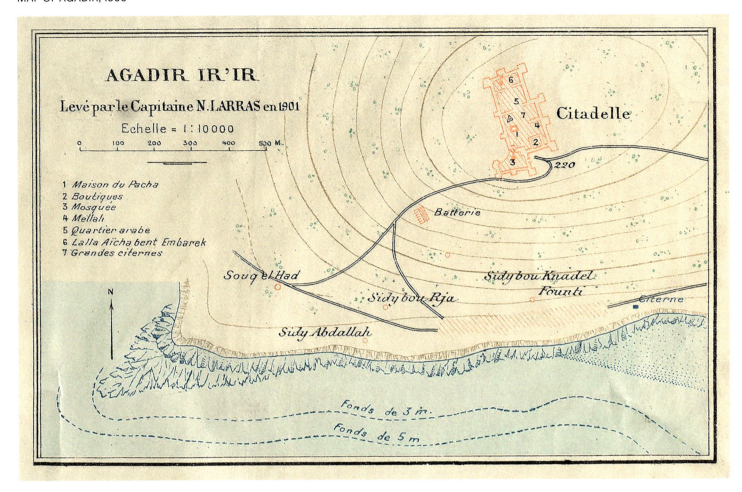

AGADIR IR'IR.

Levé par le Capitaine N. LARRAS en 1901

Echelle = 1:10000

0   100   200   300   400   500 M.

1 Maison du Pacha
2 Boutiques
3 Mosquée
4 Mellah
5 Quartier arabe
6 Lalla Aïcha bent Embarek
7 Grandes citernes

Citadelle

220

Batterie

N

Soug el Had

Sidy bou Rja

Sidy bou Knadel
Founti

Citerne

Sidy Abdallah

Fonds de 3 m.

Fonds de 5 m.

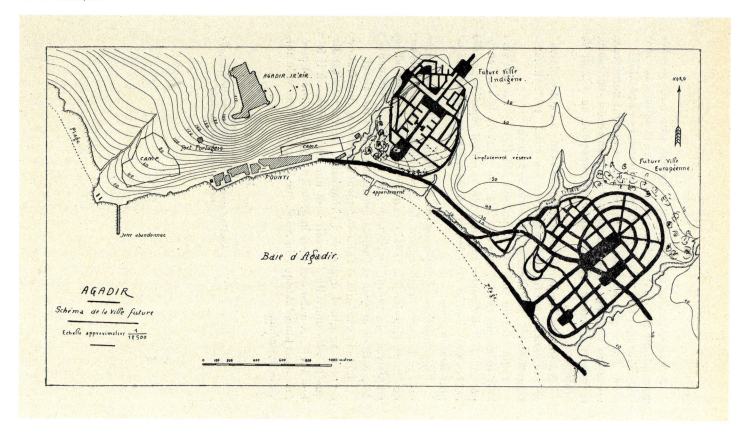

With the arrival of the French in Morocco, and the implementation of the Protectorate, established in March 1912, new urban planning concepts were applied to various Moroccan cities, including the small town of Agadir. French urban planner Henri Prost, who was dispatched to Morocco by General Hubert Lyautey in 1913, envisaged a set of urban principles for the town of Agadir typical of colonial planning of the time and identifiable in the more schematic plan of 1921 and the plan of 1924. Both show two new urban entities emerging. East of the fishing village of Founti and at the foot of the mountain where the kasbah is located, which were the only settlements in Agadir until the beginning of the twentieth century, one can see two new urban forms separated by an elevated plateau. These follow the topographical and geological characteristics of the terrain, and implement Lyautey's theory of population separation. The first urban form, labelled 'Future Ville Indigène' (Future Indigenous Town) and also known as Talborjt, on the left side of the plan was situated on the plateau of Talborjt, a Berber word meaning 'small *borj*' (small fort) borrowed from Arabic. It was planned to relieve housing pressure on the residents of the existing settlements and to accommodate the locals of Agadir. Separated by a 'reserved' plateau, on which the administrative centre would be located with administrative and military buildings, the 'Ville Européenne' (European City), also known as Ville Nouvelle (New City), intended for European residents, was planned further south, built in a horseshoe form facing the sea with large avenues. These two urban units were separated by natural riverbeds that would later be developed as gardens. This so-called 'Zone Sanitaire' (Sanitary Zone) between them is enhanced by the topography and is an attempt to rationalise the settlement of the local Moroccan residents while keeping it apart from the Ville Nouvelle. Both Talborjt and the Ville Nouvelle are characterised by straight streets and a system of boulevards, and yet they differ in their architecture. Talborjt corresponds more closely to an indigenous interpretation of European architecture and is denser, whereas the Ville Nouvelle features more classical European characteristics. Another important urban feature is the separation of Talborjt from the sea by the wide road connecting the Ville Nouvelle to the harbour. The intentional separation clearly indicates that this town plan was prepared for the primary benefit of the French settlers.

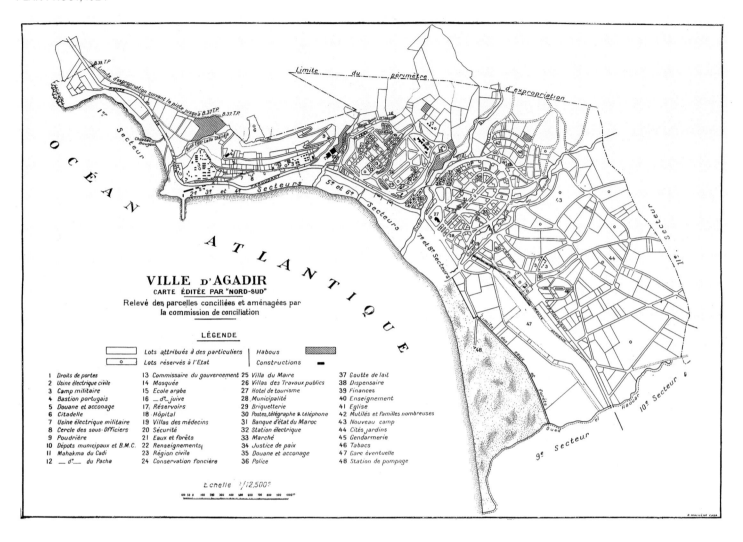

VILLE D'AGADIR

CARTE ÉDITÉE PAR "NORD-SUD"

Relevé des parcelles conciliées et aménagées par
la commission de conciliation

LÉGENDE

	Lots attribués à des particuliers		Habous
	Lots réservés à l'Etat		Constructions

1	Droits de portes	13	Commissaire du gouvernement	25	Villa du Maire	37	Goutte de lait
2	Usine électrique civile	14	Mosquée	26	Villas des Travaux publics	38	Dispensaire
3	Camp militaire	15	Ecole arabe	27	Hotel de tourisme	39	Finances
4	Bastion portugais	16	__d°__ juive	28	Municipalité	40	Enseignement
5	Douane et acconage	17	Réservoirs	29	Briquetterie	41	Eglise
6	Citadelle	18	Hôpital	30	Postes,télégraphe & téléphone	42	Mutilés et familles nombreuses
7	Usine électrique militaire	19	Villas des médecins	31	Banque d'état du Maroc	43	Nouveau camp
8	Cercle des sous-Officiers	20	Sécurité	32	Station électrique	44	Cités jardins
9	Poudrière	21	Eaux et forêts	33	Marché	45	Gendarmerie
10	Dépots municipaux et B.M.C.	22	Renseignements	34	Justice de paix	46	Tabacs
11	Mahakma du Cadi	23	Région civile	35	Douane et acconage	47	Gare éventuelle
12	__d°__ du Pacha	24	Conservation foncière	36	Police	48	Station de pompage

Echelle 1/12,500°

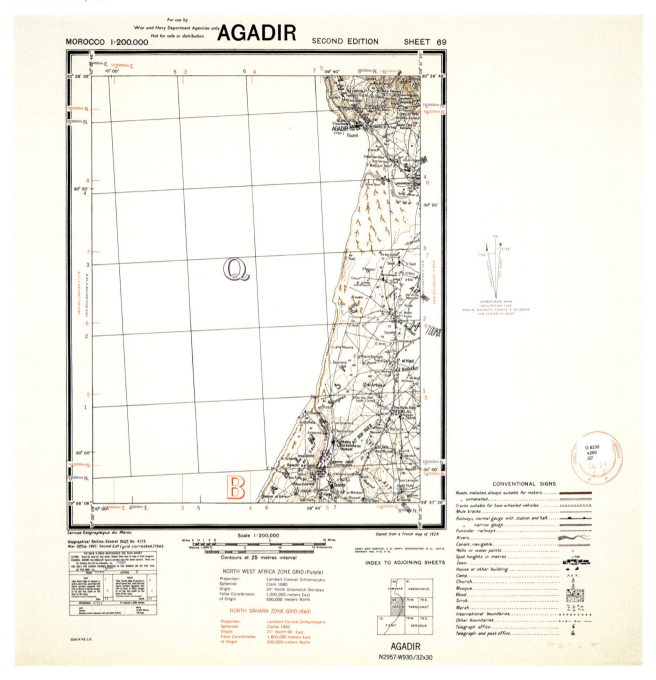

As introduced by the Service Géographique du Maroc, Morocco's territory was, as we can see on this map, subdivided into geometrical zones whereby Agadir lies at the intersection between the North-West African Grid and the North Saharan Grid. The two military maps were drawn and published by the US Army (1928, 1942). By dividing the country into zones and by giving them systematic coordinates, the maps of the region around Agadir during and after the French Protectorate can be compared with one another. They clearly show how urbanisation spread towards the south, contained by its topographical condition and the ocean. Connected with a highway and by railway, the city of Agadir is an important centre for the entire region south of the Atlas Mountains. Along the traffic corridor running towards the south, agriculture is flourishing during the twentieth century – as can be seen from the dark- and light-green areas. It is also striking how urbanisation increased rapidly around the Souss River's mouth, anticipating the densely populated area around Inezgane, south of Agadir today.

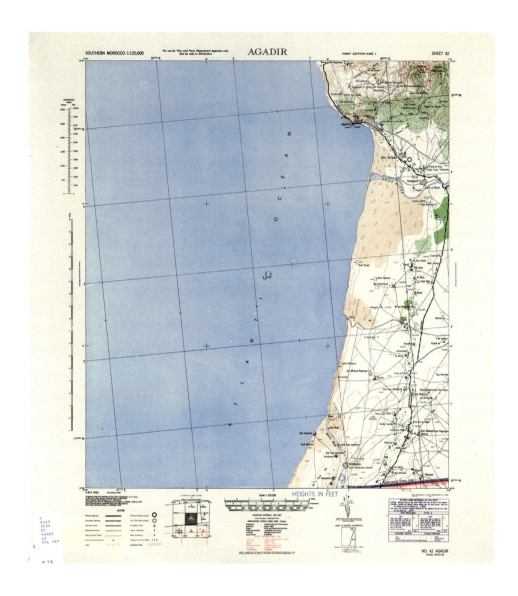

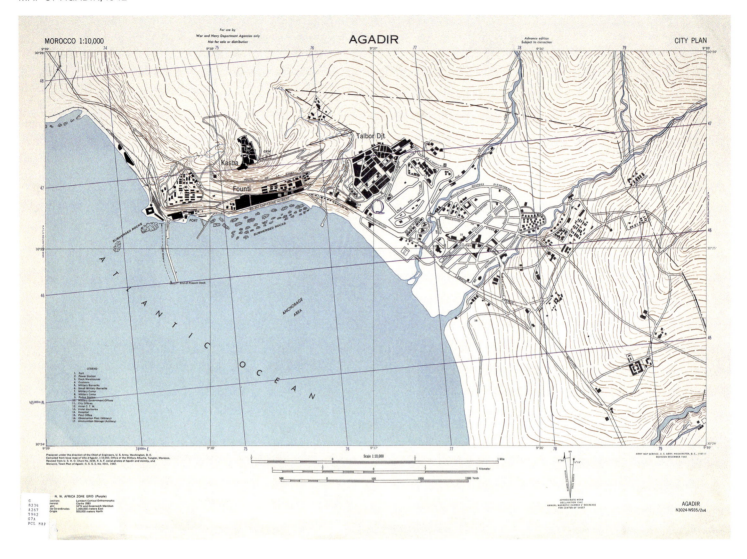

During the French Protectorate, Agadir experienced increased economic growth. The map of 1942 – prepared under the direction of the Chief of Engineers of the US Army in Washington, DC – reveals that the previously mentioned dominant urban figures of Talborjt and the Ville Nouvelle were implemented and continued to shape the development of the city of Agadir. During the 1930s and until the beginning of the 1940s, the city developed according to Prost's plan with wide streets, a sewage system and a road along the seafront. In 1946, a Plan d'Aménagement (New Development Plan) for Agadir was implemented when French architect and urban planner Michel Écochard became head of the Protectorate's Service de l'Urbanisme (Urban Planning Office). Essential features of this plan are the expansion of Agadir and the implementation of an industrial zone and workers' quarters in the east of the city, recognisable from the typical eight-by-eight-metre grid that Écochard often used. One can see that, on both plans, the different urban parts still relate strongly to the topographical conditions – and that the natural watercourses are still recognisable and continue to structure the city's development.

On the 1942 plan, and even more strongly on the 1953 plan by Écochard, an industrial extension to the south-east and the expansion of the harbour are discernible. While the two parts of the city are still separated by the riverbeds on the 1942 plan, in Écochard's plan this separation is removed by covering up the riverbeds – leading to a merging of Talborjt and the Ville Nouvelle. More significant institutional buildings like hospitals were positioned in the Sanitary Zone, which functions simultaneously as a connector and separator and was retained in both of these urban-development plans.

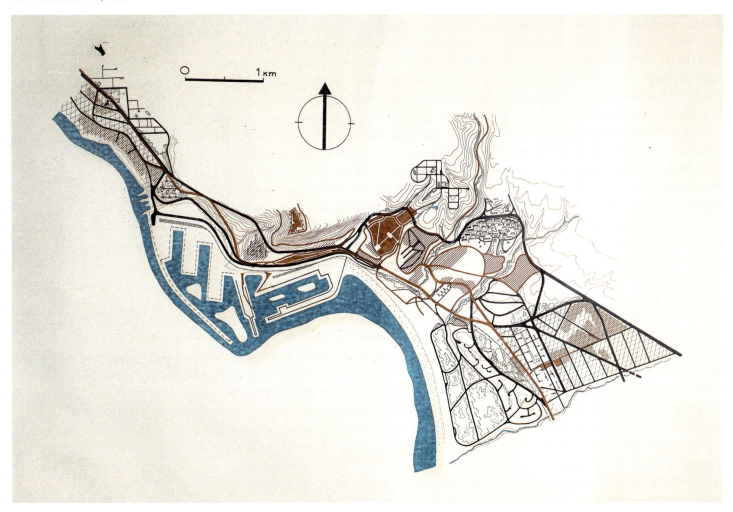

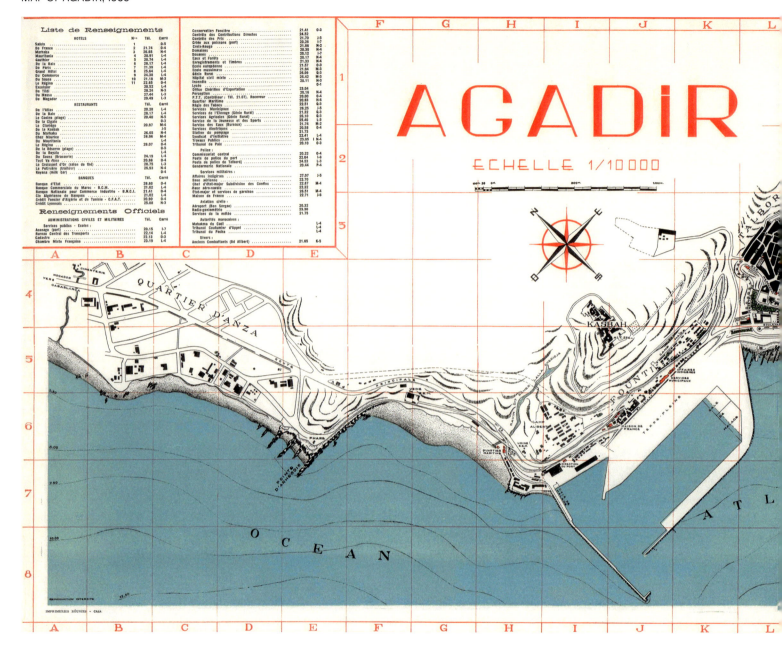

The map drawn by the Bureau Technique Bret-Leuzinger in Agadir in 1959 organises the city into square sectors and includes a comprehensive legend. The detailed coloured map, made one year before the devastating earthquake, shows the completed harbour of Agadir and the expansion of the Quartier Industriel Sud to the east. The densely built-up Talborjt, on the slope of the hill, is separated from the horseshoe-shaped Ville Nouvelle by the Plateau Administrative (Administrative Plateau).

This plain, shaped by the natural topography, accommodates more public and institutional buildings, and is interspersed with green public spaces. The Quartier Industriel Sud was created by the municipality of Agadir to meet the needs of industrialists faced with the development of the city and its industry. As the small industrial district of Anza would no longer suffice, due to lack of space, this new quarter was built at the end of the 1940s outside the city, towards Inezgane. It was contained within natural boundaries such as the mountains to the north and the river courses to the east, as well as by the Ville Nouvelle to the west. Visible on the plan is a green separation zone south of the Quartier Industriel Sud towards the sea. During the 1950s, Agadir was a prosperous city that started to open up for national and international seaside tourism – as demonstrated by the introduction of a beach and a variety of sporting facilities along the coast.

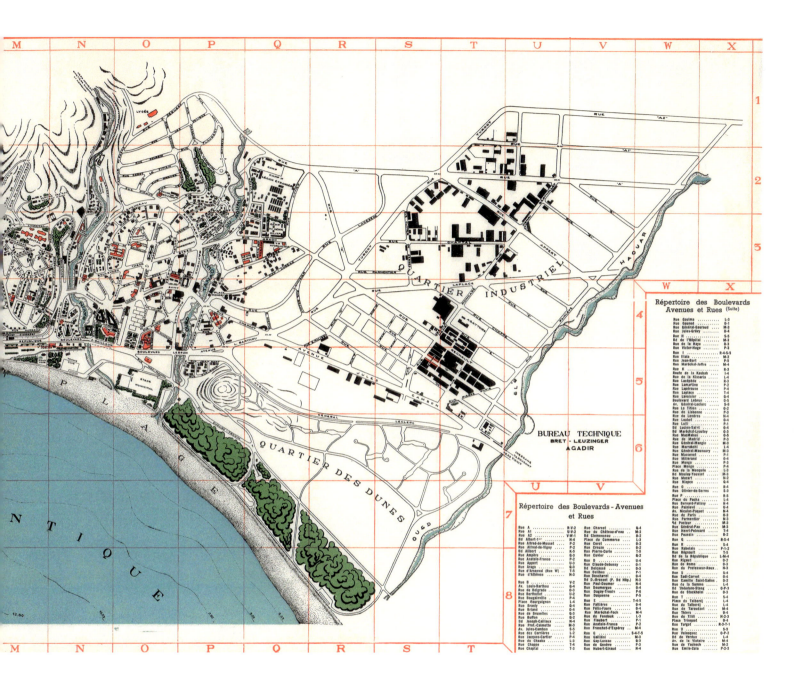

BUREAU TECHNIQUE
BRET - LEUZINGER
AGADIR

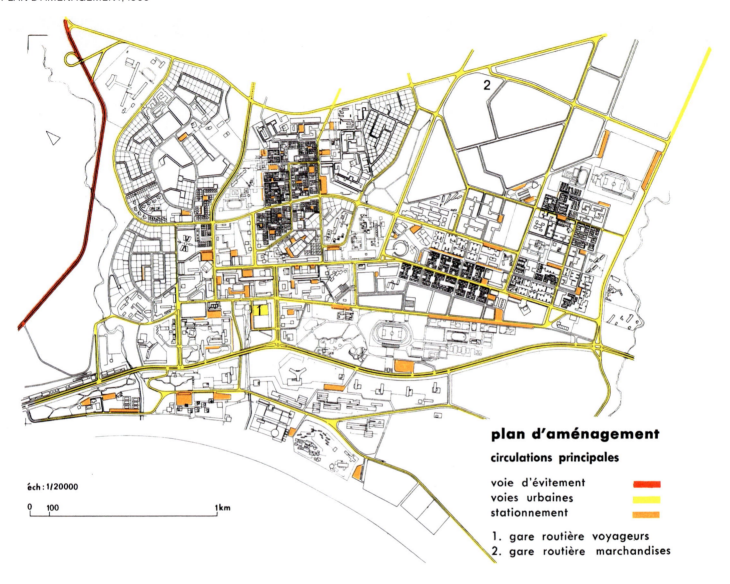

plan d'aménagement

circulations principales

voie d'évitement
voies urbaines
stationnement

1. gare routière voyageurs
2. gare routière marchandises

éch : 1/20000

0   100   1km

After the earthquake, Agadir was reconstructed in a short period of time according to urban codes and conventions. Since geological and seismic studies showed that the city could not be rebuilt on its initial site, the new Agadir was built further east. The two river courses that had formed the old site of the city were built over in the new plan. The reconstruction was elaborated according to three vital future functions of Agadir. First, the administrative importance of the city – which was at that time already the capital of the Souss-Massa economic region and had much important infrastructure, such as a harbour and an airport. Second, commerce and industry were considered essential functions that should underline the importance of Agadir as the economic centre of the region. Third, it was decided that the city would become the main tourist destination for southern Morocco, which meant that its beach was reserved for hotels. These principles would offer the basis for the reconstruction of Agadir. Due to the incompatibility of tourism and industry, the coastal area was reserved for tourist and seaside activities. Therefore, an intermediate and elevated zone was built to ensure a connection between the tourism zone and the city. The tourist sector was isolated from the industrial districts by the creation of a large connecting road, for heavy delivery vehicles, providing a direct link between the port and the southern industry. With Nouveau Talborjt, the urban designers attempted to create a new urban centre according to traditional principles. Complementing Talborjt, administrative services would be brought together in a Centre Urbain. Ensuring that the city could develop on its periphery was another key consideration. The reconstruction of Agadir was not shaped by a unifying figure but rather composed in a complementary way. Codes and conventions maintained the continuity – a gradual and balanced way of developing.

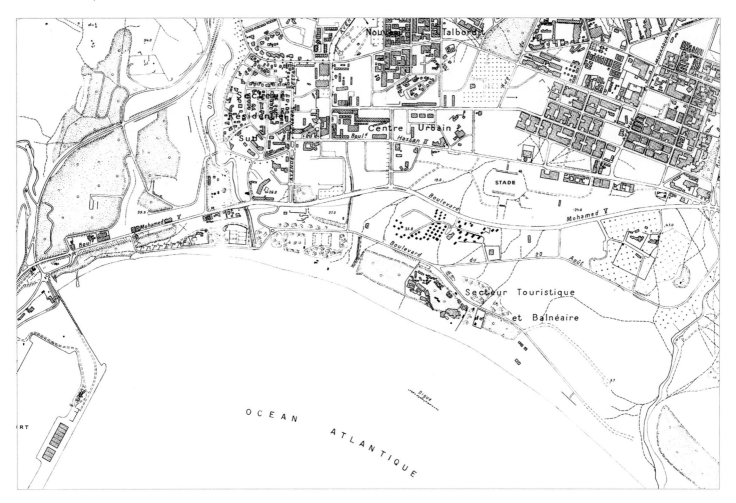

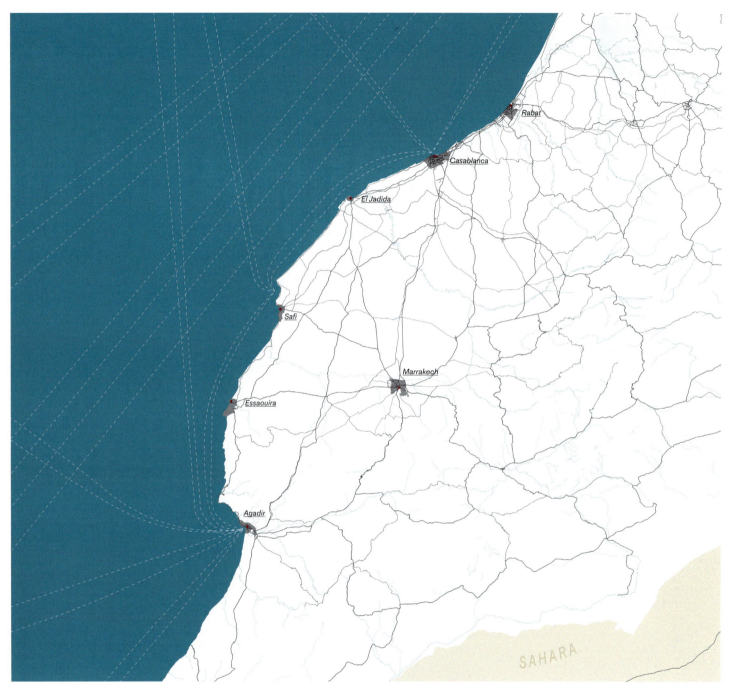

Together with Casablanca, Marrakesh and Rabat, the city of Agadir is one of the most important urban centres in the country, with its municipality counting almost one million inhabitants. It is the capital of the Souss-Massa economic region, one of the twelve regions of Morocco. Today, Agadir is considered the point of departure and access for the entire south of the country. Due to good accessibility via the main national roads and its international airport, the city of Agadir became an important national and international tourist destination during the second half of the twentieth century with a well-developed infrastructure for year-round vacationing. Moreover, due to its second industry, the fishing sector, the city is also connected by sea routes with the main international and national harbours.

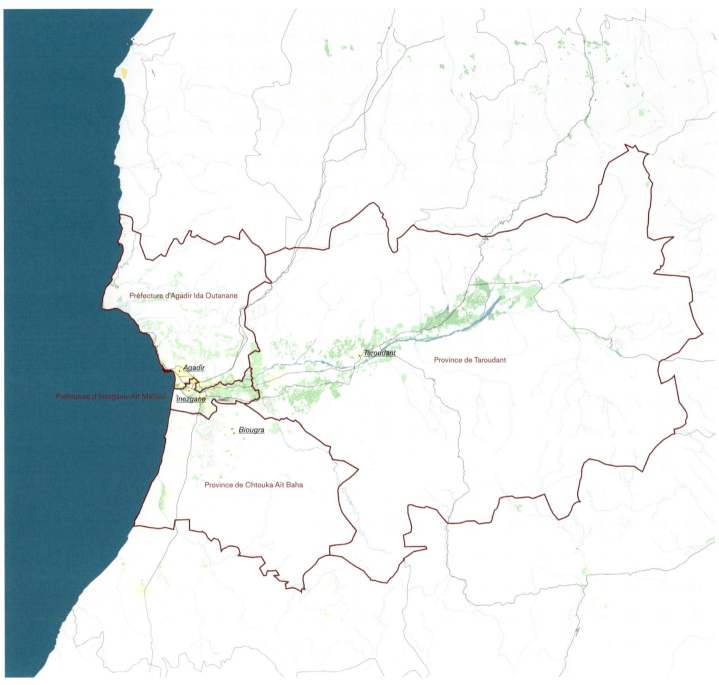

On a more regional level, Souss-Massa includes two prefectures and four provinces: the prefectures of Agadir Ida-Outanane and Inezgane-Aït Melloul and the provinces of Chtouka-Aït Baha, Taroudant, Tata and Tiznit. The city of Agadir, together with other cities such as Inezgane and Taroudant, forms an important urban and economic centre of the region and is located along the fertile lands of the Souss River, which connects the hinterland to the coast. Along the riverbed, industrial areas and agriculture are developing in addition to urbanisation. South, where desert-like landscapes begin, the road infrastructure and the urban density decrease, and artificially watered greenhouse agriculture is creating new, more informal urban centres. The coast has remained undeveloped due to the national park of Souss-Massa extending south along the coast.

Agriculture

Greenhouse buildings

Water infrastructure

Residential zone

Industrial zone

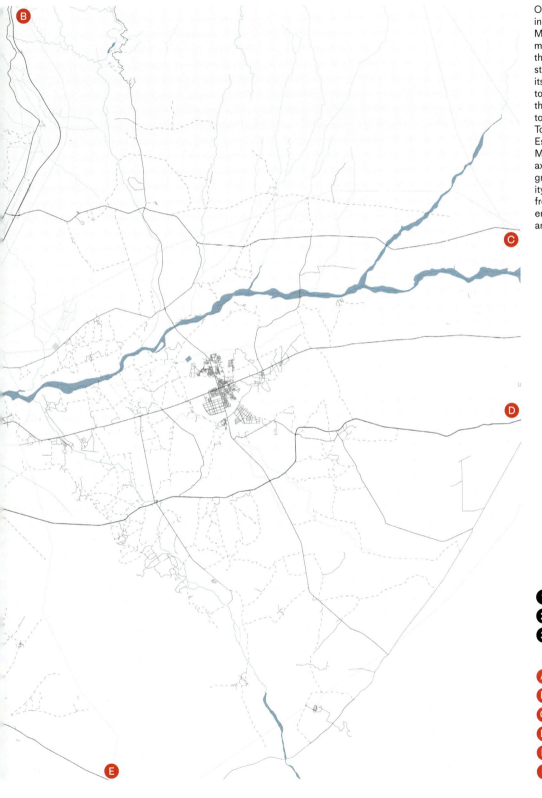

Opening up to the south-west, Agadir is located in a bay between the foothills of the High Atlas Mountains and the River Souss. These natural elements have shaped the urban development of the city to this day. The map shows the road infrastructure around the urban region of Agadir and its polycentricity. The urban concentration evolving to the south is clearly apparent, and one can see the main roads starting from Agadir and connecting to the hinterland and the south of the region. Towards the north, two roads connect Agadir with Essaouira and Casablanca and, north-east, with Marrakesh. Along the eastern and southern traffic axes, new urban centres can be recognised. The growth of the population and of the economic activity around Agadir has caused a substantial migration from the city centre to its fast-developing periphery. Also visible are the port and the airport, which are connected by main roads to the city.

1 Port of Agadir

2 Al Massira Airport

3 Military Airport of Inezgane

A towards Essaouira

B towards Casablanca

C towards Marrakesh

D towards Taroudant

E towards Biougra

F towards Tiznit

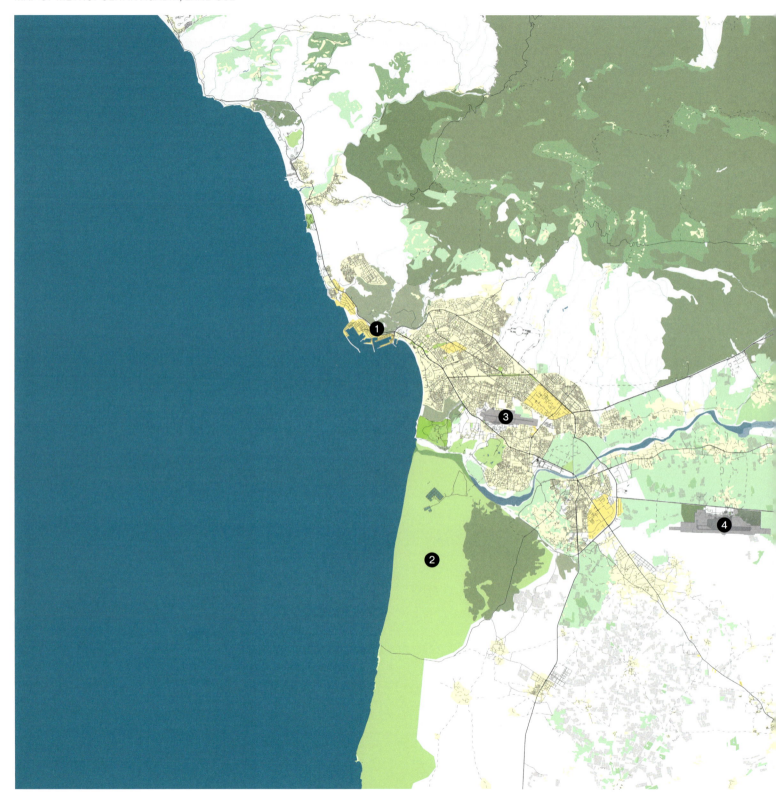

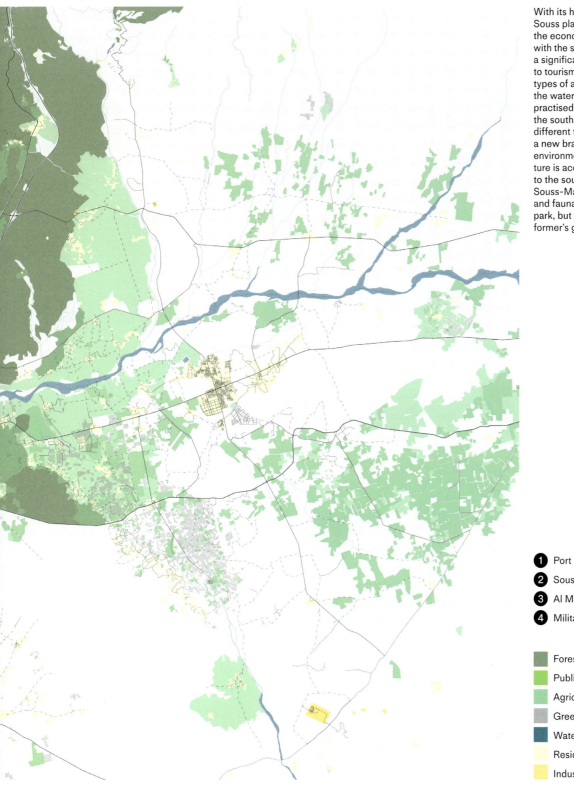

With its harbour and the hinterland of the fertile Souss plain, the city of Agadir is today the capital of the economic region of Souss-Massa and forms, with the surrounding towns Inezgane and Aït Melloul, a significant urban and political centre. In addition to tourism, the region is also characterised by various types of agriculture. This cultivation is related to the watercourses of the Souss River to the east and practised in the mountain regions to the north. To the south, one recognises – from the grey colour – a different type of agriculture: greenhouses, creating a new branch of the economy in a desert-like environment. The growth of this greenhouse agriculture is accelerating the rapid urban development to the south. The coast is undeveloped due to the Souss-Massa National Park, which protects flora and fauna. The city is also shaped by the national park, but the latter is under pressure due to the former's growth.

1 Port of Agadir

2 Souss-Massa National Park

3 Al Massira Airport

4 Military Airport of Inezgane

- Forest / scrub
- Public greens
- Agriculture
- Greenhouse buildings
- Water infrastructure
- Residential zone
- Industrial zone

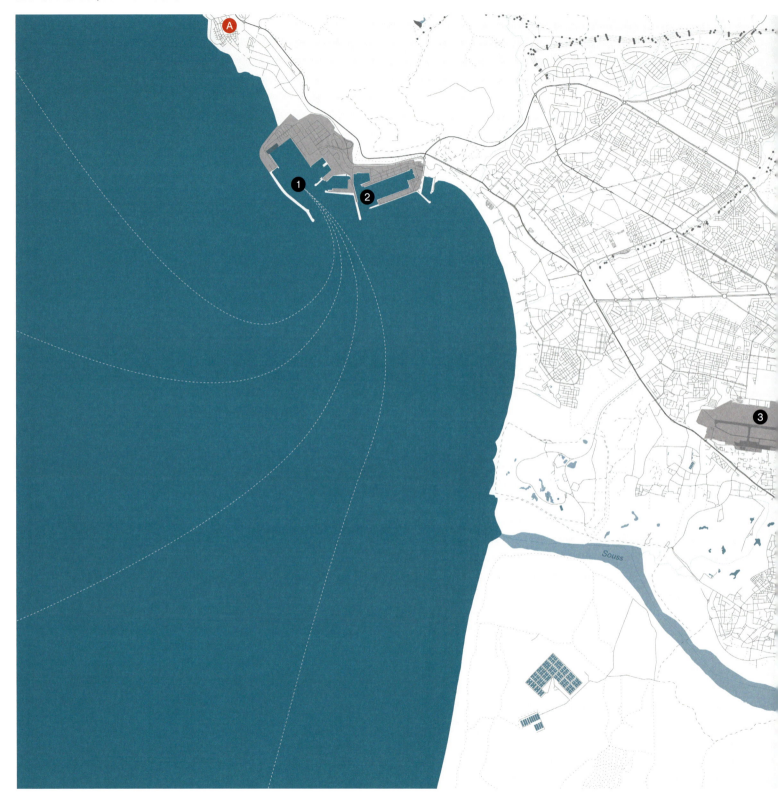

The infrastructural map of the urban centre of Agadir
shows the original structure of the city, moulded
by the hills and coast, and its emerging expansion
towards the south-east. The two new centres of
Inezgane and Aït Melloul, together with the city of
Agadir itself, are beginning to form a new polycentric urban fabric, which is limited and diverted in
the south by the river. In addition, to the east, along
the already-large road infrastructure, one can
see the emergence of new urban neighbourhoods,
which continue to enlarge the polycentric metropolitan area of Agadir.

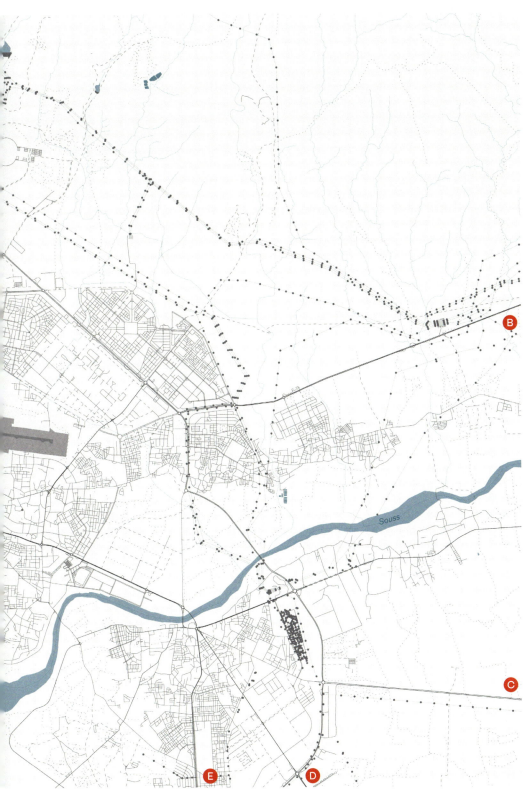

1 Commercial Port

2 Fishing Port

3 Military Airport of Inezgane

A towards Essaouira

B towards Casablanca / Marrakesh

C towards Taroudant

D towards Biougra

E towards Tiznit

Souss

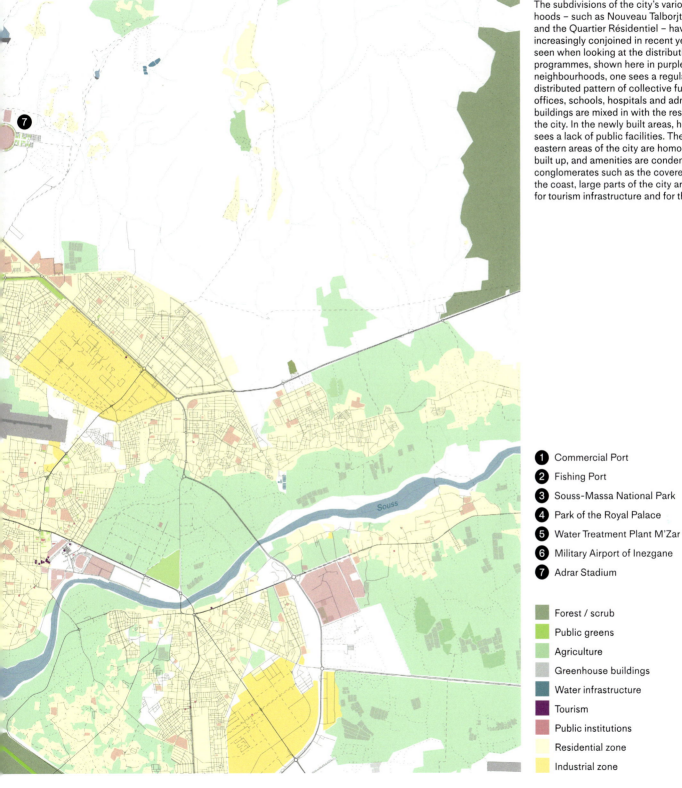

The subdivisions of the city's various neighbour-hoods – such as Nouveau Talborjt, Centre Urbain and the Quartier Résidentiel – have become increasingly conjoined in recent years. This can be seen when looking at the distribution of public programmes, shown here in purple. In the original neighbourhoods, one sees a regular and equally distributed pattern of collective functions. Public offices, schools, hospitals and administrative buildings are mixed in with the residential areas of the city. In the newly built areas, however, one sees a lack of public facilities. The northern and eastern areas of the city are homogeneously built up, and amenities are condensing into large conglomerates such as the covered souk. Along the coast, large parts of the city are reserved for tourism infrastructure and for the national park.

1 Commercial Port
2 Fishing Port
3 Souss-Massa National Park
4 Park of the Royal Palace
5 Water Treatment Plant M'Zar
6 Military Airport of Inezgane
7 Adrar Stadium

Forest / scrub
Public greens
Agriculture
Greenhouse buildings
Water infrastructure
Tourism
Public institutions
Residential zone
Industrial zone

FOUNDATIONS

THE CITY AND THE 1960 EARTHQUAKE

Lahsen Roussafi

This interview with Lahsen Roussafi, survivor of the earthquake, took place in a café on the terrace of a hotel whose Berber name is Afoud ('knee') in recognition of the fact that in 1960 the city was brought to its knees. At the request of Tom Avermaete, the interview focused on three themes:

1. The earthquake as witnessed by Lahsen Roussafi;
2. The reconstruction project, especially with reference to the role of the Haut Commissariat à la Réconstruction d'Agadir (High Committee for the Reconstruction of Agadir), which was in charge for the first ten years (distributing financial aid and selecting the architects, both Moroccan and foreign, according to established guidelines); and
3. The continuation of the work from the time that the office of the Haut Commissariat was dissolved up to the present day.

Despite reconstruction needing to be done so urgently that there was no time to deploy an urbanistic vision, a couple of positive assets did emerge: (a) administrative facilities, which no longer exist, were created, giving the Haut Commissariat centralised decision-making power to choose, finance and authorise the projects; and (b) the first buildings, designed by famous architects, were of high quality, original, and at the same time earthquake-proof.

The last part of the interview is dedicated to the current state of Agadir: a city centre that has been emptied; a city government deprived of the means to intervene in and influence decisions taken by real-estate developers; and a lack of essential infrastructure, like roads and railroads, that would have allowed durable economic development. As a result, Agadir has remained largely a holiday destination for tourists where speculators and the private sector dominate. The Centre Urbain, as planned and constructed in the time of the Haut Commissariat, is now in decline – and in a few decades it will be entirely empty, with the city's largest agglomerations of buildings located in other zones.

THE CITY AND THE EARTHQUAKE

What was it like to live through the earthquake as a young person? Agadir was in what kind of state in the hours and days after the earthquake? You can begin with your personal memories.

I certainly did live through the earthquake. I was twenty years old and felt it all. At the time I was a student in the French high school, standing with my French friends when I felt the first tremors. None of us was afraid. At first, we were amused. Our grandparents told us that each year God placed the earth on the horn of a bull. When the bull was tired, he shifted the globe to his other horn and that act caused the earth to tremble. We weren't afraid; we were thinking of this old tale told by our grandparents, and we were joking.

The night of the earthquake. In the evening toward 11.30 I had been in bed for half an hour when the earth trembled again very hard. The roof flew off and landed some distance away. Several rooms in our house, made of earth and *torchis* (straw bricks), were flattened by the falling roof.

In what state was your village after the earthquake?

I lived in the village of Yachech, which was inhabited only by people from the south of Morocco. The village had a population of 7,000. Suddenly there were only 3,000 left. The other 4,000 were underneath the stones. The village was [later] flattened by bulldozers. The temperature was very hot, about 42 to 45 degrees Celsius at 7 the following morning, and the corpses were already beginning to smell. You couldn't pull the people from the rubble with your bare hands.

In our home we lost eleven people. They were the renters living in rooms we leased out. We also lost a member of our family, the husband of my sister, and his sister disappeared, too.

We [at first] believed we were the only ones in our village to survive the catastrophe.

Towards 3 p.m., I asked my mother for permission to go see what had happened in the Ville Nouvelle where my teachers lived. I saw the rubble. My mother asked me to find out if 'her bridge' was still standing. She had built this bridge with my father and a few others, so I was born thanks to this bridge. She wanted to know if there were another way to get to the other side of this canalised stream, but the bridge had not, in fact, fallen. In the Talborjt everything, or almost everything, was destroyed. My mother was nevertheless happy because the bridge was still standing.

Did you stay in the destroyed village?

We stayed there for two days. We pulled some things out from under the rubble. The army came with trucks. We were then removed to Inezgane, where there was only sand and eucalyptus. We stayed there seventeen days.

There was nothing left in Agadir and the city was inaccessible. All was closed in an effort to avoid epidemics and thieving. You needed a military escort in order to go from the south to the north. The soldiers were under orders to shoot at anything that moved. There were people who were killed in this way while trying to steal.

Did you live in tents at the time?

No, we lived in the open air under the trees because the tents hadn't arrived yet. In two days, aid organisations did arrive. They were carrying gifts from all the countries of the world, [like] Switzerland, France, America, Germany, Belgium, even Israel.

The international community came to take care of the wounded?

These organisations offered on-the-spot help to the wounded in the form of dressing, shots . . . In the morning, the army gave us a meal; at midday and in the evening, these other organisations provided the food. They were cold meals, and water tanks were brought in to provide water. After seventeen days, we were placed in a camp with big tents meant to hold ten families sleeping on folding cots. In each tent, there were at least ten families.

Who built this camp – the army or other organisations?

The army built them with international help. People came from many different countries. Franciscan sisters slept there with us. We all ate the same meals, either in a cheap restaurant or wherever else we could find food; we ate under the tent; we received medical treatment there; we waited . . . The majority of the people came from Agadir and waited to be rehoused. But the others could leave if they had family elsewhere.

What happened to young people? Were they able to continue their studies?

At the time, I was doing technical studies. There weren't any more schools; everything was closed. With four other students, I was transferred to a boarding school in Rabat. Belgium financed the schools in Rabat through the intervention of a Belgian envoy collaborating with Moroccan Princess Aicha. Through the princess's office, the Belgian envoy established connection with many places where there were refugees. We stayed two months in Rabat in order to finish the school year. Then, three months of holiday.

When you returned from Rabat to Agadir two months later, what did you find?

Nothing at all. There were prefabricated barracks. People were lodged in prefabricated campgrounds while waiting for the reconstruction to begin – though they weren't given meals any more, but just the foodstuffs. With flour and powdered milk, they got by. There was a sanitary block with six taps for each housing complex, plus six male and six female toilets. Two little rooms per family, parents and children. With electricity.

Where were these temporary barracks located?

We left the tents and they built temporary housing in the Quartier Industriel Sud, near today's souk. They gathered together all the survivors, who already constituted a sort of village. The social connection was very important, to have people you already knew nearby.

I lived seven years in the neighbourhood of Amsernat. Beginning at the end of 1960, we first made an emergency settlement which Mohammed V inaugurated before his death. The people of Talborjt were first housed there – that is, traders and the better-off people who had the means of paying. We, the more modest folk like masons and fishermen, were the last to leave Amsernat. They rebuilt using Écochard's model.

URBANISME SOLIDAIRE: CODES AND CONVENTIONS AS PROJECT FOR A NEW CITY

Tom Avermaete

It is up to the architects to discover why some buildings have withstood the test better than others. It is highly desirable that as complete as possible documentation be collected on each of the city's important constructions: statistical sheets with the behaviour of essential elements in the earthquake would certainly provide very fruitful information for the realisation of future earthquake-resistant constructions.[1]

With these words, the French seismologist Jean-Pierre Rothé summarised his article 'The tragic toll of the 1960 earthquake is largely the result of poor quality buildings' after visiting Agadir. Rothé remarked that the Agadir earthquake was brutal and constituted 'a terrible blow, and yet each year more than one 150 earthquakes exceeded the energy released in the Agadir earthquake'.[2] He noticed that the quake in the French city of Orléansville was thirty-three times stronger, the one in San Francisco in 1906 5,000 times – while the Lisbon earthquake in 1755 (which was felt in Morocco) was 80,000 times stronger than the one in Agadir. The Frenchman remarked that well-constructed buildings such as the post office in the Talborjt neighbourhood of Agadir had been spared, even though they were located very close to the epicentre. In contrast, the rest of this district, erected in poor-quality masonry, was in ruins (Fig. 1). The urgent need to think in a different way about the architecture of the city was, for a seismologist such as Rothé, crystal clear.[3]

RECONSTRUCTING URBAN AND POSTCOLONIAL CONDITIONS

Only a few days after the earthquake of 29 February 1960, Moroccan King Mohammed V and his son Prince Moulay Hassan, who was appointed to lead the rescue operations,

Fig. 1
King Mohammed V
visits the ruins of Agadir
after the earthquake.
Fig. 2
Effects of the earth-
quake: destroyed
buildings in red and
repairable buildings
in black.

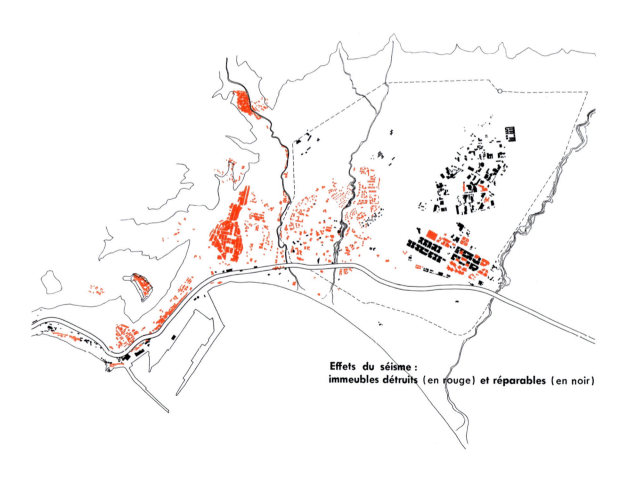

Effets du séisme :
immeubles détruits (en rouge) et réparables (en noir)

publicly announced the start of the reconstruction works in Agadir (Fig. 2).[4] When, on 2 March 1960, the first rescue activities were over, the crown prince declared that a new city would be built in a time span of a single year and that this would be achieved with the help and 'spirit of solidarity' of other nations (Fig. 3).[5] An editorial in the Moroccan newspaper *Al-Istiqlal* maintained a few days later that this reconstruction would not only encompass 'a new Agadir but also, and above all, a new Morocco'.[6]

French critics of decolonisation, such as the writer André Figueres, were full of scepticism about Morocco's capacities to reconstruct the annihilated city. In the French newspaper *Le Figaro*, Figueres maintained that Morocco's first French resident-general, Hubert Lyautey, 'had conjured Agadir out of the marvellous but deserted sands of the Moroccan South' and had single-handedly brought the discipline of urbanism to the Moroccan territory.[7] He wondered, now that the country's governance had been handed over to what he called 'the archaic feudal regime', if anything would remain of Lyautey's legacy? The French critic loudly enquired whether 'Morocco did not still need Lyautey?'[8] Figueres' discriminatory comments illustrate the way in which some neocolonial voices in France looked upon the reconstruction of Agadir not only as a 'stress test' for the young independent Moroccan nation state but also as an opportunity to reinstate colonial relations.

Within days of the first announcement of the reconstruction of Agadir, the Moroccan government approached the French Republic to request assistance.[9] Four years after independence, mutual relations between the two states remained very intense. Morocco's Ministère des Travaux Publics (Ministry of Public Works) and its Service de l'Urbanisme (Department of Urbanism) were still dependent, even at the highest levels, on French coopérants. These 13,000 French professionals worked for the Government of Morocco

under the terms of a bilateral convention. Their presence meant that strong diplomatic relations were maintained between the two countries. These implied not only that France was well informed about Moroccan political viewpoints but also was deeply involved in so-called 'technical assistance' for the realisation of concrete modernisation projects in the former colony.

Within the context of this specific postcolonial condition, two high-level French coopérants – the secretary-general to the minister of public works and the engineer-in-chief of the Service de l'Urbanisme – travelled to Paris on 7 March 1960 to request reconstruction aid from the former coloniser. They made an explicit plea to the French government to send a team of highly qualified urban designers to develop a reconstruction plan for Agadir and define seismic building standards for the reconstruction. In addition, they enquired about the possibility of providing technicians to reinforce the Moroccan Ministry of Public Works as well as of commissioning expert firms that had gained experience with the reconstruction of Orléansville to make an inventory of the remaining buildings and roads. Though the total cost of all of these aid measures was considered very high, estimated at 16 million French francs, the French government initially agreed upon the idea of providing aid – if only because it wanted to maintain its influence in the realm of technical assistance in Morocco.

URBAN PLANNING AS COLD WAR POLITICS

However, the reconstruction of Agadir was coloured not only by the legacy of French colonialism but also by Cold War geopolitics. Next to France, the United States had long made attempts to increase its influence in Morocco with a military presence at Port Lyautey and three strategic airbases elsewhere in the country. As a result, American forces, alongside French and Moroccan army troops, could play a prominent role in the immediate rescue and aid actions after the Agadir earthquake. US soldiers were amongst the first to rescue casualties and to provide survivors with goods and infrastructure. The provision of aid during the initial days following the earthquake, but also for the reconstruction, was explicitly looked upon by American politicians as a way in which to obtain a more significant foothold on Moroccan territory. Conversely, Morocco's leaders – especially Minister of Public Works Abderrahmane ben Abdelali and Crown Prince Moulay Hassan – regarded this American interest in Morocco as ideal ground on which to construct a path to greater independence from the former French coloniser.

Given this international interest in Morocco, the reconstruction of the city of Agadir would become a truly geopolitical battleground on which architecture and urban design played a key role. A month after the earthquake, the French ambassador in Morocco officially invited the renowned Swiss-born French architect Le Corbusier to visit Agadir, hoping to convince him and the Moroccan government to collaborate on the reconstruction project. This rapprochement was, however, short-lived. The Moroccan officials rejected Le Corbusier's ideas for reconstruction – his request for 'carte blanche' in the reconstruction design, in particular, encountered stiff opposition. Already during his short stay in Morocco, it had become clear that he would not be given the commission. Nevertheless, Le Corbusier found a way to leave his mark on Agadir by pointing out, in a radio interview during his travels, that the most crucial aspect for the success of the reconstruction project would be active concertation between the different and various urban planners – a feature that he called urbanisme solidaire (an urbanism of solidarity) (Fig. 4).[10]

The idea that independent Morocco would not solely rely on the former coloniser's urban design and architectural expertise was clear

from the very beginning. A few days after the earthquake, on 4 March 1960, Prince Moulay Hassan had already outlined the idea of a joint international reconstruction to the US ambassador, Charles Yost. The prince imagined that experts from several countries – including the US, France and some other unspecified nations – would contribute towards rebuilding the city by working on different neighbourhoods and different buildings. In an attempt to further emancipate the country from the French metropole, Prince Moulay Hassan invited the US ambassador to solicit a vast amount of help from American experts. A formal request was made to appoint an innovative and modern American urban planner to Morocco – preferably José Luis Sert, the Spanish-born dean of the Graduate School of Design at Harvard University. In addition, the minister of public works, Abderrahmane ben Abdelali, asked for the services of American experts in the domains of seismology, geology, housing and architecture. This intense solicitation of American aid represented not only Morocco's will to establish a critical distance from the former coloniser. It also illustrates how strategic engagement with international aid by Moroccan leaders allowed them to position the young sovereign nation in the context of broader geopolitical power relations and models of modernisation.

Hence, it was no coincidence that the commission for the reconstruction plan of Agadir was awarded in April 1960 to the American firm of Harland Bartholomew and Associates, who had been responsible for the urban planning of the Washington Metro and the St. Louis waterfront.[11] As a chairman of the National Capitol Planning Commission, urban planner Harland Bartholomew epitomised the American approach to planning and modernisation. The US State Department paid his firm to prepare a plan for the reconstruction of Agadir. However, his design soon became contested. Moroccan officials considered his firm to be insufficiently engaged with the local realities of Agadir and evaluated its

Fig. 3
Prince Hassan II and
an urban designer
discussing the plans
for a new Agadir,
14 March 1960.
Fig. 4
Le Corbusier's
encounter with
Prince Hassan II.

URBANISME SOLIDAIRE: CODES AND CONVENTIONS AS PROJECT FOR A NEW CITY

plans as too abstract and too costly. Provoked by the key roles that the government had given to American experts, such as George Schobinger in the realm of housing and Harland Bartholomew in the domain of urban planning, the Moroccan architects and urban designers who worked at the national Service de l'Urbanisme started to develop an alternative vision for the reconstruction of Agadir. In reaction to these plans, the Moroccan king and government discontinued collaboration with Harland Bartholomew and Associates after a few months. They thereby also weakened the diplomatic relationship with the United States. Nevertheless, the reality remained that the reconstruction of Agadir could only be realised with the aid of numerous foreign experts.

THE HAUT COMMISSARIAT À LA RECONSTRUCTION

In order to combine the large variety of foreign and local urban design expertise into a concerted reconstruction process, the Moroccan government created the Haut Commissariat à la Reconstruction d'Agadir (High Committee for the Reconstruction of Agadir, HCRA) on 21 July 1960.[12] This large and powerful technical administration was legally installed for the duration of the reconstruction of Agadir.[13] It was headed by a high commissioner, who was typically a senior civil servant – the first post-holder being Mohamed Imani, an engineer from the Ponts et Chaussées (Bridges and Roads) Department.[14]

The Haut Commissariat was given sweeping power in various domains of the reconstruction: it developed all the main urban principles and plans, it managed allotments and building permits on behalf of the municipality, it inspected construction sites, it handled all general and aid budgets, it decided on the demolition of non-authorised buildings and was mandated to expropriate land whenever needed for public use. In addition,

the body was also responsible for informing the disaster-stricken population about all issues relating to new urban planning and reconstruction. Finally, it combined the role of public commissioner and designer with that of the controller of private reconstruction initiatives. The Haut Commissariat initiated and designed public buildings and facilities such as public spaces, public housing, schools, markets and health centres. As a manager of building permits, it still also fully controlled the design of private commissions such as single houses, private apartment buildings, shops and factories. Every architect operating in the city of Agadir, local or foreign, had to engage with it. In other words, the omnipotent Haut Commissariat decided on the design of literally every building for the reconstruction of Agadir.

To achieve all of these tasks, the Haut Commissariat was divided into various departments.[15] The development of urban principles and plans for the reconstruction, as well as the granting of building permits, was the responsibility of the Service de l'Urbanisme – a satellite office of the national administration with the same name. The Bureau de Contrôle (Control Office) monitored the strict application of building permits and regulations, controlling all the building sites and supervising tenders. The Service des Affaires Foncières (Land Affairs Department) assisted citizens with acquiring new building plots, while the Service Voiries et Réseaux Divers (Department of Roads and Networks) was in charge of highway and technical infrastructures. Checking the stability of buildings and their compliance with anti-seismic regulations was the responsibility of the Société de Contrôle Technique et d'Expertise de la Construction (Company for Technical Control and Construction Expertise, SOCOTEC). All departments of the Haut Commissariat were supported by the Service de Comptabilité (Accounting Department). As Bruce Falconer reported in 1966, the Haut Commissariat counted no fewer than 407 employees and was housed amid the building activities, in temporary structures in the midst of the city centre of Agadir (Fig. 5).[16]

OF OPEN PLANS AND LANDSCAPE

The enormous powers endowed upon the Haut Commissariat laid the foundations for a new approach to urban design. The basis for this novel urban design attitude lay in the experiences and skills that a group of urban planners, landscape architects and architects had acquired at the national Service de l'Urbanisme.[17] Within this colonial administration, vast knowledge had been generated on how to think about urban design as a more dynamic matter than hitherto. For instance, the French architect Michel Écochard, who led the Service de l'Urbanisme between 1946 and 1952, made a clear distinction between the short-term temporality of architecture and the enduring legacy of urban design: 'Put the factors into order: Urbanism (permanent) in the first place, Construction (transitory) afterwards.'[18] The city's architecture was considered part of a process of continuous change; hence, Écochard wrote, 'Moroccan Habitation, like any object of mass consumption, follows the cycle: conception, production, distribution, utilisation, elimination. One must consider this fact, and one must be far-seeing.'[19] From such a perspective, the colonial Service de l'Urbanisme had been developing various urban design instruments – amongst others, a specific urban grid – that allowed for various simultaneous architectural initiatives and constant transformations in the built environment while retaining a certain urban coherence.

This dynamic approach to urban design would become a shared experience for many architects working at the colonial Service de l'Urbanisme in the late 1940s and the beginning of the 1950s. When in 1960 the Service de l'Urbanisme became a department in the postcolonial Haut Commissariat – directed by

Moroccan architects Abdeslem Faraoui and, subsequently, his successor Mourad Ben Embarek – this shared experience became an important guide (Fig. 6).[20] Some of the long-time collaborators with the Service de l'Urbanisme – like the urban planner Pierre Mas, the architects Éliane Castelnau and Claude Beurret, and the landscape architect Jean Challet – would use this shared experience to lay the foundations of an alternative approach to modern urban design.

A key feature of this new approach was the fact that the reconstruction of Agadir did not take the form of a blueprint for an ideal future, as was the case with many new towns that were being planned concurrently in Europe. Instead, the urban design for this city of 50,000 inhabitants on a site of 500 hectares took a more open character, allowing for different architects to work simultaneously on the reconstruction. This more open attitude was based on a combination of various urban design instruments. A Plan Directeur (General Plan) by the Service de l'Urbanisme established the foundation and consisted of three parts: first, an economic analysis of the city, province and hinterland; second, a study of the topography, climate, cultural practices and densities in the city of Agadir; third, an evaluation of the temporary accommodation constructed immediately after the disaster, combined with a report on the different viewpoints that politicians, urban planners and architects had been developing for the future reconstruction of the city. The conclusions of the three parts were summarised in a new urban plan, which determined in very broad brushstrokes the various zones of the city – including an administrative zone, a commercial and industrial sector, a touristic area and several residential zones.

Based on the General Plan, a process of consultation with various Moroccan and foreign architects was begun by the Service de l'Urbanisme, which allowed the further development and concretisation of these urban

Fig. 5
The offices of the Haut
Commissariat à la
Reconstruction d'Agadir
(in barracks) in the midst
of Agadir's city centre.

Fig. 6
Prince Hassan II during
an official audience
with Morrocan archi-
tects led by Abdeslem
Faraoui and Mourad
Ben Embarek.

Fig. 7
Model of the 1961 Plan
d'Aménagement by
Pierre Mas and Jean
Challet of the Service
de l'Urbanisme.

Fig. 8
The new public realm as
a continuous landscape.

ideas into a so-called Plan d'Aménagement (Development Plan) by the end of 1961 (Fig. 7). Though this Plan d'Aménagement had the intention of being more precise, it was understood as an initial stance that was entirely negotiable. It mainly defined general principles, such as the use of a clear, orthogonal urban grid. Still, its most innovative characteristic resulted from the involvement of several landscape architects at the Service de l'Urbanisme. They were instrumental in articulating a conception of urban design that did not start from traditional urban elements such as the street and the square. Instead, they considered the landscape as the prime organising urban feature.

On a large-scale level, the topographical, natural and cultural characteristics of the landscape were used as regulators of urban development. The Service de l'Urbanisme specified that the main parts of the city should be situated in the higher areas, and reserved lower parts and thalwegs for public gardens, woodland and sports grounds.[21] The low coastal landscape was conceptualised as an untouched natural zone, which would allow the city to accommodate modern coastal tourism and offer a buffer zone for high sea waves after any future earthquake. The Oued Tanaout (Waddi Tanaout) landscape, which before the earthquake had marked the boundary between the European quarter and the industrial area where the Moroccan working-class population lived, was channelled and bridged. The erasure of this geographical boundary symbolised the political will to leave behind the cultural distinctions of the colonial era and to build a modern city based on principles of equality.

On a smaller-scale level, the landscape architects of the Service de l'Urbanisme developed a new conception of public space. From this novel perspective, the public realm was no longer understood as the counter-form of the built spaces in the city but rather as a continuous landscape that was prolonged – in the form of passages, interior streets and gallery spaces – within the various buildings of the city. Taking its point of departure from the specific topographical conditions, the Service de l'Urbanisme designed a landscape of large open plazas, platforms and terraces that were continued in covered public galleries, interior plazas and arcades as well as in gardens and parks. (Fig. 8) The Service de l'Urbanisme maintained that this would introduce a modern public realm in Agadir, fostering new social relations.

Both on large- and on small-scale levels, the articulation of the landscape would become an essential instrument of urban design, which allowed the Service de l'Urbanisme to combine clear definition with openness to future urban development. As one of its landscape architects, Jean Challet, summarised,

> [t]he landscape plan helps to specify protected areas (natural reserves, archaeological or historical heritage), areas for agriculture and forestry, for tourism and recreation, for urban development, and for industry. [. . .] But, it also intervenes directly in the internal structure of neighbourhoods. It allows to create, or prepare, a coherent and organised framework that can influence the development, the composition and the architecture of the neighbourhood.[22]

The Plan Directeur and the Plan d'Aménagement, with its reliance on the landscape, offered a general framework for urban development. Various architects from Morocco and abroad could start designing buildings within the context of these openly defined plans and thus simultaneously contribute to the vast project of the reconstruction of Agadir.

NORMES AGADIR 1960: HIDDEN IDIOM OF A MODERN AFROPOLIS

How could such openly defined plans, which were interpreted by various architects from different backgrounds and nationalities, be combined into a consistent image for a new city? The answer lies in a third urban design instrument that complemented the Plan Directeur and the Plan d'Aménagement: the Normes Agadir 1960. On 21 December 1960, Crown Prince Hassan II signed the so-called Dahir (Royal Decree) No. 2-60-893.[23] Based on norms developed in countries like Japan, the USA, and Italy, this decree defined a set of anti-seismic building standards that became applicable to all construction within the urban perimeter of Agadir. Normes Agadir 1960, a thirty-four-page document, was de facto a new building code for the city that contained, next to specifications about the quality of the soil and the solidity of foundations, no fewer than seven pages on particular requirements about the materials and the construction methods of the buildings.

On the level of load-bearing structure, the Agadir code specified that

> buildings have simple structural forms in plan and elevation. The structural forms of buildings must permit the incorporation of adequate bracing (by panels or frames) for the full height, and in two principal horizontal directions. Ties are required between all foundation elements. Complete structural separation of a minimum of 5 cm (2 inches) distance is required between adjoining buildings, and also between discrete structural entities of long buildings, and at the junctional parts of buildings of complex shape (U, L, T etc.).[24]

However, not only were the layout and construction methods of the buildings the subject of this new building code; the character and extent of their materials were also defined in considerable detail:

> Masonry may be of burnt clay brick, concrete block or of stone, unreinforced, but must be contained in panels supported around the perimeters by reinforced concrete work. The supporting concrete work may be the frame of a building supplemented where necessary by intermediate concrete members of wall thickness. Panels are limited in size so that specified intervals of support, horizontally and vertically, are not exceeded. Masonry walls, if presumed in design to support vertical loads, must include additionally a supplementary reinforced concrete support member longitudinally at the mid-storey height. Support members must have both primary and stirrup [shear-resistant] reinforcement.[25]

Intended originally as a set of technical standards that could avoid major damage in case of future seismic activity, in reality these specifications started to outline a particular architectural idiom. Normes Agadir 1960 defined an architecture of fair-faced concrete beams, columns and frames combined with infills of plastered masonry and natural stone as a common architectural language to rebuild the city's various public and private buildings – as well as its public infrastructures such as fountains, ramps and stairs. This idiom functioned as a common code for the numerous architects working on the reconstruction of the centre of Agadir, including the French Émile-Jean Duhon, Henri Tastemain and Éliane Castelnau; Moroccans Élie Azagury and Mourad Ben Embarek; and the Moroccan-born French architect Jean-François Zevaco. Though their buildings in the reconstructed centre of Agadir differed largely in terms of typology, layout and attitude towards public space, time and time again the Normes Agadir 1960 assured a certain coordination of materiality, tectonics and expression. Constructed in a very short time and by numerous architects simultaneously, the city of Agadir acquired, due to this common code, an urban consistency (Figs. 9, 10, 11 & 12).

Figs. 9–12
Buildings designed by different architects were constructed with similar materials and technologies that correspond to the Normes Agadir 1960.

URBANISME SOLIDAIRE: CODES AND CONVENTIONS AS PROJECT FOR A NEW CITY

Fig. 13
Buildings and walkways in the Cité Administrative, defined in a common language of concrete beams and columns.

Figs. 14–16
The Normes Agadir 1960 specified an idiom of *béton brut* that allowed different architects to articulate the various forms of the modern Afropolis.

Such consistency in the way of building also depended upon the capacity to produce materials locally. As several reports maintain, in a short time period the construction sector in Agadir transferred to a way of building that complied with the Normes Agadir 1960 (Fig. 13).[26] Portland cement was manufactured by factories in the northern industrial area of the city. At the same time, coarse aggregate was sourced by specialised companies from the hard-limestone quarries sixteen kilometres north-west of the city centre, and sand was obtained from the dunes along the shore. Small construction firms mixed these different components mechanically and poured the concrete from wheelbarrows into the formwork of the various buildings. They also made the concrete blocks for partitions on site and sometimes finished them with plaster, either naturally white or painted. This availability of practical and material knowledge that corresponded to the specifications of the Normes Agadir 1960, combined with architects designing within the confines of the new building code, offered a powerful basis from which to construct Agadir as a consistent urban artefact of *béton brut* (raw concrete) (Figs. 14, 15 & 16).

ASSISTED URBAN DESIGN

To assure that the Normes Agadir 1960 were implemented and to coordinate the reconstruction of Agadir with its numerous private commissioners, as well as its multiple architects and construction companies, the Haut Commissariat developed a model of what could be called 'assisted urban design'. This peculiar modus operandi entailed the Haut Commissariat playing the role of an engaged *régisseur* (director) in the design process and exercising firm control over all reconstruction phases.

This role of *régisseur* ensured that the Haut Commissariat, in an initial phase, preselected designers and offered commissioners the possibility to choose their architects from a panel of about twelve preferred offices and in clear agreement with the Haut Commissariat. Subsequently, the architectural office had to discuss the initial design of its building with the Service de l'Urbanisme before undertaking construction drawings and writing specifications. All structural plans and drawings of reinforced-concrete work or steelwork were to be made by an engineering office, which could be selected from a panel of six firms that the Haut Commissariat approved.

Throughout the construction phase of the various buildings, the Haut Commissariat continued to play a central role. It directly selected construction firms and subcontractors in consultation with the architect and commissioner. Its functionaries also led the negotiations about price rates with contractors and subcontractors. When construction was ongoing, they supervised the quality of the work. While the architect was considered responsible for the general site supervision, all structural-engineering supervision was undertaken by SOCOTEC.

From the conception to the construction phase, the Haut Commissariat thus played for private commissioners the roles of regulator, coordinator and administrator. Above all, however, it functioned as *régisseur* of the reconstruction of Agadir – which ensured time and time again that the various buildings complied with the building codes of the Normes Agadir 1960 but also, above all, assisted commissioners and architects to work within the conventions that had been decided upon for the reconstruction of the city. In combination with its role as commissioner and designer of public buildings and infrastructures, the Haut Commissariat kept strong control over the reconstruction of Agadir without relying on static blueprints and while allowing for negotiation and dynamism. The result of this assisted urban design is astonishing. While numerous commissioners and multiple architects contributed to the reconstruction

Fig. 17
Aerial image of the
reconstructed city
centre.

of the city, Agadir stands to this day as an example of a modern city simultaneously characterised by diversity and unity (Fig. 17).

URBANISME SOLIDAIRE: ANOTHER APPROACH TO URBAN DESIGN

Seismologist Jean-Pierre Rothé could probably not have imagined that his recommendations for buildings that could survive new seismic challenges would evolve into a new paradigm for planning and realising a modern city. Based on anti-seismic concerns and propelled by the necessity to rapidly provide new housing and communal services for the inhabitants of the destroyed city, local politicians, urban planners, landscape architects and architects developed during the ambitious reconstruction process of Agadir a new mode in which to design a city.

The Normes Agadir 1960, their interplay with the Plan Directeur and the Plan d'Aménagement, and the intense assistance of the Haut Commissariat offered a new definition of urban design. In this other urban design approach, the city is not regarded as a condition that can be controlled by a single planner or by a static plan that offers a perfect blueprint for future urban development. Instead, the design of the city is considered a matter of collective labour that needs to be constantly adjusted, accommodated and negotiated. In Agadir, the base for this collective labour was provided by the public landscape defined in the Plan d'Aménagement. The Normes Agadir 1960 offered the idiom – a language that allowed different architects to articulate the forms of the modern Afropolis – while the Service de l'Urbanisme of the Haut Commissariat played the role of engaged *régisseur*.

Against this backdrop, the statement about the need for an *urbanisme solidaire* by Le Corbusier seems to have been prophetic. While the French-Swiss architect may have thought about the city's urban design as the sum of various acts of solidarity and mutual aid, in the actual practice of the city of Agadir the notion received a completely new definition. *Urbanisme solidaire* came to represent an approach by which various designers, through the juxtaposition of large architectural projects, cooperatively constructed the city as a large collective artefact (Fig. 18). Such an approach could only exist because of the presence of material and construction expertise and of the use of specific urban planning tools. The combination of definition and openness, which is to be found in the Plan d'Aménagement and the Normes Agadir 1960, provided the framework for the concerted contribution of various architects assisted by the conventions of the Haut Commissariat. Against this backdrop, the rebuilding of Agadir not only stands as a tantalising saga of the swift realisation of a modern Afropolis; it also represents a unique approach to urbanism, based on codes and conventions.

Fig. 18
A variety of different
housing typologies that
are bound by a common
architectural idiom.

1
Rothé, Jean-Pierre, 'Le tragique bilan des séismes de 1960', *La Nature*, no. 3305 (1960), pp. 378–87 (p. 379). [Translation by the author.]

2
Ibid.

3
Rothé's argument about the necessity of a different architecture was repeated in successive studies such as Clough, Ray W., *The Agadir, Morocco Earthquake, February 29, 1960*, New York: American Iron and Steel Institute, 1962.

4
King Mohammed V announced his plans for a new Agadir and proposed his son as a coordinator in a speech delivered on 1 March 1960, parts of which were republished in multiple newspapers such as *Al Aman*.

5
'Agadir détruit aux trois quarts par un terrible tremblement de terre nocturne', *Le Figaro*, 2 March 1960. 'Prince Moulay Hassan, who was appointed by King Mohammed V to lead the rescue operations, told me this evening. "The city will have to be razed to the ground to build another one. You foreign journalists, you should be our interpreters to other nations so that they show their spirit of solidarity and that we can rebuild Agadir within a year".' [Translation by the author.]

6
'Des problèmes qui demeure', *Al-Istiqlal*, 12 March 1960. See also, 'Il faut reconstruire Agadir', *Al-Istiqlal*, 5 March 1960. [Translation by the author.]

7
André Figueres, 'Le crime d'Agadir', as cited in Segalla, Spencer D., *Empire and Catastrophe: Decolonization and Environmental Disaster in North Africa and Mediterranean France since 1954*, Lincoln NE: University of Nebraska Press, 2020, p. 129 / JSTOR, www.jstor.org/stable/j.ctv10crdt6 (accessed 7 July 2021).

8
Figueres, 'Le crime d'Agadir', as cited in Segalla, *Empire and Catastrophe*, p. 129.

9
These paragraphs are strongly informed by the highly detailed description of this process of soliciting international aid by Segalla in *Empire and Catastrophe*.

10
The radio interview can be consulted on the website of INA.fr – Institut National Audiovisuel: boutique.ina.fr/audio/P13276317/le-corbusier-a-propos-de-la-reconstruction-d-agadir.fr.html (accessed 27 July 2021).

11
Harland Bartholomew and Associates. *Agadir Master Plan*, Rabat, 1960.

12
On 21 July 1960, King Mohammed V decreed the creation of a High Commission for the Reconstruction of Agadir (HCRA) placed under the authority of the crown prince by Dahir (Royal Decree) no. 1-60-165 of 26 Muharram 1380 (21 July 1960) with a high commissioner in charge of informing the prince on the execution of the reconstruction plan of Agadir and on all the questions related to it.

13
The Haut Commissariat would exist between 1960 and 1972.

14
He was succeeded by Mohamed Bel Hadj Soulami, another engineer from the Ponts. From 1965 onwards, the Governors-General Bel Larbi and M. A. Ben Hammou held the position of high commissioner.

15
Collaborators with the Haut Commissariat include engineer Michel Pariat, in charge of the technical aspects of earthquake reconstruction; administrators Janin and Marty, responsible for accounting; architects Philippon, Berthelet, Sylvie, Torres and Reis; and building engineers Bombezy, Wuillaume, Etienne, Hedde, Lucas, Coupois, Lary and Donguy.

16
Falconer, Bruce H., 'Agadir, Morocco, reconstruction work six years after the earthquake of February 1960', *Bulletin of the New Zealand Society for Earthquake Engineering*, vol. 1, no. 2 (1968), pp. 72–91.

17
For an introduction to the work of the Service de l'Urbanisme in colonial Morocco, see Avermaete, Tom and Maristella Casciato, *Casablanca Chandigarh: A Report on Modernization*, Zurich: Park Books, 2014.

18
GAMMA architects, Habitat for the Greatest Number Grid, Panel series: 'The Problem', unpublished presentation at CIAM IX, Aix-en-Provence, 1953. Phototheque Ecole Nationale d'Architecture de Rabat.

19
Ibid.

20
Mas, Pierre. 'Plan Directeur et Plans d'aménagement', *A+U: Revue Africaine d'Architecture et d'Urbanisme*, 5 (1966), pp. 6–17 (p. 6); Péré, M., 'Agadir, ville nouvelle', *Revue de Géographie du Maroc*, no. 12 (1967), p. 57. [Translation by the author.]

21
Mas, 'Plan Directeur', p. 11. [Translation by the author.]

22
Challet, Jean, 'Urbanisme et Paysage', *A+U: Revue Africaine d'Architecture et d'Urbanisme*, 3 (1965), pp. 16–22 (p. 21). [Translation by author.]

23
Dahir no. 2-60-893 of 2 Rajab1380 (21 December 1960) applied to constructions inside the municipal perimeter of Agadir and the development zone defined by the dahir of 27 Rabi II 1371 (25 January 1952). See adala.justice.gov.ma/production/html/Fr/120597.htm (accessed 29 July 2021).

24
Falconer, 'Reconstruction work six years after the earthquake', p. 79.

25
Ibid.

26
Ibid., p. 87.

THE CONTACT ZONE OF AGADIR'S EMERGENCY AID OPERATIONS

Cathelijne Nuijsink

For a mere few seconds during the night of 29 February 1960, the third night of Ramadan, the earth beneath Agadir city trembled – an earthquake measuring a modest 5.7 on the Richter scale had hit the city. However, what followed was nothing short of a tragedy. The exceptional violence of the earthquake, followed by a second shock and a fire, devastated the city in minutes (Fig.1). A total of 15,000 lives were lost, 25,000 citizens were injured, and most survivors lost their homes.[1] The old kasbah – the citadel strategically situated 230 metres above sea level on a hill overlooking the ocean, which had served to protect the city and its port from possible foreign invasions since 1540 – was razed to the ground despite its metre-thick walls.[2] Other areas also largely built from traditional masonry and rammed earth, such as the Founti quarter adjacent to the beach and the poor inland district of Yachech, were instantly wiped out, burying thousands of Moroccans in the rubble.[3] The structural weaknesses of the modern-looking buildings in Agadir's city centre, normally hidden behind their plastered walls, were exposed after the sudden, violent shocks. Once the commercial heart of Agadir, Talborjt, was now, according to an eyewitness, 'nothing more than a bloodletting in a sea of stones, where the dead and the living rub shoulders in the midst of an awful inventory of punctured carpets, babouches, onion baskets, cardboard suitcases, children's carriages'. At least 60 per cent of the buildings were destroyed.[4] Even the newly built Ville Nouvelle, constructed in 1947 by French colonisers between Ancien Talborjt and the beach, and the touristic area Front-de-Mer (Seafront), adjacent to the beach, could not withstand the quake. Many of the modern apartment buildings housing the Europeans were half standing but ripped open and terribly damaged. Moreover, the luxurious resort hotels at Front-de-Mer – the accommodation for tourists arriving at 'the Miami of North Africa' – could not resist the shocks of what was the most

Fig. 1
The exceptionally
violent earthquake
devastated the city
in minutes.
Fig. 2
Ruins of the luxurious
Saada resort hotel in
Agadir.

destructive 'moderate' earthquake of the twentieth century, and the deadliest earthquake in Morocco up to that point (Fig. 2).[5]

FIRST AID DISASTER-RELIEF OPERATIONS

Soldiers and sailors stationed in the vicinity of Agadir were quick to fetch help and kick-start the rescue operations. Despite political tensions – Morocco was still in the process of decolonialisation four years after gaining formal independence from France on 2 March 1956 – the French Navy provided immediate assistance.[6] Since the Moroccan Army troops were paralysed – desperately looking for their own relatives while simultaneously suffering heavy losses in personnel and equipment – it was the French Army that assumed the lead in the immediate rescue operations.[7] Within an hour of the earthquake, the first of the 1,500 French soldiers stationed at the undamaged aero–naval base just south of Agadir arrived on site, followed by French civilian and military doctors, to rescue citizens from the ruins and treat as many injured people as possible.[8] When King Mohammed V arrived by plane from Rabat the next morning to observe the damage, the immediate on-the-ground rescue operations took new directions.

After conducting his inventory, Mohammed V placed his son, Prince Moulay Hassan, in charge of the rescue operations; in response, the prince started to direct a massive rescue effort and ordered Moroccan troops from all parts of the country to come to Agadir and search for survivors under the ruins (Fig. 3).[9] Besides the French and Moroccan armies, American soldiers stationed near Casablanca also played a crucial role in the very first aid operations. With Morocco's own air force still in its infancy, the deployment of foreign aircraft in the relief operations made a significant difference.[10] On the eve of the first day after the quake, the US Embassy in Rabat provided two transport planes that flew an initial delegation of the League of Red Cross Societies, as well as stretchers and the relief workers, to Agadir. This initial rescue flight would come to mark the start of a comprehensive, worldwide humanitarian-aid campaign on an unprecedented scale.[11]

INTERNATIONAL SOLIDARITY

The League of Red Cross Societies in Geneva took a pivotal role in the coordination of the international aid campaign. Following an urgent appeal from the Moroccan government for help, the League, on 2 March, called on Red Cross and Red Crescent societies worldwide with a plea to send doctors, nurses, medical supplies and funds (Fig. 4).[12] The Red Cross societies of Belgium, Great Britain, the Netherlands and Switzerland assembled their own medical teams and immediately dispatched surgeons and nurses to Morocco (Fig. 5). A second plea launched by the League of Red Cross Societies the next day requested specific medical supplies as well as food, clothing, blankets, camp beds and tentage. An overwhelming number of sixty-one sister societies responded to the call, and the French and American aid workers were soon joined by those of West Germany, England, Spain, Portugal, Italy and Yugoslavia, bringing food, medicines, vaccines, blood plasma, surgeons and nurses. The Swiss Red Cross assembled its own medical team and dispatched – together with food, medicine, blankets and clothes – a care team to Morocco to work in local hospitals.[13] The German Red Cross launched a successful relief-and-donation campaign, collecting hundreds of thousands of German marks for the benefit of the earthquake victims while sending reconstruction experts and development experts from the Federal Office for Civil Protection to Morocco.[14] Other countries had doctors on standby at home to answer calls from medical staff at hospitals in Agadir (Fig. 6).

On 2 March, an efficient air bridge between Casablanca and Agadir was set up to accommodate the influx of medical staff and medical goods. A fleet made up of fifteen transport airplanes from the United States Air Force – together with another forty-five aeroplanes donated by Britain, France, Portugal, Spain and West Germany – formed a professional emergency corridor of people and goods between the two cities. The air bridge allowed not only an influx of medical specialists, stretchers and relief goods but also the evacuation of injured people out of Agadir to hospitals elsewhere (Fig. 7). French planes, for example, used it to bring stretchers, bandages and medicines to Agadir while on their way back evacuating the seriously injured to hospitals across Morocco, in Marrakesh, Casablanca and as far afield as Paris, Toulon and Marseilles.[15] With no airbase nearby, West Germany's sympathy for the victims translated into sending a Bundeswehr (Armed Forces) medical unit. No fewer than thirty-six Noratlas transport aircrafts left Cologne-Wahn Airport to bring doctors and medical staff to Agadir – as well as a complete field hospital, medical supplies and food.[16] The mission of the Bundeswehr was politically charged as this goodwill 'exercise' was the very first of its kind. Since the Second World War, no German soldiers had been deployed abroad out of fear of their actions being misconstrued – yet their humanitarian mission was much appreciated in Morocco.[17] The Bundeswehr set up its very own military hospital, a modern, fully equipped main dressing station that was ceremonially handed over to Morocco after the mission was completed.[18]

Another effort to aid Agadir came through the establishment of a sea bridge between Agadir and Casablanca. Upon hearing the news of the destructive earthquake, a squadron of French, Spanish and Italian warships and merchant ships in the waters of the Canary Islands immediately set sail for the city.[19] Anchored near Agadir, these vessels were converted into floating military hospitals.

The Dutch naval Smaldeel (squadron), on a mission in the Mediterranean Sea, changed course from its journey home and headed for Agadir with four warships.[20] Within the day, they reached Agadir and anchored close to the coast to discuss with the local Moroccans what help they could offer. 'If we could search for survivors in the poor district of Founti', was the local response, since 'nothing was left of that district', reported one of the sailors, Rinus Sporken.[21] Rescue teams were then assembled on board, and with cloths dipped in Dettol for their noses and mouths, some 750 young Dutch sailors – some of them trainees aged only sixteen or seventeen – went ashore to search for survivors amid the ruins during the following three days. Together with Moroccan soldiers spared by the earthquake, these French, Spanish, Dutch and Italian sailors participated in the initial salvage work.

MEDIA COVERAGE

Media coverage of the Agadir catastrophe in the local and international press generated a spontaneous wave of international solidarity and aid for its victims. Spanish fishing vessels anchored in Agadir harbour were the first to report the news of the devastating earthquake.[22] In the early morning of 1 March, Europe learned the news via a concise message from a teletypewriter stating that 'a violent earthquake took place at 1 a.m. in Agadir. Part of the European city was destroyed. Connections are cut with the city.'[23] By 10 a.m., a second news flash reported 'hundreds of deaths and wounded' – numbers that would rise to 20,000, or half of the city's population – over the next few days.[24] Locally, the francophone daily newspaper in Morocco, *La Vigie Marocaine*, and the Moroccan-based newspaper *Le Petit Marocain* started to cover the disaster with richly illustrated daily reports, showing the unfolding of the emergency aid in the immediate aftermath – from the ruins to the soldiers and sailors trying to

Fig. 3
Soldiers searching
for survivors under the
ruins.
   Fig. 4
Report of plea from
the League of Red
Cross Societies
to national Red Cross
organisations.
   Fig. 5
Nurses dispatched
to Morocco.
   Fig. 6
Stretchers from the
Red Cross assembled
in a hangar.

Earthquakes, Morocco, Agadir 29th February 1960

LIGUE DES SOCIÉTÉS DE LA CROIX-ROUGE
40, RUE DU 31 DÉCEMBRE — GENÈVE

Relief Bureau   Geneva
Circular No. 120   8th March, 1960

AGADIR EARTHQUAKE DISASTER - 29th FEBRUARY, 1960

Arising out of the above tragic disaster an appeal was launched by
the League on March 2nd, 1960, to 36 National Societies closest to Morocco, some
of whom were asked for a limited number of surgeons and nurses whilst others
were approached for medical supplies for the urgent treatment of burns and
trauma, and, where possible for funds to meet the emergency in other directions.

The following day a more specific appeal was made for dressings,
antibiotics, antitetanus serum, saline solution, splints, blankets, camp beds,
clothing, tents, rice, lentils, sugar, edible oil, milk, canned vegetables,
coffee and tea. From latest reports it would appear sufficient medical personnel and hospital material have now been made available, but blankets,
bedding, camp beds, tentage and all the food items mentioned above are still
needed.

All shipments should heretofore be addressed as under, and the goods
clearly marked as a gift for "Victims of Agadir":-

                    League of Red Cross Societies
                    for Moroccan Red Crescent,
                    84, Boulevard Joffre,
                    CASABLANCA.

Any National Society in a position to assist the Moroccan Red Crescent
in its present hour of trial, with three separate relief operations taking place
in that country concurrently -- namely for the Paralysis Victims, Algerian
Refugees, and now Agadir Earthquake Survivors -- is requested to provide the
League Secretariat as quickly as possible with exact details of the assistance
already or to be provided, how shipped, date of departure and value, to enable
our staff in Morocco efficiently to trace all donations.

Medical aspects of the operation are being co-ordinated in Rabat with
the Moroccan Red Crescent and the Moroccan Government by Dr. Jean-Jacques
LAURIER, made available by the Canadian Red Cross, and Miss Lilli PETSCHNIGG
of the League Nursing Bureau, while in Casablanca Mr. A.E. REINHARD is responsible for the relief action on behalf of the able-bodied survivors.

        Edward Winsall   Henry W. Dunning
        Director, Relief Bureau   Secretary General

P.8713/mh.

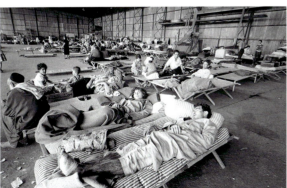

Fig. 7
Foreign planes evacuating seriously injured people to hospitals.
Fig. 8
Agadir's boulevard turned into a graveyard.

Fig. 9
Makeshift homes.
Fig. 10
Soldiers using trucks to spray chloride of lime disinfectants over the ruins.

rescue people with shovels, picks and jack-hammers, to the king's visit to the disaster site, to the clearing of the rubble.[25] The French newspaper *Le Figaro* featured, on 2 March 1960, an article from envoy André Lagny who reported that an entire city had been 'wiped off the map of Morocco' with 'thousands of inhabitants still under the rubble'.[26] Panic-stricken inhabitants – an estimated 30,000 of them homeless – were fleeing the ruins. The French-language weekly news magazine *Paris Match* made the earthquake its cover story, explaining it as 'a tragedy of the walls' since most dwellings had lacked the rigidity to withstand the earthquake and had simply collapsed like houses of cards.[27] A report on the cover of *The New York Times* of 2 March 1960 described the scene of destruction as a 'rubble heap', reporting how the tragedy had led to at least 1,000 deaths and thousands of injuries in the Moroccan resort town, among whom were also Americans.[28] A fierce critical review of the international rescue operation in Agadir came from the influential German weekly magazine *Der Spiegel*, some five months after the earthquake.[29] Referring to the conclusions of a report carried out by the French government, it stated that the international rescue operation was marred by corruption on the part of the Moroccan authorities. It blamed the Moroccan government for down-playing the role of foreign help, for placing foreign aid under the control of the Moroccan Army and for demanding that foreign rescuers subordinate themselves in favour of Prince Moulay Hassan's popularity.

VILLE INTERDITE (PROHIBITED CITY)

Although Moroccan soldiers, French and Dutch sailors, and American troops were all on the scene to rescue people from the ruins, their success was limited. Thousands of victims were engulfed by tonnes of concrete rubble, and Agadir's four-kilometre-long stretch of boulevard soon became a graveyard (Fig. 8).[30]

Survivors fled the horror site and crafted their own makeshift homes with whatever they could salvage on the outskirts of the destroyed city (Fig. 9). Others were brought to emergency shelters and camps at the French military base that was equipped with tents, beds and some furnishings, and were supplied with food by the Red Cross and Red Crescent societies.[31] On the fifth day, Crown Prince Moulay Hassan came to pay one last visit to the various teams working in the ruins. By now, emergency aid was no longer a matter of searching for living, injured people but increasingly a task of taking corpses to mass graves on the outskirts of the city. The atmosphere in Agadir at this point was absolutely inhuman, as radio broadcaster Annemarie Schwyter reported from the field: a city 'shattered, crushed, atomized, smashed by a tremendous force'.[32] The many lifeless bodies in combination with extremely warm temperatures had resulted in a rapid putrefaction of corpses and created fear of an outbreak of typhus, plague or cholera that could have had effects far beyond Agadir. Seeing the sailors and soldiers physically and mentally exhausted, Moulay Hassan decided on 4 March to stop the clearing work and to block all the exits from the city with a sanitary cordon, hermetically sealing it off to declare Agadir a dead city. The Ville Interdite came under the rule of the Moroccan Army, allowing only troops and those with a special permit to access the deserted city. With heavy construction equipment from the US Army, which had arrived from West Germany by airlift, the scant remains of the city were razed to the ground. Bulldozers levelled the few walls that remained standing and cleared the roads to make room for the decontamination crew. For the sake of containment and disease prevention, thousands of unsaved victims thus went to their graves at the site of the disaster.[33] With the help of lorries and helicopters, soldiers sprayed chloride disinfectants over the ruins and put the city to sleep (Fig. 10). From this ground zero, plans for a new Agadir were soon made – a solidarity project that the king had promised his people on the day immediately after the earthquake, but which he was obviously not able to undertake on his own.

REBUILDING AGADIR: THE SWISS CASE

Until the implementation of the new urban plan starting from Spring 1961, a programme for the permanent or provisional rehousing of the victims was drawn up that included the construction of emergency housing as well as prefabricated dwellings in the Quartier Industriel Sud.[34] Different administrations, as well as primary- and secondary-school classrooms, were temporary housed in spacious barracks in the Ville Nouvelle. Another temporary prefab city was built in the neighbouring town of Inezgane, consisting of several thousand semi-permanent homes of lightweight, prefabricated construction. Yet even before the construction of these temporary dwellings could start, King Mohammed V had – a mere four months after the disaster – already laid the first stone of the new Agadir construction site (Fig. 11).[35] The costs of rebuilding were to be partly covered by a newly implemented 'national solidarity tax' that was levied on everyday items and indirectly made every Moroccan a financial contributor to the reconstruction project. These national revenues were complemented by international aid money from countries that had also supported the immediate humanitarian aid. Take the case of Switzerland: besides being a generous donor of emergency aid, Switzerland also provided extensive reconstruction aid and self-initiated the idea of constructing a new neighbourhood in Agadir. Initially, the Swiss donor organisation Glückskette – responsible for collecting money for humanitarian and social projects for populations affected by disasters and humanitarian crises abroad as well as in Switzerland – collected more than a million francs in a couple of weeks after the disaster to support the Swiss nationals living in Agadir. The Swiss Red Cross collected another 1.4 million francs

to help Agadir victims. Since there was still a considerable amount of money left after the emergency phase, a 'Swiss Committee' made up of representatives of the Swiss Embassy in Rabat, the Swiss Consulate in Casablanca, Swiss residents living in Morocco and the Swiss Red Cross was set up to study the question of what to do with the remaining funds. A few weeks after the disaster, the Swiss consul in Casablanca, Joseph Birchler (1907–1987), announced the idea of building a new part of the city with the remaining donations collected in Switzerland.[36] The project initially targeted 150 housing units, twenty shops, twenty-five garages and a youth centre – and the committee assumed that land for the construction of housing units would be made available free of charge by the city of Agadir. Brief minutes of one of the meetings reveal that the committee had decided that the housing units would become the property of the tenants after a period of fifteen years, allowing the dissolution of the management body that they had been obliged to set up.[37] The implementation of the building project was entrusted to the Cité Suisse d'Agadir Foundation, created on 9 May 1961, a collaborative project of the Glückskette, the Swiss Red Cross and the Lausanne newspaper *Feuille d'Avis*.[38] Together, they donated 1.5 million Swiss francs for the making of a new neighbourhood: Cité Suisse (Swiss Neighbourhood).[39] In an 'explanatory note concerning the construction of housing units in Agadir' issued on 26 July 1960, Cité Suisse was presented with a model incorporating eighty housing units, eight shops and a youth centre for the disaster victims.

Morocco-based Swiss architect Albert U. Froelich, a resident of Agadir and himself a survivor of the 1960 earthquake, was part of the Agadir Working Committee and was placed in charge of the architectural design of Cité Suisse because of his knowledge of the terrain and the Moroccan way of life (Fig. 12).[40] Guided by expert reports on earthquake resistance, as well as his own experiences of the Agadir quake, Froelich designed bungalow-type

Fig. 11
King Mohammed V
symbolically laying the
first stone of the new
Agadir construction site.
Fig. 14
Plan of courtyard-type
dwellings in Cité Suisse.

Fig. 12
Plan of Cité Suisse.
Fig. 13
Model of courtyard-type
dwellings in Cité Suisse.

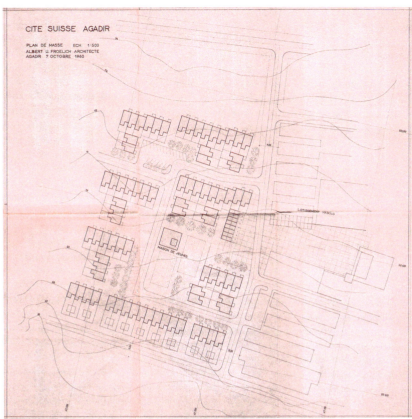

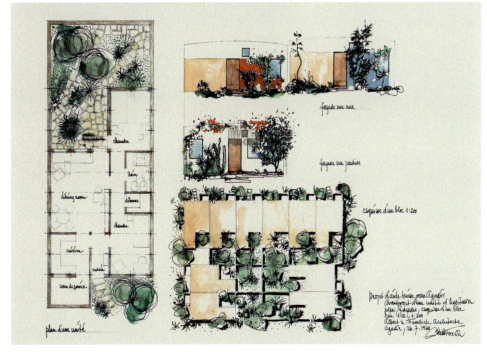

Fig. 15
Aerial view of the
hospital complex.
 Fig. 16.
Plan of the hospital
complex.

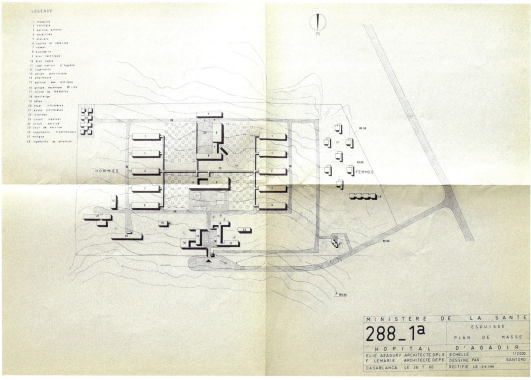

dwellings with special care for their seismic qualities. He opted for a construction system with a semi-rigid frame in which exterior walls and interior partitions made use of a new material composed of sea sand, shells, pulverized cement and lime (Fig. 13). An internal corridor allowed family members to reach all the rooms and the garden without the need for a living room (Fig. 14).[41] More than merely reconstructing new housing targeting Moroccan families, the Cité Suisse was thought of as a project that could support Agadir in the long run. Rents were not only used for maintenance of the buildings but also to cover a programme training young Agadir residents in an artisanal profession and to grant scholarships to students without the resources to attend high school.[42] Cité Suisse was officially opened on 30 July 1965 as a small neighbourhood unit consisting of fifty-six three-room houses, six shops, and a youth centre. Donations from readers of *Feuille d'Avis* were used specifically to build an additional youth centre there.[43] The social aspects of Cité Suisse were linked to the use of this Maison des Jeunes (Youth Centre). It was initially planned as a professional training centre for young Moroccans, but during the construction it was decided to donate the building to the local section of the Red Crescent Youth.[44]

Another key project in the longer-term international aid campaign was the building of a new hospital. Agadir's only such facility had been reduced to a pile of rubble in the earthquake, and alternative premises such as airport hangars temporarily took over the role of hospital during the immediate rescue efforts. Thanks to generous support from the national Red Cross, Red Crescent and Red Lion and Sun societies, relief funds were still available after the first emergency phase. The League of Red Cross Societies played a key role in the design and construction of the hospital by inviting those national Red Cross societies that still held unexpended relief funds for Agadir to contribute towards it. More than a single building, the complex was, from

the start, envisioned as a 'city' that, besides a 500-bed hospital, included laboratories, a nursing school, an administrative centre, a provincial pharmacy, a nurses' home, a boarding school and living quarters for staff on permanent duty (Fig. 15). The hospital was designed as a collaborative project between the Paris-born, Agadir-based architect François Louis Lemarié (1902–1996) and the influential Moroccan architect Élie Azagury (1918–2009) in accordance with the latest anti-seismic methods. The architects opted for a series of ten single-storey pavilions, each with a capacity of fifty beds, separated from each other by a courtyard or gardens for the patients (Fig. 16).[45] Another requirement with which the architects worked was that 'the architecture must be simple in every case avoiding all elliptical or circular construction, either inside or outside, and must be restricted to the classical rectangular style, whether for the technical, operational buildings or those intended for hospitalisation purposes' (Figs. 17 & 18).[46] The Hôpital Hassan II (Hassan II Hospital) came to symbolise global solidarity with the victims of Agadir – and in particular, the Red Cross's international cooperation in rebuilding the city. No fewer than fifty-three national Red Cross organisations contributed to this vast new complex – either through monetary means or with equipment or technical know-how – covering 60 per cent of the construction budget, while the Moroccan government paid the remainder.

RESONANCE OF AID OPERATIONS

This chapter has aimed to illustrate the fact that the emergency aid operations in the wake of the 1960 Agadir earthquake constituted a 'contact zone' between local and international rescuers, experts, citizens, organisations and governments. Only a few years out of the colonial situation, Morocco did not passively wait for aid but showed agency by actively reaching out for help internationally. The tension between the urgent need for assistance, on the one hand, and the negotiations between foreign-aid and Moroccan authorities about the distribution of the aid money, on the other, was present at many levels and also transpired in the built environment. The idea that the development aid was not unconditionally accepted is a typical process of transculturation. As aid receivers, Morocco dared to channel developments in a certain way and at times even reject, refute or push away elements of knowledge exchange. Take the League of Red Cross Societies. Acting as coordinators of the international aid operations, they always had to negotiate with Moroccan authorities and justify their expenses. The 'contact zone' of Agadir's emergency aid operations equally elucidates that its architecture was not merely a matter of stylistic development and formal considerations. The architecture resulting from the collaborations between local and foreign architects and engineers was tied up to a considerable extent with questions of trauma caused by the earthquake and the potential for architecture to provide safe shelter. While rebuilt Agadir showed characteristics that resonated with 'Brutalist' architecture elsewhere in the world, the idea of creating an architecture of stability, protection and credibility dominated to a greater degree. Finally, analysing the aid operations through the lens of 'contact zones' allows us to consider the resonance of development aid in the long term. Widely covered in the media, the destroyed Agadir received an overwhelming volume of aid from across the world. This grand solidarity with the victims of the earthquake was 'monumentalized' in projects such as the Hassan II Hospital, which came to set an example for collaborative aid programmes globally. Undoubtedly, the reconstruction of Agadir was a very fertile moment for architectural production that introduced new urban models into Morocco. Yet the long-term legacy of this architecture can be questioned. Contemporary housing developments on the outskirts of Agadir show little of the great attention to detail and collective spaces that projects like Cité Suisse introduced back in the 1960s.

Fig. 17
The hospital under
construction.
Fig. 18
Exterior of the hospital
complex.

THE CONTACT ZONE OF AGADIR'S EMERGENCY AID OPERATIONS

1

The number of deaths and injuries remains imprecise because only European residents were registered at that time.

2

Howespecial, Marvin, '1,000 feared dead as quakes wreck Moroccan resort; Agadir is heap of rubble—tidal wave and fire hit port city on Atlantic thousands are injured Americans among missing—power and water failure hinder rescue work Agadir is turned into rubble heap tidal wave and fire wreak havoc in beach resort—Americans are missing', *The New York Times*, 2 March 1960.

3

Hicks, David T., 'Rebuilt Agadir', *Architectural Review* 142 (1967), p. 294.

4

Schwyter, Annemarie, 'Agadir ist Tot', *Das Schweizerische Rote Kreuz*, 69, Heft 3 (1960), p. 5.

5

Despite being moderate on the Richter scale, the earthquake was so destructive because its epicentre was located right under the surface of the city. Additionally, few buildings had been built to seismic codes. 'The Agadir, Morocco earthquake February 29, 1960', *American Iron and Steel Institute*, New York (1962), pp. 12–15. On citation, Commandant Ferwerda, '29 February 1960', *Stichting Agadir 1960–2000*, website: wj-gerrits.com/agadir/html/29_februari_1960.html (accessed 8 July 2021). See also, US Geological Survey, 'Historical Earthquakes', http://earthquake.usgs.gov/regional/world/events/1960_02_29.php (accessed 19 April 2021).

6

Historian Spencer Segalla contextualises the 1960 Agadir earthquake as a cataclysmic environmental intervention in the decolonisation process and argues that the French relief efforts were part of this contested decolonisation process. Segalla, Spencer D., *Empire and Catastrophe: Decolonization and Environmental Disaster in North Africa and Mediterranean France Since 1954*, Lincoln, NE: University of Nebraska Press, 2020, p. 129 / JSTOR, www.jstor.org/stable/j.ctv10crdt6 (accessed 7 July 2021). When Morocco officially gained independence on 2 March 1956, Agadir counted an estimate of 40,000 inhabitants, of which 30,000 were Moroccans and 10,000 were of European descent (of which the majority were from France, followed by Spain, Italy, and Portugal). Diverres, François, 'François Diverres', in Le Toullec, Roger, *Mémoires d'un séisme: Agadir, 1960*, Nantes: Marines Editions, 2002, p. 9.

7

Segalla, *Empire and Catastrophe*.

8

Sine nomine, 'Die Rotkreuzhilfe für Agadir', *Das Schweizerisches Rote Kreuz*, 69, Heft 3:9 (1960). According to French sources, the French naval air base employed nearly 1,200 civilian and military personnel and had about fifty aircrafts. Article published in *Le Figaro*, 2 March 1960, www.lefigaro.fr/histoire/archives/2015/02/27/26010-20150227ARTFIG00256-29-fevrier-1960-agadir-detruite-en-15-secondes.php (accessed 8 July 2021).

9

Until the Moroccan Red Crescent Society took over on 17 May 1960, the Moroccan Army was made responsible for caring for the survivors. MacAulay, John, 'Telegraph Licross-Geneva'. League of Red Cross Societies. 11 July, 1960. Box R510407825: Health Hospitals – General Documents Agadir 1960 to 1969 Parts 2. IFRC Archives. Courtesy of Grant Mitchell.

10

Besides French colonialism, scholar Spencer Segalla situates the international disaster response in the wake of the 1960 Agadir earthquake amid Cold War politics. With strategically located military bases in Morocco, both American and French diplomats hoped that the disaster aid would bring them political goodwill. Segalla, *Empire and Catastrophe*, p. 112.

11

Sine nomine, 'Die Rotkreuzhilfe für Agadir', p. 9.

12

Ibid., p. 10.

13

Winsall, Edward and Henry W. Dunning, *Agadir Earthquake Disaster – 29th February, 1960*, Relief Bureau Circular No. 120, Geneva, 8th March, 1960. Box R510536792: Disasters Earthquake – Agadir Morocco 1960 Part 2. IFRC Archives. Courtesy of Grant Mitchell. On 2 March, the Eidgenossisches Politisches Department (Federal Political Department) in Bern sent a plea to the Swiss Federal Council to help the victims of the Agadir earthquake. In the letter, they give an immediate assessment of the situation in Agadir, the measures that needed to be taken straightaway and a proposal to send a sum of 50,000 Swiss francs to support the Swiss Red Cross with medical equipment and on-site medical help. On 4 March, the Swiss Federal Council confirmed the request from the Political Department and donated 50,000 Swiss francs as part of the 11.5 million francs reserved for international help. See also, Letter of the Swiss Red Cross to the Department for International Organizations of the Federal Political Department concerning aid for the victims of the earthquake in Agadir, March 2, 1960, in: E 2003 (A), 1971/44, Az. o.222.1, Action d'entraide pour Agadir, vol. 103. Federal Council Decree on aid to the victims of the Agadir earthquake, 4 March 1960, in: E 2003 (A), 1971/44, Az. o.222.1, Action d'entraide pour Agadir, vol. 103, www.communautejuiveagadir.com/index.php?page=Aide-Suisse-au-Seisme (accessed 8 July 2021).

14

Hampe, Erich, *Agadir: Eine Internationale Rettungsaktion, Ziviler Bevölkerungs-schutz*, vol. 60, no. 4 (1960), p. 2.

15

Sine nomine, 'Die Rotkreuzhilfe für Agadir', pp. 9–10.

16

A total of 102 soldiers went into action, including six physicians (two of them surgeons and one hygienist), two pharmacists and forty-seven medical orderlies. They were supported by ten ABC-Abwehr (Atomic, Biological, Chemical) defence specialists, eleven airlift specialists, four field cooks, two interpreters and sixteen naval personnel who were to set up a radio station on site. Hartmann, Volker, 'Erdbebenhilfe in Agadir 1960 – Wie alles begann', Wehrmedizin, wehrmed.de/humanmedizin/erdbebenhilfe-in-agadir-1960-wie-alles-begann.html (accessed 8 July 2021).

17

Ibid.

18

The field hospital was given to Morocco on 21 March 1960. Ibid.

19

Sine nomine, 'Die Rotkreuzhilfe für Agadir', p. 10.

20

Margés, Joost, 'Agadir Blijft Je een Leven Lang Bij', *Alle Hens Magazine of Ministerie van Defensie 8*, magazines.defensie.nl/allehens/2016/08/08_noodhulp-agadir (accessed 8 July 2021).

21

Ibid.

22

US Geological Survey, 'Historical Earthquakes'.

23

Camus, Marie-Hélène, Daniel Camus and Jack Garofalo, 'La Tragedie des Emmures', *Paris Match* 560, 1960.

24

Ibid.

25

www.communautejuiveagadir.com/index.php?page=le-petit-marocain (accessed 8 July 2021).

26
Lagny, André, 'Agadir (Maroc) détruit aux trois quarts par un terrible tremblement de terre nocturne', *Figaro*, 5, 2 March 1960. Retrieved from the republication: www.lefigaro.fr/histoire/archives/ 2015/ 02/27/26010-20150227ARTFIG00256-29-fevrier-1960-agadir-detruite-en-15-secondes.php (accessed 20 August 2021).
27
Camus, Camus and Garofalo, 'La Tragedie des Emmures', p. 41.
The French made up the largest foreign community in Agadir. According to French sources, around 6,000–7,000 of the 35,000 residents of Agadir were of French nationality, https://www.lefigaro.fr/ histoire/archives/2015/02/27/26010-20150227ARTFIG00256-29-fevrier-1960-agadir-detruite-en-15-secondes. php (accessed 8 July 2021).
28
Howespecial, '1,000 feared dead', p. 1. Howespecial, Marvin, 'Agadir a scene of destruction; residents flee shattered city', *The New York Times*, 18, 2 March 1960, p. 18.
29
Editoral, 'Agadir-Hilfe', *Spiegel*, 28, 5 July 1960, p. 36, www.spiegel.de/politik/aga-dir-hilfe-a-567da0ae-0002-0001-0000-000043066202?context=issue (accessed 8 July 2021).
30
By a miracle, one walled-up victim was found alive on the twelfth day.
31
Schwyter, 'Agadir ist Tot', p. 5.
32
'Agadir ist tot; zertrümmert, zermalmt, atomisiert, von einer ungeheuren Kraft zerschlagen'. Ibid., p. 5.
33
See avengers-in-time.blogspot. com/2017/01/1960-news-earthquake-in-agadir-morocco.html (accessed 8 July 2021).
34
Gazay, Marc, 'Action de Secours d'Agadir', Inezgane (Sept 15, 1960). Box R510536792: Disasters Earthquake – Agadir Morocco 1960. IFRC Archives. Courtesy of Grant Mitchell.
35
The first stone was laid on 30 June 1960. Hicks, 'Rebuilt Agadir', p. 203.
36
'Das Erdbeben von Agadir vom 29. Februar 1960 und die "Cité Suisse"', *Schweize-risches Bundesarchiv*, www.bar.admin.ch/ bar/de/home/service-publikationen/ publikationen/geschichte-aktuell/das-erdbeben-von-agadir-vom-29--februar-1960-und-die-cite-suisse.html (accessed 8 July 2021).

37
Cité Suisse did not come without a dose of national pride. The project was set up with the idea that the Swiss residents in Agadir appeared responsible for the construction and management as a way to satisfy the Swiss doners. Kurzprotokoll des Arbeitskomitees Agadir, 23 May 1960. *Schweizerisches Bundesarchiv*. in: E 2200.275 (B), 1980/125, Az. G.65.40.0. *Agadir, Aide suisse aux sinistres d'Agadir*, Bd. 5.
38
Brief protocol of the Agadir working committee, 23 May 1960, in: E 2200.275 (B), 1980/125, Az. G.65.40.0. *Agadir, Aide suisse aux sinistres d'Agadir*, vol. 5.
39
The Swiss Red Cross donated 600,000 Swiss francs, and Glückskette another 900,000. Sine nomine, 'Bau eines Schweizer Quartiers in Agadir', *Das Schweizerische Rote Kreuz*, 70 (1961), p. 38.
40
Froelich was also chosen as he was the only Swiss national of the three architects living in Agadir, although his competences in design were, in the process, questioned.
41
Froelich, Albert, E2200, July 26, 1960: p. 275. (B), 1980/125, Az. G.65.40.0. *Agadir, Aide suisse aux sinistres d'Agadir*, vol. 5.
42
'The aim of the project is to promote the vocational training of young people through scholarships and on-site training', reports the Swiss Red Cross journal. The granting of scholarships started in 1966, under the direction of a Swiss–Moroccan control committee. Courtesy of Swiss Red Cross historian Patrick Bondallaz.
43
Sine nomine, 'Bau eines Schweizer Quartiers', p. 38.
44
The Red Crescent Youth could not be formed in time, so the youth centre was first used by a local sports club and then served as a workhouse for local girls. The 'Maison des Jeunes' was made available to the Moroccan Red Crescent in the early 1970s. Fondation Cité Suisse D'Agadir. *Visite sur les lie par le président* (1965), p. 9. Swiss Red Cross Archives. Courtesy of Patrick Bondallaz.

45
'Souvenez-vous d'Agadir ...', *La Croix-Rouge Suisse*, Band, 73, Heft 2 (1964), p. 3, doi.org/10.5169/seals-682993 (accessed 8 July 2021).
Paris-born Lemarié was registered as an architect-topographer in Agadir in 1949, where he lived with his wife in the old Talborjt neighbourhood until the 1960 earthquake. He designed several villas and executed an extension and renovation of the Lyautey Hospital in Agadir in the 1950s. Moreover, he actively participated in the reconstruction of Agadir as an archi-tect and as an expert – which included, besides the Hassan II Hospital, the rebuilding of two hotels, a girls' school in New Talborjt and the Rialto cinema. Lemarié remained in Agadir until his death in 1996. Morvan-Lemarié, Annie, 'François Louis Lemarié (1902–1996), Architecte DPLG', mfd.agadir.free.fr/sitetalb/Plateau %20administratiff/Hopital/Fran%E7ois %20Louis%20LEMARIE.html (accessed 8 July 2021).
46
Ben Abbes, Youssef, 'Notes on the product for a new hospital complex in Agadir', Box R510407825: Health Hospitals – General Documents Agadir 1960 to 1969 Parts 1 and 2. IFRC Archives. Courtesy of Grant Mitchell.

BRUTALISM: THE GEM OF MOROCCO'S CONTRIBUTION TO WORLD CULTURE[1]

Laure Augereau, Imad Dahmani, Lahbib El Moumni

From the beginning of the twentieth century, the Sherifian kingdom of Morocco grew increasingly open to global influences. Its architecture and urbanism were particularly affected by the French Protectorate installed in 1912. Thereafter, new architectural forms appeared in Morocco – imported first from elsewhere in North Africa (Algiers, Tunis) and Europe, and later from the Americas.

Over the course of the twentieth century, Morocco experienced massive urbanisation – and so its cities provided fertile sites for the application of ideas and philosophies like those encompassed by the term 'modernism'. European architects, mainly based in Casablanca, responded to the needs of clients who wanted to advertise their modernity through the form, modern conveniences and materials that they chose for their buildings. Examples by French practitioners include the Assayag Building designed by Marius Boyer in 1930; the Suraqui Frères' eponymous building, also of

1930; and the Fraternelle du Nord apartment block designed by Marcel Desmet in 1931. We are talking here about an architectural style that evolved quickly and became more refined over time.

Because Morocco was developing economically in the first half of the twentieth century and suffered from no major destructive conflicts, it was an ideal laboratory for architects. Although they had been academically trained (at the École des Beaux-Arts in Paris), they were filled with new ideas like those presented in the 1925 exposition of decorative arts in Paris and those published in the pages of specialised journals then proliferating, such as *L'Architecture d'Aujourd'hui*. Generations of architects would sustain this creative and innovative spirit, and would prove to be remarkably productive.

After beginning his career in Syria and Lebanon (1931–1944), French architect and urbanist

Michel Écochard arrived in Morocco in 1946. He was named director of urbanism there, Écochard also served as a member of the Congrès Internationaux d'Architecture Moderne, CIAM (the International Congresses of Modern Architecture), and was active in the modernist movement. He engaged his team, then planning Morocco's cities, in implementing the ideas developed in the Athens Charter.[2] At the same time, Le Corbusier's collaborator, Vladimir Bodiansky, was creating ATBAT Afrique (Atelier des bâtisseurs Afrique; Builder's Workshop Africa) in 1951 with Georges Candilis, Shadrach Woods and Henri Piot.[3] They would all bring to life the ideas of modern architecture – particularly in constructing multi family housing in Casablanca. Écochard presented his Moroccan experience at the CIAM IX meeting at Aix-en-Provence in 1953 as a representative of Groupe des architectes modernes marocains, GAMMA (Group of Modern Moroccan Architects), which he had founded in 1949, thereby publicising Morocco's achievements on the world scene.[4]

The relative stability of Morocco, and especially of its administration, allowed its architectural forms to evolve along the lines of international currents. At the time, Morocco was situated at the crossroads of twentieth-century Western and Eastern ideas about architecture. The new generation was developing its style with reference to international models – notably, American and Japanese ones. In this context, 'Neo-Brutalist' architecture began to appear in Morocco in the 1950s and would go on to characterise the local architectural idiom until the beginning of the 1980s.[5] This style enjoyed two high points before it disappeared: it appeared in the form of international Brutalism, then it developed in a more regionalist form. Here, we will first present the context in which Neo-Brutalism appeared in Morocco, then we will try to understand the political, economic and cultural environment in which it blossomed into the country's own signature style.

THE BIRTH OF 'INTERNATIONAL' BRUTALISM IN MOROCCO, 1950–70

Modernism had been well embedded in Moroccan architecture during the first half of the twentieth century. By the time the first Neo-Brutalist buildings appeared in Casablanca in the 1950s, Michel Écochard had left Morocco. He had already played a determining role in anchoring the country to modernism via the international exposure that he had engineered as well as through his inspiration to younger architects. To understand the birth and development of this Brutalist architecture in Morocco, we must get to know this new generation of architects.

The first Moroccan architects were Élie Azagury, Isaac Lévy, Abdeslem Faraoui, Mourad Ben Embarek, Armand Amzallag and Mustapha Farès, plus Moroccan-born French architects such as Jean-François Zevaco and Patrice de Mazières, and Moroccan-born Spanish architect Claude Verdugo. During their childhoods, they had lived through the development of the large Moroccan cities and the blossoming of new styles of architecture like Art Deco. They were thus heavily influenced by these new forms, as well as by the new ways of living that those buildings housed.

Several of these architects were eventually involved in the ateliers of the master architects of the time. Claude Verdugo worked with Marius Boyer, and all of them studied in France – either at the École des Beaux-Arts or the École Spécial d'Architecture, both in Paris.[6] There – following the examples of Isaac Lévy, Élie Azagury and Jean-François Zevaco – they mixed in workshops and agencies with the big names of the period such as Auguste Perret, Eugène Beaudouin and Marcel Lods. They would be the first to return to Morocco just after the Second World War, when Michel Écochard was director of urbanism. They worked alongside him and his team. These young architects created their first works in the Golden Age of the modernist movement,

Fig. 2
Double-height living
room of the villa and
studio of Élie Azagury.

while incorporating their own architectural influences (Figs. 1 & 2).

This new generation expanded with the arrival of French architects and planners – Henri Tastemain, Pierre Mas, Jean Chemineau – who moved to Morocco because they were called to join Écochard's team, in addition to those who came on their own initiative such as the French architects Achille Dangleterre and Louis Riou, and Baku-born Léon Aroutcheff, as well as those who took advantage of other professional offers such as Georges Candilis and Vladimir Bodiansky. These architects, whether they belonged to CIAM or simply adopted the theories developed by the group, grew in number – and it was the symbiosis of their developing ideas that gave rise to new forms of architecture in Morocco. They were in harmony with modernist urbanism and they intended their buildings to reflect their times, adapted to the local context. This young generation joined with the GAMMA group, sharing the same ideas. They were aware of the late work of Le Corbusier at Marseilles – that is, the Unité d'Habitation with its rough concrete.

At the beginning of the 1950s in Morocco, the country's first Brutalist architects were dreaming up their ideas within this climate of confidence in the future of architecture. In the words of Jean-Louis Cohen and Monique Eleb, 'these architects enjoyed a privileged situation' because they had, as architect Robert Maddalena noted, 'the rare opportunity of being able to work in total freedom [in Morocco]'.[7] Examples include the re-education centre in Tit Mellil, conceived in 1953 by Jean-François Zevaco, and the 1954 infirmary and food market in Settat (now destroyed). Other exemplary buildings include the 1953 Stadium of Honour and the 1954 church of Notre Dame de Lourdes, both designed by Achille Dangleterre. The first primary schools in this style also went up in 1954 – such as the Longchamp school complex in Casablanca by Élie Azagury, Isaac Lévy and Léon

Aroutcheff, and the Omar Khayyam school in Rabat designed by French architects Henri Tastemain and Éliane Castelnau.

These first Proto-Brutalist projects may be characterised as pure forms made from raw materials (without cladding), with stone being gradually replaced by formed concrete. Zevaco's 1953 Tit Mellil re-education centre is an example of this type. It includes dormitories, staff housing, a dining area, workshops and an amphitheatre. The ensemble is organised like a Roman city on two axes with common public spaces and recreational areas located where these axes cross. In order to adapt to the shape of the site, its structures were composed of many smaller buildings. Harmony with the environment is accentuated by the use of stone for the walls, punctuated by panels of raw concrete blocks. Some facades possess large openings to let in light and air. The exceptionally fine amphitheatre is made of large panels of white concrete, which soar towards the sky (Figs. 3 & 4). The particular lyricism of this design by Jean-François Zevaco was celebrated by Michel Ragon.[8] Further, a black-and-white photograph of the structure by Marc Lacroix was chosen as the cover illustration for a book on new African architecture by Udo Kultermann in 1963, as if it were the standard-bearer for the whole continent.[9]

More generally, this generation may be characterised as having 'a sort of common language, combining stilt-like pillars, sunscreens, and expansive walls, all playing with the contrast between glass bricks, screens, exposed stones and rough or coated concrete'. Cohen and Eleb add that the context brings about 'an encounter between the clients' explicit desires and a Neo-Brutalism imbued with Mediterranean references'.[10]

It must be remembered that the political context allowed these young architects to rise rapidly to commanding positions. The French Protectorate administration was having to mobilise itself in the face of a nationalist movement that was growing ever stronger. Erik Labonne, named resident general in 1946, had to apply 'to North Africa a policy of modernization and industrialization, employing new means of dealing with health, education, and housing'.[11] It was to achieve success in these policies that he had recruited Écochard in the first place. From the 1950s, housing and infrastructure projects were made the subject of competitions set up among architects. At that time, GAMMA played the role of ideologically uniting the generations. Among the younger generation, Écochard's team was, throughout the 1950s, particularly invested in taking part – to the point of supplying its main actors: Élie Azagury represented GAMMA during the CIAM XI meeting at Otterlo in 1959.

After Morocco gained its independence in 1956, a certain continuity in the country's policies was observable – especially in the housing sector. To boost construction, a policy to provide educational and sanitary infrastructure was developed.[12] A school at Roches Noires, conceived by Élie Azagury in 1959, is an example of the new orientation in educational infrastructure. The architect designed three parallel pavilions that were successively recessed or set back in order to allow space for individual playgrounds based on hygienic principles of having plentiful air and natural light. Because the concept was focused on use and comfort, the resulting buildings were refined envelopes, albeit usually made from raw materials (Fig. 5).

From 1960, France participated in the development of school infrastructure by calling on the services of young architects. Élie Azagury and Jean-François Zevaco played a leading part in the 'Mission Française' district-school project, 'constructing several Brutalist complexes of reinforced concrete that received wide acclaim in Europe, notably via Marc Lacroix's photographs. Renaudin, Pierre Coldefy, Fleurant, Maddalena and Zéligson likewise worked on similar commissions,

at least up to 1962'.[13] Nevertheless, the Neo-Brutalist style had only sporadically been adopted before Agadir was destroyed by an earthquake on 29 February 1960 and it became imperative to reconstruct the city. This catastrophe allowed a new generation to put into practice on a large scale the latest stage in the evolution of modern architecture.

The experience of working in Agadir proved to be a catalyst for generations of architects who practised in this unique style: they defined Brutalist forms that responded to Morocco's needs and also contributed to its international heritage (in England, Japan and Brazil). Mourad Ben Embarek, Louis Riou, Henri Tastemain, Jean-François Zevaco, Élie Azagury, Claude Verdugo, Abdeslem Faraoui, Patrice de Mazières and Armand Amzallag were the principal architects in the city's reconstruction.

One can explain the catalytic effect of Agadir by making three points. First is the challenge that it posed to the Moroccan team when King Mohammed V's cabinet announced that an American firm would prepare a planning study for the reconstruction. The Moroccan team was swiftly mobilised on the ground to work on a counter-project that it would present to the king at the same time as the Americans.[14] The Moroccan project won royal consent.

Second, the team participated in drawing up the regulatory documents. These documents emerged from discussions reuniting the experiences of working for Écochard with the theories of CIAM's Athens Charter. They all defined an architecture that had to respond to the need of reconstructing Agadir while taking into account the collective trauma and the local style of the time: local regulations imposed constraints on the design and use of a property, thus determining which colours and materials could be used.[15]

Third, beyond the rules emerging from fruitful exchanges within the team as they confronted the necessity of reconstructing Agadir lay the

Fig. 3
The auditorium of the
Tit Mellil rehabilitation
centre that stands out
from the ground.
Fig. 4
Composition demon-
strating the duality
between the massive
and the light surfaces of
the rehabilitation centre
of Tit Mellil.

BRUTALISM: 'THE GEM OF MOROCCO'S CONTRIBUTION TO WORLD CULTURE'

Fig. 5
The main facade of the
Roches Noires school
with a rhythmic pattern
of brick and plain
surface.
Fig. 6
Main entrance of the
Faculty of Medicine
with the dominant
volume of the library.
Fig. 7
Concrete strips of
the gallery connecting
the auditoriums of
the faculty of science
in Rabat.

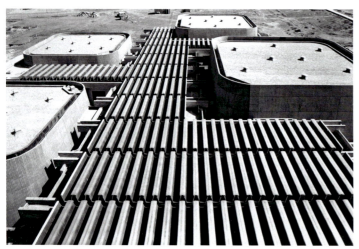

fact that each architect produced their drawings very rapidly. Even though the projects were distributed to different architects, unity of action characterised the team even down to their individual projects.[16] The architects went on to build what we call 'Brutalist' architecture today. While they themselves called it 'contemporary architecture', it was indeed, as Patrice de Mazières likes to remember, a deliberate and emphatic Brutalism (Figs. 6 & 7).

This period was thus marked by a grand opening up of local willingness to work in unison with the international. The architects of the time were as influenced by what was happening internationally, through reading architectural journals, as they were by their own local networks. There is abundant evidence that international architectural journals were present in the workplace of Jean-François Zevaco. In his archives, held at the École Nationale d'Architecture in Rabat, there are copies of *L'Architecture d'Aujourd'hui*, the *Architectural Forum* and *Japan Architect*.[17] Élie Azagury testified in a lecture that he was nourished by his friendships with architects and painters whom he had encountered during his studies in Paris and Marseilles as well as on his travels in Sweden, Brazil, the USSR and Latin America.[18]

This openness was connected to international recognition of Moroccan architecture. For example, as early as 1955, the English architects Alison and Peter Smithson wrote,

> We regard these buildings in Morocco as the greatest achievement since Le Corbusier's Unité d'Habitation at Marseilles [. . .] The importance of the Moroccan buildings is that they are the first manifestation of a new way of thinking. For this reason, they are presented as ideas; but it is their realization in built form that convinces us that here is a new universal.[19]

Furthermore, in March 1960, when Le Corbusier cut short his visit to Morocco without securing the commission to plan Agadir's reconstruction, he left his comrades the following note: 'The solidarity of architecture and urbanism. (Yes, with all that implies!) Oh yes, make a beautiful Agadir. Good luck!'[20]

The appreciation and diffusion of Moroccan models is equally apparent in specialist journals. For example, *L'Architecture d'Aujourd'hui*, edited by André Bloc, devoted an issue to Morocco in May 1951 and published articles on the architecture of Jean-François Zevaco a dozen times.[21] In the light of this cultural and international recognition, the members of the younger generation developed confidence in their personal orientation – one that they went on to develop by incorporating influences that were decidedly local.

MATURING TOWARDS A 'REGIONAL' BRUTALISM, 1965–1980

After having proven their good sense in their collective work in Agadir, the architects assimilated the style. That is, strengthened by their experience they mastered its conception (design, expression) as well as its achievement (technique, quality of construction) due to their close collaboration with local construction firms. They expressed their evolving expertise in other areas of Morocco as well – all the while remaining true to the guiding principles that they had recently developed.

Brutalist architecture in Morocco therefore evolved very rapidly towards a style intended to be much more regional, albeit with local specificities. Sigfried Giedion showed that this was a widespread tendency at the time, when writing in 1960:

> one finds in all contemporary architecture of quality [. . .] the concern to respect climatic and geographical conditions of a given region, without considering them as obstacles but as springboards for the artistic imagination. We have given the

name 'new regionalism' to their adaptation to the climatic and social particularities of their building sites. Thanks to current spatial conceptions and to contemporary modes of expression, one can re-establish today a fertile dialogue with the past.[22]

The numerous public commissions, combined with an interest in new technologies and materials that were not yet widely diffused or accessible, allowed Brutalist architects in Morocco to experiment with building in reinforced concrete and with rough materials – paralleling avant-garde developments in other countries.

The post-independence period was marked by economic planning aiming to boost the country's development. Morocco faced exponential demographic growth and a high rate of urbanisation. The three-year plan of 1965 and the five-year plan of 1968 set priorities in the fields of agriculture and tourism, plus a policy of building infrastructure such as, first, schools and courts and, subsequently, universities and hospitals. The large number of important commissions and the scarcity of qualified architects meant that the architects discussed above were in high demand.[23] They had experienced Agadir through companies formed under the strong constraints of operating in a territory prone to earthquakes. They had thus acquired familiarity with concrete, building good-quality walls with a rigorous technique. The strong aesthetic standards that they had gained there would be expressed in subsequent projects.

The techniques of prefabrication or curtain walls – plus the availability of new materials like aluminium, developed in Europe after the Second World War – had not previously been subject to such rapid development in Morocco. The architects thus had to judiciously express their ideas by relying on the knowledge of *maalems* (local artisans).[24] Industrialised building construction in a developing country like Morocco was not a priority, and the economic context did not, in any case, permit it: modern infrastructural development was limited, handicrafts were available and inexpensive, and local industrial materials were limited to the essentials (bricks, concrete).

A traditional method of construction was maintained.[25] This reliance perhaps contributed to the continued construction of Brutalist-style buildings as the architects tried to evolve and, at the same time, to pay respect to the modern movement to which they belonged: an architecture without embellishment, whose structure rang true in both its form and its function. The result was an architecture of raw concrete or brick, whose diverse surfaces reflected the geographical context of the place in which they were used.[26] The fact that the texture varied as the strong light changed was part of its decorative appeal.

The desire to be more closely aligned with local usage and culture forced this architectural style to evolve. Appropriating a modernist style allowed local architects to mature by varying its forms and the ways in which they used its materials according to the country's different regions (Fig. 8). One sees a return to the use of *zellij* (mosaic tilework), which had been practically absent from Moroccan architecture since the 1940s, as well as woodworking – which was revived, rejoining the metalworking that had never disappeared. A couple of architects – Abdeslem Faraoui and Patrice de Mazières – developed local architecture in collaboration with artists. Their initial efforts were strengthened in 1967 when architects from the Faraoui and de Mazières agency encountered a group of artists from Casablanca composed of Farid Belkahia, Mohamed Melehi and Mohamed Chebaa, among others.[27]

Contemporary art, as the members of the so-called 'Casablanca School' asserted, had to take its place in daily life. They wanted to develop an art that would serve as a counterpoint to the traditional art valorised by

Fig. 8
The hotel Ibn Toumart in harmonious integration within the landscape of Taliouine.
Fig. 9
The reception of the hotel including 'the integrations of the artists' (wooden claustra and ceiling lights of Mohamed Chabaa and the carpet of Claudio Bravo).

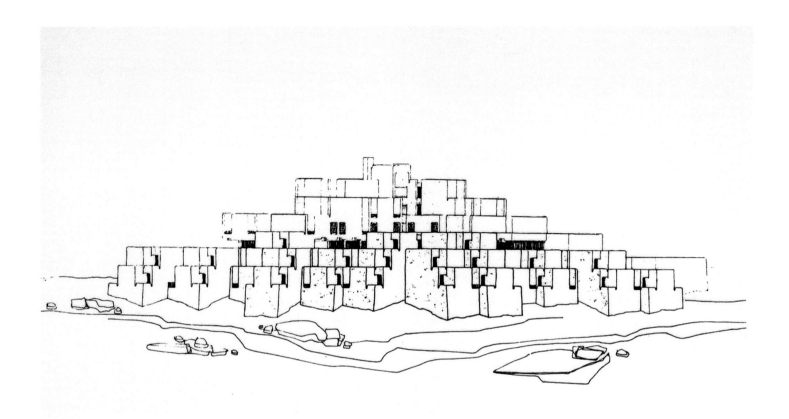

Fig. 10
The compact composi-
tion of les Gorges du
Dadès hotel inspired by
the kasbahs of southern
Morocco.

the protectorate government. For them, this valorisation had obscured part of Moroccan culture. Thus, they were hoping to integrate this missing dimension into their teaching and their practice, conforming harmoniously with Moroccan culture. They were more interested in the form of art that is part of daily life, not just present in galleries or in the pictorial representation of only a certain part of the Moroccan population.[28]

Architects and artists began this collaborative approach on hotel projects planned by the Faraoui and de Mazières agency. Unbeknownst to the project managers, they integrated creations such as a ceiling painted by Mohamed Melehi into the hotel Roses du Dadès (1971–2), wooden lamps by Mohamed Chebaa at a hotel in Taliouine (1972–4), and the copper doors by Farid Belkahia at a hotel in Marrakesh (1972) (Fig. 9) built under the control of the National Tourism Office. For instance, the Dadès hotel represents an attempt to integrate modern architecture, without pastiche, using vernacular references in a region where traditional architecture was still alive. The architects set out to respect the essential elements of this local architecture: modest and differentiated volumes, adaptation to the site's materials and colours (Fig. 10).

In the case of the Dadès hotel, Moroccan artists such as Mohamed Chebaa were associated with the project from the beginning. The hotel's interior fixtures introduced a new aesthetic alongside traditional Moroccan craftsmanship, such as wooden panels and ceramic flooring in the lobby as well as wooden signs. Subsequently, many frescos and other decorations appeared on projects such as banks, post offices and businesses. This stylistic collaboration, called *intégrations*, was adapted to the local context, while the principles of modern architecture were maintained in their pure form in which nothing is hidden. In addition, there was more woodwork, and building materials with more varied textures and volumes were used – such as

zellij in the interior as well as on the exterior of buildings. All of the above added a touch of colour that had not been used in the first Brutalist buildings, which had been characterised, rather, by their large white spaces with wood only in the interiors in contrast to their rough concrete exteriors. Cultural reappropriation was part and parcel of this regionalism by virtue of local ways of life being integrated into these contemporary architectural plans. For example, Jean-François Zevaco embedded local usage and lifestyle into his buildings via their interiority and their *entrée en chicane* (offset entrances), as in the villa that he completed in 1975. He took particular care to design openings that took into account the intense light of Morocco: see the courthouses of Beni Mellal (1960) and of Mohammedia (1958).

In another example, Armand Amzallag's Club Mediterranée in Ouarzazate, one sees a massive and compact building turning inward like the neighbouring *ksour* (fortified village). Amzallag created this design in a warm and dry climate that was cut off from easy access to building materials. He therefore dreamt up a complex on two levels whose structure is made of stone walls and concrete walls and flooring (Fig. 11). This idea shares a bond with Sigfried Giedion's observation about the development of architecture in Japan. Referring in particular to Kenzo Tange and the annex for the 1964 Olympic Games in Tokyo, Giedion wrote, 'The secret of their architecture is to maintain close contact with the lived past while maintaining the desire to make something new.'[29] In Morocco, this approach gave rise to an architecture without mimicry or the pastiche of traditional forms.

L'Architecture Marocaine and *A + U* contained the sole writings by Morocco-based architects during this period. *A + U*, the African review of architecture and urbanism created in 1964 by Mourad Ben Embarek, appeared three times a year for distribution nationally and throughout Africa (Fig. 12). The editorial committee made it a space for reflection and the exchange of ideas. It disseminated news about local projects along with international references, and fostered a new recognition of African architecture. Unfortunately, after six issues, the journal folded in 1970. At the same time, Moroccan architects contributed less frequently to other architectural reviews including *L'Architecture d'Aujourd'hui*.

When CIAM has dissolved in 1959, there was no longer a space for the exchange of ideas – such as GAMMA had been at the national and international levels.[30] The group of architects who had participated in the reconstruction of Agadir took GAMMA's place. Their title, *Ecole de Rabat*, employed by Thierry Nadau, comes from the fact that this group, located in Rabat but also in Casablanca, produced work in a modern idiom with a unity of tone and national expression.[31] Nevertheless, without a real space for exchanging ideas it was in no way a school that developed theories – perhaps because its members were too busy dealing with their own commissions. However, one can note that the Aga Khan Prize for architecture raised international awareness of Moroccan architecture in the 1980s: Jean-François Zevaco's courtyard houses (1964) won the prize in 1980, then the housing project Dar Lamane by Moroccan architects Abderrahim Charai and Abdelaziz Lazrak (1983) won in 1986. One senses a change of mood at this time, as Moroccan practitioners became less interested in the production of architecture as part of the global architectural movement.

THE AFTERLIFE OF BRUTALISM

Brutalist architecture was able to develop in Morocco from the 1950s because a new generation of local architects had come of age there. They were trained in the culture of modernism and they had gained professional experience working alongside the modernist masters. Their participation in GAMMA ensured that their work continued to be inspired by modernist ideology. Members of this generation were quite open to the rest of the world by virtue of their own travels and their access to architectural magazines. They adapted their building materials, techniques of construction and skills to the needs of the moment and to the aesthetic demands of modernism. The experience of working in Agadir allowed them to realise the aims of this style in the 1960s, and they followed up with large infrastructural projects in the 1970s. Furthermore, one senses that they genuinely adapted their architectural forms to the local culture, territory and geography. Perhaps in reaction to having lived as children through the protectorate period, these architects were on a personal quest to express their identity through their architecture. They developed a more regional architectural style partly because they had to respond to local cultural needs and partly because they were genuinely engaged in dialogue with vernacular styles, as they had to rely on available materials and technologies.

This last point perhaps limited the development of Brutalism in Morocco and led to its end, especially when a policy of economic Moroccanisation was adopted after 1973. Did this policy weaken the industrialisation of building construction? What was the policy's impact on the disappearance of certain industries, as well as on the slowing down of the building sector's growth? The 1980s in Morocco were a period in which numerous restraints were placed on economic and cultural development: social crises had a great impact in diminishing public and private demand, thus slowing down the infrastructural development of the country. There were many fundamental reorientations within Moroccan life during this period. It is easy to enumerate them, but difficult to fully understand their impact on the evolution of the nation's architecture. The first shift was apparent in King Mohammed V's address to architects on 14 January 1986. His speech, on regaining Moroccan identity in architecture, was interpreted by administrations and their

Fig. 11
Alternating between the
vacuous and the solid
on Club Mediterranée
hotel in Ouarzazate.
Fig. 12
Cover of the second
issue of A+U magazine.

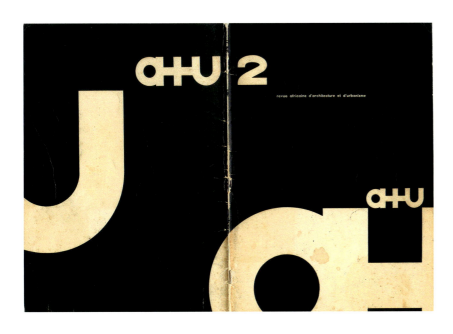

BRUTALISM: 'THE GEM OF MOROCCO'S CONTRIBUTION TO WORLD CULTURE'

functionaries through the implementation of formal elements such as the arcade, columns and glazed-tile roofs. Most administrators from the protectorate period had been replaced in the 1970s, and the baton of modernist urbanism was not passed on to their successors.

Morocco was, by then, gaining international visibility with large royal projects – such as the Grande Mosquée of Casablanca (1986–93, French architect Michel Pinseau) or the Moroccan Pavilion at the Seville Expo in 1992 (also Pinseau) – which recycled architectural motifs from previous dynasties such as lobed arches, *zellij* panels, glazed tile roofs and Andalusian gardens. This representation of Moroccan style contradicted the direction of almost all the architecture produced in the independence era, and it rejected modernism as a marker of contemporary Moroccan identity.

At the same time, there was a change in the way in which projects were managed. Previously, there had been a period of acculturation that Paul Bowles had called in 1966 'implicit hybridisation' and that Cohen and Eleb expressed as a 'kind of interplay between values and bodily motions [. . .], explaining the ease with which Casablancans can change from a jellaba into tight pants or move from a living room into an Arab salon'.[32] From the 1980s, the Moroccan middle class had difficulty accepting modern architecture. They distanced themselves from the Westernisation that had formerly been an acceptable face of modernisation. By the same token, projects were being managed more and more often by 'developers [who wanted to be] free from all pressures and cultural influences'.[33]

What remains is to take account of changes within the profession itself. First, the new generation of Moroccan architects such as Abdelaziz Lazrak and Hafid El Awad were trained in schools of architecture in France that had, since 1968, been separated from

art schools; this was also the case in Morocco in 1980, when the first National Architecture School was founded in Rabat. Working in an unpromising administrative context and training with many more fellow students than hitherto (perhaps a thousand of them), many of these architects gained limited access to the profession – some working in the administration to apply the 'Moroccanness' evoked in King Mohammed V's speech; others becoming architectural functionaries, simply endorsing documents. 'The practice of the profession according to artistic and ethical rules became more and more difficult', according to Fouad Akalay and Selma Zerhouni.[34]

All these changes led to the creation of a new school of thought among the younger generation, which had at its disposal different expressive objectives and different technologies of construction from those of its predecessors. This new generation, which had not participated in the rebuilding of Agadir, began to analyse the critical feedback on, and sometimes the poor reception of, the city's new buildings by the local population.

One must also remember that, in international circles, post-modernism developed in opposition to modernism. Post-modernists saw the modernist style not as appropriate but, on the contrary, as ostentatious and full of self-promoting vanity.[35] For modernists, on the other hand, post-modernism amounted to pastiche and was opposed to their sense of what was required. The younger generation seized upon post-modernism because it would allow them to integrate arcades and columns, and thus fashion a contemporary response to the request for 'Moroccanness'. After the golden age of Moroccan architecture extending from the 1950s to the 1970s, Brutalism went into decline in the 1980s.

Today, because Brutalist architecture is on the brink of disappearing through a variety of means – being disfigured, abandoned, even demolished – a movement is afoot among the younger generation of architects to safeguard examples of this style, like the Postal Sorting Center in Casablanca designed by Faraoui and De Mazières and the Thermal Station of Sidi Harazem designed by Jean-François Zevaco. Morocco is beginning to appreciate its own Brutalist architecture, which is already accepted in international circles. After several buildings have now been defaced due to ignorance or misunderstanding, is it possible that the experience of Agadir can become an inspiring point of reference for the future for today's young Moroccan architects?

1
This subtitle is based on the expression: 'Le fleuron de la contribution du Maroc à la culture mondiale' in Nadau, Thierry, 'La Reconstruction d'Agadir, Ou Le Destin de l'architecture Moderne Au Maroc', in Culot, Maurice and Jean-Marie Thiveaud (eds), *Architectures Françaises Outre-Mer: Abidjan, Agadir, Alep, Alger, Bangui, Beyrouth, Brazzaville, Cansado, Casablanca, Conakry, Dakar, Damas, Hanoi, Libreville, Niamey, Orléansville, Ouagadougou, Riyadh, Tananarive, Tunis, Yaoundé*, Collection Villes, Liège: Mardaga, 1992, p.163.
[Translation by the editors.]
2
The Athens Charter was the foundational text produced during a sea voyage between Marseilles and Athens in 1933 by CIAM IV (Congrès Internationaux d'Architecture Moderne, fourth meeting) under the aegis of Le Corbusier on the theme of the 'functional city'.
3
ATBAT [L'atelier des bâtisseurs] was a design firm created in 1947 in Tangier by Le Corbusier, Vladimir Bodiansky and André Wogenscky. It extended its reach throughout North Africa from 1951 to 1955 as a collective linking architects Georges Candilis and Shadrach Woods and engineers Vladimir Bodiansky and Henri Piot.
4
'During the CIAM IX conference held at Aix-en-Provence in 1953, the Moroccan contribution on housing presented by Michel Ecochard and his GAMMA team was of central importance and shocked the most radical members at the meeting. GAMMA, the Moroccan branch of CIAM, was created in 1949 and was composed of Michel Ecochard, Claude Béraud, Vladimir Bodiansky, Georges Candilis, Georges Godefroy, Bernard Kennedy, Pierre Mas, and Shadrach Woods.' Tom Avermaete and Maristella Casciato, *Casablanca Chandigarh, A Report on Modernization*, Montreal: Canadian Centre for Architecture, 2014, p.110 [French edition].
5
Critic Rayner Banham used the term in his book *The New Brutalism: Ethic or Aesthetic?* (1966) following its use since 1954 by English architects Alison and Peter Smithson.
6
Marius Boyer (1885–1947) worked as an architect in Morocco from 1919 to 1947. His firm was taken over after his death by Émile-Jean Duhon.

7
Cohen, Jean-Louis and Monique Eleb, *Casablanca, Mythes et figures d'une aventure urbaine*, Paris: Hazan, 1998, p.419. [All subsequent references are also to the French edition of this book.]
8
Ragon, Michel and Henri Tastemain, *Zevaco*, Paris: Éditions Cercle d'Art, 1999.
9
Udo Kultermann, *Architecture Nouvelle en Afrique*, Brussels: Prismes Éditions, 1963.
10
'[U]ne sorte de langage commun, combinant les pilotis, les brise-soleils et les pans de murs jouant avec le contraste des briques de verre, des claustras, des pierres apparentes et du béton brut ou enduit. Une rencontre entre les souhaits des clients éclairés et un néo-brutalisme nourri de références méditerranéennes semble ainsi s'opérer', Cohen and Eleb, *Casablanca, Mythes et figures*, p.391. [Translation in the English version.]
11
Ibid., p.290.
12
The Independence Manifesto was made public on 11 January 1944.
13
Cohen and Eleb, *Casablanca, Mythes et figures*, p.437.
14
Diouri, Younès, 'Mourad Ben Embarek – L'architecte du nouvel Agadir', online video, 2011.
15
Beurret, Claude, 'Architecture et aménagements publics', *A + U*, Agadir, no.4 (1964), p.34.
16
Cohen and Eleb, *Casablanca, Mythes et figures*, p.437.
17
Hofbauer, Lucy, 'Transferts de modèles architecturaux au Maroc', *Les Cahiers d'EMAM*, 20/2010, p.73.
18
'Conférence de Elie Azagury au Collège des architectes, 09/03/1991', p.3, in Archives of Amal Barrrada.
19
From Alison and Peter Smithson, 'Collective Housing in Morocco', *Architectural Design*, vol.25, no.1 (January 1955), p.2. Quoted in Cohen and Eleb, *Casablanca, Mythes et figures*, p.332.
20
Note on Le Corbusier ms. dated 26 March 1960.
21
Ragon and Tastemain, *Zevaco*, p.8.

22
'[O]n retrouve dans toute architecture contemporaine de qualité [. . .] le souci de respecter les conditions climatiques et géographiques d'une région donnée, en ne les considérant pas comme des obstacles mais comme des tremplins pour l'imagination artistique. [. . .] Nous avons donné ailleurs le nom de "nouveau régionalisme" à cette adaptation aux données climatiques et sociales. Grâce à la conception actuelle de l'espace, grâce aux modes d'expression contemporains, on peut rétablir aujourd'hui un dialogue fécond avec le passé.' Sigfried Giedion, *Espace, temps, architecture*, Paris: Éditions Denoël, 1990 [first French edition published in 1968], p.18.
[Translation by Diana Wylie.]
23
'There were 200 European architects during the Protectorate; after independence there were only 80.' Michel Ragon, *Histoire mondiale de l'architecture et de l'urbanismes modernes*, vol.2, Tournai: Éditions Casterman, 1972, p.348.
24
In Morocco, the *maalem* was an artisan who was part of a corporation in which knowledge was transmitted by initiation into rituals that had been kept secret by families of elite artisans. Many of these secrets are now at risk of disappearing.
25
Aoun, Mustapha, 'Etude comparée entre les modes de construction en traditionnel et en préfabriqué, le Colloque d'Agadir, UIA', *Habitation, revue trimestrielle de la section romande de l'Asociation Suisse pour l'Habitat*, no.41 (1968).
26
'Zevaco wielded his baton with a lot of style. Concrete blocks with distressed texture, sculptured walls, rough surfaces. Ribbed and textured the way granite contains sand and pebbles.' Ragon and Tastemain, *Zevaco*, p.8.
27
Farid Belkahia was director of the École des Beaux-Arts in Casablanca from 1962 to 1976. Melehi and Chebaa taught there.

28
'For 15 years the architects Abdeslam Faraoui and Patrice de Mazières collaborated with artists to create a typology of works and objects termed Les Intégrations (Integrations) specially designed for public infrastructure, thus promoting art's participation in the renewal of Morocco's society and urban fabric. In the face of an academic tradition inherited from colonialism, the artistic interventions implemented by the firm Faraoui and de Mazières highlighted Morocco's counter-cultural spirit, one where transdisciplinary cross-pollinations between literature and poetry, the visual arts, and design and architecture did not crystallize so much in aesthetic claims as give substance to the possibility of an emancipatory modernity, participating in the subordination of art-time to life-time.' Houssais, Maud 'Les Intégrations: Faraoui et de Mazières, 1966–1982, Du Temps de l'Art au Temps de la Vie', 2018, www.bauhaus-imaginista.org/articles/2387/les-integrations-faraoui-and-mazieres-1966-1982 (accessed 8 July 2021).
29
'Le secret de leur architecture, c'est de maintenir un contact étroit avec un passé demeuré vivant tout en ayant le désir de faire du neuf.' Giedion, *Espace, temps, architecture*, p. 20.
[Translation by Diana Wylie.]
30
The dissolution of CIAM was organised by Team X in 1959 at Otterlo, the Netherlands.
31
Nadau, Thierry, 'La reconstruction d'Agadir, ou le destin de l'architecture moderne au Maroc', in Culot and Thiveaud, *Architectures Françaises Outre-Mer*, p. 147.
32
Paul Bowles (1910–1999) was an American composer, writer, and traveller who lived for a long time in Morocco.
'[L]e jeu avec les temporalités permettant ainsi de passer de la djellaba au caleçon et du living-room au salon arabe, ce qui modifie autant la gestuelle que les valeurs', in Cohen and Eleb, *Casablanca, Mythes et figures*, pp. 443–4.
[Translation by Diana Wylie.]
33
Akalay, Fouad and Selma Zerhouni, 50 ans d'architecture au Maroc ou la politique des ruptures, *Architecture du Maroc*, Casablanca, 2005, p. 41.
34
Ibid., p. 38.
35
Elie Azagury, lecture at the Collège des architectes, 9 March 1991; and Jean-François Zevaco, lecture at the Complexe culturel d'Anfa, 26 October 1991.

BUILDING AGADIR

Maxime Zaugg

An earthquake destroyed vast parts of the city of Agadir during the night of 29 February in 1960. Due to the terraced topography that characterised Agadir, the destruction was enormous. It resulted in a high number of casualties as well as the displacement of the survivors. This tremendous social and physical annihilation would soon be followed by the almost complete reconstruction of Agadir within a very brief period. The rebuilding of the city's new neighbourhoods was declared by King Mohammed V to be a national emergency task. Initial plans were made by the Haut Commissariat à la Reconstruction (High Committee for the Reconstruction, HCRA) to rebuild Agadir, focusing on administrative, commercial and touristic functions. To meet the need for rapid reconstruction, the architecture of the new city was conceived according to specific codes and norms that various designers could implement. Renowned national and international architects were employed to design urban and architectural projects, and many of them were realised within a few years. This chapter presents previously unpublished images and plans, the majority of which were developed by the Haut Commissariat during Agadir's reconstruction period in the first half of the 1960s.

Our intensive research in Agadir, undertaken in 2019, revealed that the entire planning record of the reconstruction by the Haut Commissariat had long been lying unnoticed in the basement of the Hôtel de Ville (Town Hall) as a sort of 'hidden archive'. At our request, the mayor of Agadir granted us access to his basement – and we were able to take our first look into this rich record of an unparalleled urban design venture. The following thirty-seven projects do not form a conclusive documentation of all buildings of the reconstruction of Agadir but they constitute, rather, an initial cross-section of what we discovered during our research in the archives. The plan documentation found in the hidden archive is supported by historical photographic documetation from the period immediately following the reconstruction, which we retrieved from the personal collections of Lahsen Roussafi, Marie-France Dartois and Régine Caïs-Terrier, and Omar Ech-Chafadi and Hassan Bouziane.

This chronologically ordered catalogue thus offers a first overview of projects planned and built by the Haut Commissariat during the short period of the reconstruction. The will to rebuild the city of Agadir as quickly as possible and the resulting, extremely short, time span in which all the projects were planned and realised can be perceived in the standardised presentation of the plan material. Though many architects from different countries and cultures were at work simultaneously, the plan material seems to speak of a common idiom.

The projects differ widely in terms of programme and scale. They cover a large part of the new city of Agadir and range from the Centre Urbain to Nouveau Talborjt, the Secteur Résidentiel and the Quartier Industriel Sud. The pace of reconstruction was rapid. At the end of 1966, in the Centre Urbain, sixty new residential buildings were completed and eighty were being designed or under construction; 109 shops were completed, and sixty-two were planned or under construction. As a result, 52 per cent of the planned reconstruction work was already completed. Most of the buildings in the Centre Urbain were built of béton brut (raw concrete), rendered or painted in white, with wooden elements for windows; doors; and, occasionally, interior walls.

For each of the projects presented on the following pages, information has been found in the archival documents themselves, in the register of the Haut Commissariat or in personal collections. Each project is labelled with essential information – including floor area and cost in Moroccan dirhams (DM) – and an extended caption summarising some of its most significant urban and architectural properties. The projects reveal largely unknown architects, typological and constructive experiments, and interesting compositional features. The project catalogue Building Agadir is intended to serve as a starting point for further research into the previously unknown material regarding the reconstruction of Agadir.

BUILDING AGADIR

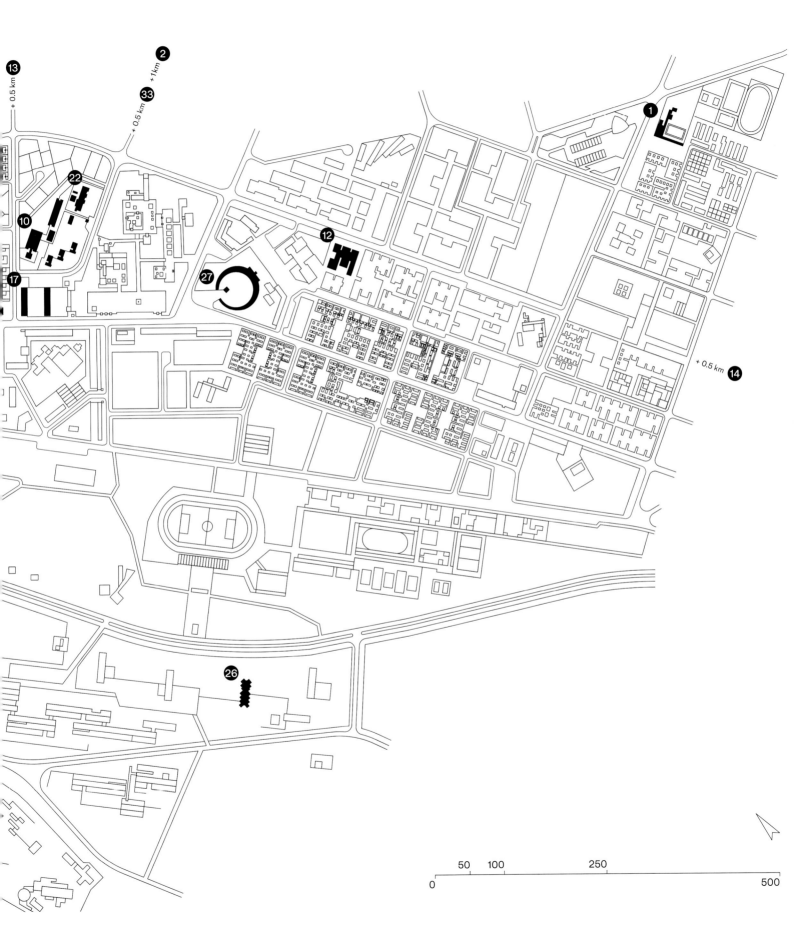

MAISON DES JEUNES

ARCHITECT: Albert U. Froelich
YEAR: 1961
LOCATION: Quartier Industriel Sud
FLOOR AREA: 375 m^2
CONSTRUCTION COST: 95,000 DM
COMMISSIONER: Division de la Jeunesse
et Sports Agadir

The Maison des Jeunes (Youth Centre) was designed in 1961 by the Swiss architect Albert U. Froelich and commissioned by the Division de la Jeunesse et Sports Agadir (Youth and Sports Division Agadir). Froelich, who was already working as an architect in Agadir in the 1950s, realised several buildings during the reconstruction period – such as a Unité d'Habitat Collectif in Agadir and other projects together with the Moroccan architect Élie Azagury. Today known as the Maison de la Jeunesse Hay Hassani, the building is located at the intersection of Rue Berthollet (today, Avenue El Mouqwama) and Rue Laplace (today, Rue de Souks) in the Quartier Industriel Sud. This youth centre was built along-side other functional *équipement* (collective infrastructure) – e. g. two mosques, a cinema and three schools – and it lies close to the public square marked by the distinctive cupola of the Marché en Gros (Wholesale Market) designed by French architect Pierre Coldefy and Moroccan-born Spanish architect Claude Verdugo. For the recon-struction of the city of Agadir, the intention was to build a Maison des Jeunes in each new neighbour-hood – thus creating a new type of centrality in the various parts of the city. The Maison des Jeunes is understood as a building type that encompasses outdoor and indoor leisure spaces. With various functions such as sports, workshops and libraries, it produces a centrality for a new category of young citizens. It is a conglomeration of various buildings, all conceived as rational and repetitive portal constructions in concrete. The spaces housing these different functions are connected by a continuous gallery, and arranged around the outdoor sports terrain and garden.

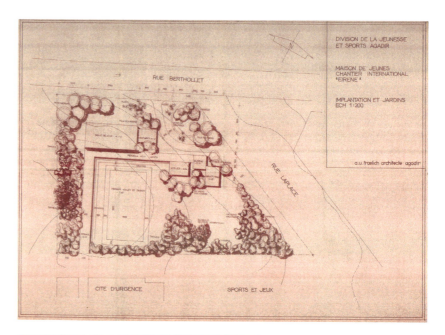

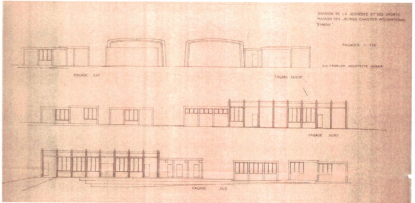

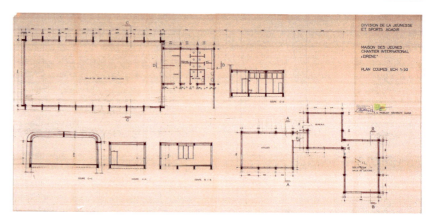

HÔPITAL HASSAN II

ARCHITECT: Élie Azagury, François Louis Lemarié
YEAR: 1960–4
LOCATION: Secteur Résidentiel
FLOOR AREA: 17,190 m²
CONSTRUCTION COST: 12,598,300 DM
COMMISSIONER: Ministère de la Santé Publique

The Hôpital Hassan II (Hassan II Hospital) was designed in 1960 by the French architect François Louis Lemarié and the Moroccan architect Élie Azagury, with construction starting in 1963. It is built in the periphery of the new city of Agadir, next to the Secteur Résidentiel and in proximity to the road linking the harbour to the district of Tikiouine. This hospital comprises a set of ten pavilions located in rows on the site and connected via a central pathway. They are built following the anti-seismic standards of the time and are all south oriented. Each pavilion is equipped with fifty beds and is connected to the neighbouring pavilions by covered galleries. The single-storey pavilions are organised in regular segments that are laid out along a linear corridor to avoid obstructing the hospital's workflow. The complex of Hôpital Hassan II also includes a diagnosis centre, laboratories, a nursing school, an administrative centre, a provincial pharmacy, a boarding school and living quarters for staff on permanent duty.

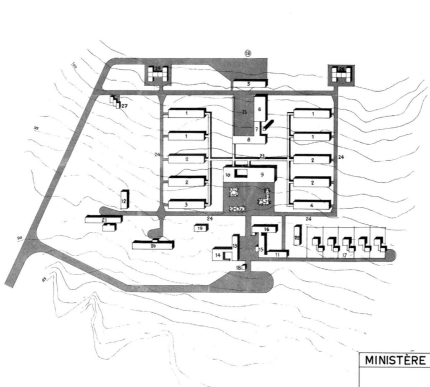

LÉGENDE

1 Médecine
2 Chirurgie
3 Service enfants
4 Maternité
5 Ateliers
6 Cuisine et réserves
7 Vapeur
8 Buanderie
9 Bloc technique
10 Bloc radio
11 Labo. institut d'hygiène
12 Logements brevetés
13 Action provinciale
14 Pharmacie
15 Service des entrées
16 Groupe technique 30 lits
17 Villas
18 Concierge
19 Halles
20 Foyer des infirmières
21 École d'infirmières
22 Internes
23 Circuit médical
24 Circuit service
25 Cour de service
26 Logements traditionnels
27 Morgue
28 Réservoir d'eau 250 m³

MINISTÈRE DE LA SANTÉ PUBLIQUE	
	ESQUISSE
	PLAN DE MASSE
HOPITAL D'AGADIR	
E.AZAGURY ARCHITECTE D.P.L.G. F.LEMARIE ARCHITECTE D.E.P.E.	
AGADI. LE 7 AÔUT 1960	ECHELLE 1:2000

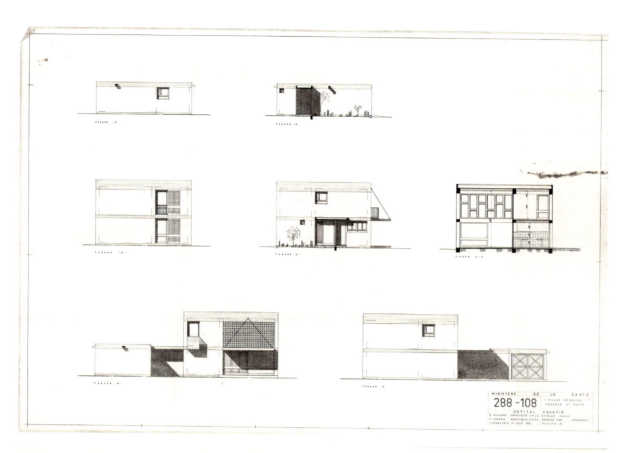

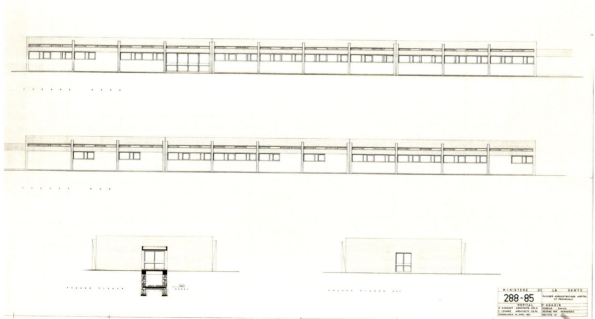

IMMEUBLE D

ARCHITECT: Abdeslem Faraoui, Patrice de Mazières
YEAR: 1962–3
LOCATION: Centre Urbain
FLOOR AREA: –
CONSTRUCTION COST: –
COMMISSIONER: État Marocain, Haut Commissariat
à la Reconstruction

The residential building Immeuble D (Building D) was designed by the Moroccan architect Abdeslem Faraoui and the Moroccan-born French architect Patrice de Mazières between 1962 and 1963, and commissioned by the Haut Commissariat à la Reconstruction. Immeuble D is located parallel to Avenue du Prince Moulay Abdallah in the new Centre Urbain and – together with other buildings, such as Immeubles H1–3 and Immeubles O1–2 – creates a coherent urban ensemble. The apartments of Immeuble D, intended for the administrative staff of the Agadir municipality, show a rational and well-developed modern typology that is adapted to the local climatic conditions. The residential Immeuble D is conceived as a slab with concrete beams that protrude on its facade, creating shadow and cross ventilation. Spacious staircases

with *mashrabiya*-like screens can be found in the communal parts of the building. The apartments are characterised by a wide variety of outdoor spaces such as loggias, balconies and front gardens, as well as service balconies to the rear. Together with the spacious internal layouts of the apartments themselves, these offered the white-collar workers, who had to move from great distances to Agadir in order to work in the various administrations, a very high standard of living.

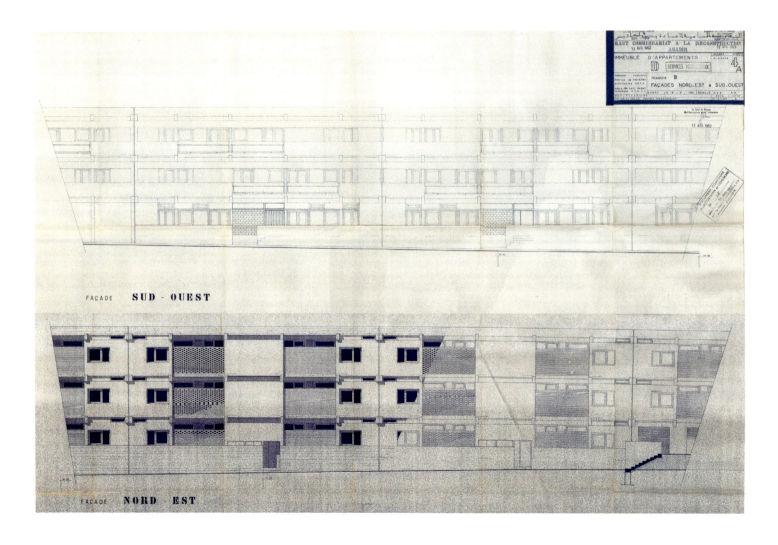

FAÇADE **SUD - OUEST**

FAÇADE **NORD - EST**

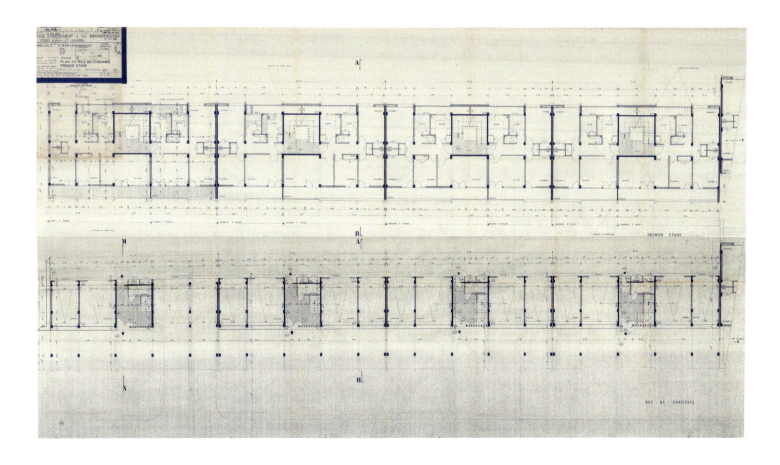

115

IMMEUBLE H1

ARCHITECT: Abdeslem Faraoui, Patrice de Mazières
YEAR: 1963
LOCATION: Centre Urbain
FLOOR AREA: 488 m²
CONSTRUCTION COST: 450,000 DM
COMMISSIONER: État Marocain

The residential Immeuble H1 (Building H1) was designed by the Moroccan architect Abdeslem Faraoui and the Moroccan-born French architect Patrice de Mazières in 1963. The three-storey Immeuble H1, together with the five-storey Immeubles H2 and H3 and the single-storey commercial building (known as 'Chaffeï'), form a complex perpendicular to Avenue du Prince Moulay Abdallah. Built in 1963, Immeuble H1 was, along with Immeuble D on the opposite side of the street, among the first buildings to be erected in the Centre Urbain at the beginning of the 1960s. The floor plans of Immeuble H1 feature compact and well-organised apartments with continuous loggias on their front sides (towards the courtyard) and staircases and kitchens with directly connected loggias to the rear (towards the street). The two apartments at both ends of Immeuble H1 additionally offer a generous living space. Historic photographs reveal an additional building on the street corner at the end of Immeuble H1, which does not appear on the plans. The typical architectural appearance of sand-coloured *béton brut* elements and white-rendered surfaces is applied differently for the front and rear facades. The elevation facing the street is closed, with small horizontal rows of windows, while the facade facing the courtyard is more open, with continuous horizontal balustrade elements.

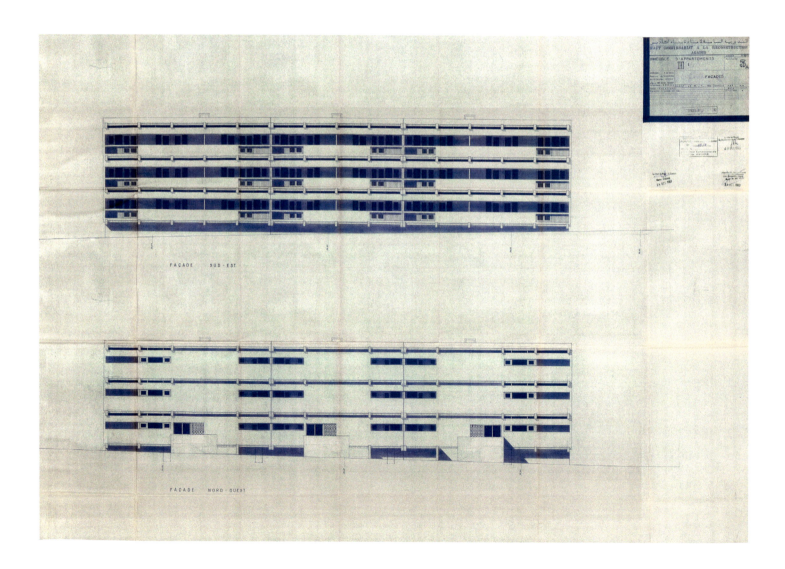

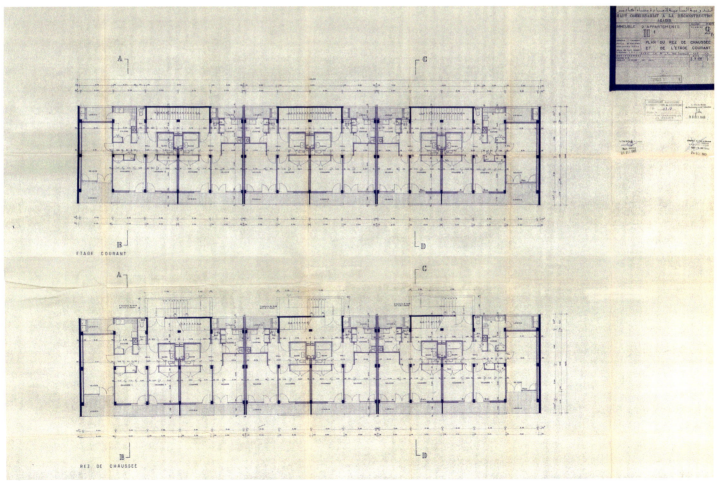

IMMEUBLE COMMERCIALE U1

ARCHITECT: Albert U. Froelich
YEAR: 1962 (opening of the construction site: 2 October 1962)
LOCATION: Centre Urbain
Floor area: 276 m²
CONSTRUCTION COST: 93,373 DM
COMMISSIONER: M. Lyazid Nadim

There is very little information about Immeuble Commerciale U1 (Commercial Building U1), which is located in the Centre Urbain at the intersection of Avenue des Forces Armées Royales and Boulevard Hassan II. It was commissioned by Lyazid Nadim and designed by the Swiss architect Albert U. Froelich. Construction work began in 1962. The single-storey Immeuble Commerciale U1 is situated between a pair of four-storey residential buildings. Its double orientation towards the street and interior courtyard assure a continuation of public life from the street into the inner courtyard. Even in these simple buildings, the construction details show that the architecture was designed to respond to climatic conditions. The facade is characterised by a strip of perforated openings situated above the windows, which allows for ventilation. A series of

brise-soleils (sun shades) is incorporated in a concrete beam underneath. The building is divided into five units. The rational structure, with sanitary installations located centrally, allows a flexible organisation. The shops either run across the entire depth of the building or are paired back-to-back.

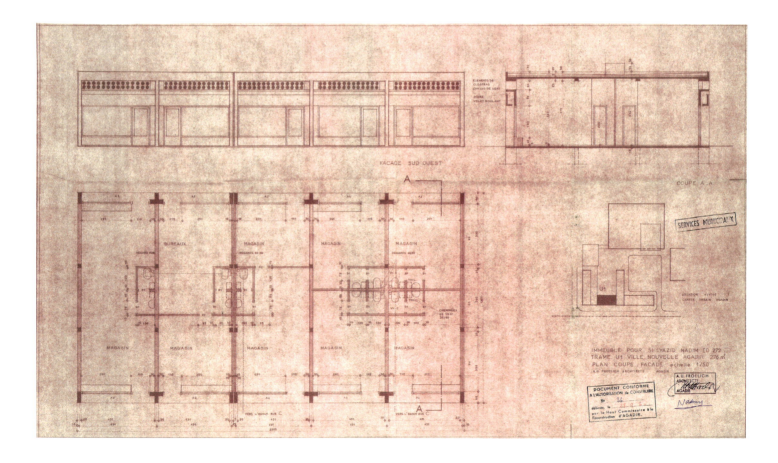

8 VILLAS EN BANDE

ARCHITECT: Pierre Coldefy, Claude Verdugo
YEAR: 1962–3
LOCATION: Secteur Résidentiel
FLOOR AREA: –
CONSTRUCTION COST: –
COMMISSIONER: État Marocain, Haut Commissariat
à la Reconstruction

The eight Villas en Bande (Terraced Villas) were designed by the French architect Pierre Coldefy and the Moroccan-born Spanish architect Claude Verdugo between 1962 and 1963. Originally planned as a staggered configuration of six and two units, connected on the site by an internal pathway, the Villas en Bande were realised as one staggered block of eight. Located in the Secteur Résidentiel between Boulevard E (today Rue Président Kennedy) and Rue D (today Rue des Nations Unies) the typology of the Villas en Bande belongs to a widespread type of housing in this neighbourhood. The floor plan reveals that the single-family villas are organised around a patio in an attempt to incorporate an intricate relationship between external and internal dwelling space, characteristic of Moroccan culture, into a modern typology. Next to the spacious living room, which is directly related to the patio, we encounter three bedrooms, a kitchen, a bathroom and two toilets. The generosity of the villas is supplemented by two enclosed exterior spaces (with terraces) on both sides of each unit. The section indicates a response to the climatic conditions of Agadir: a sophisticated system of cross ventilation connects the rooms continuously to the patios and outdoor spaces.

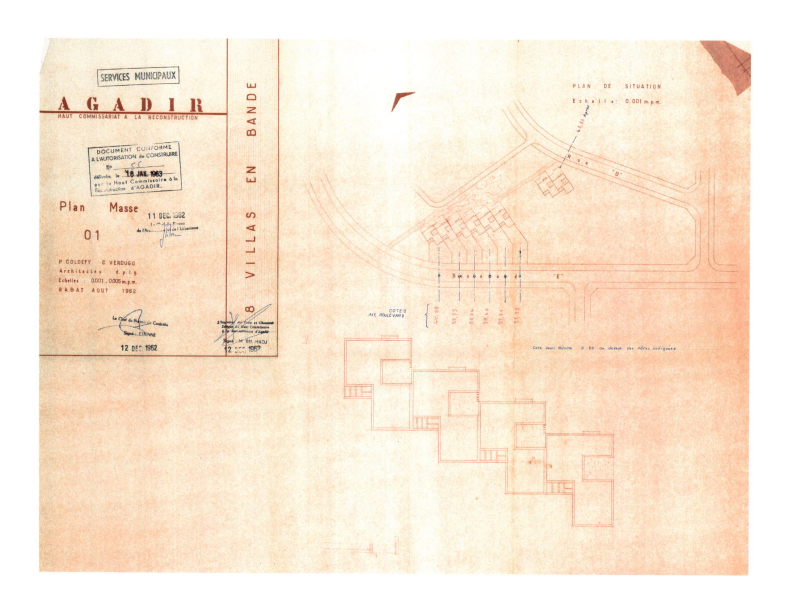

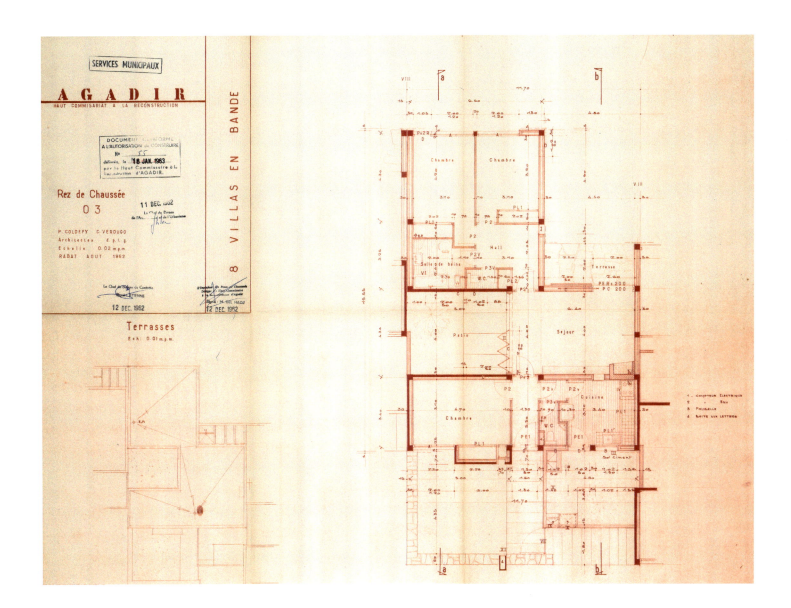

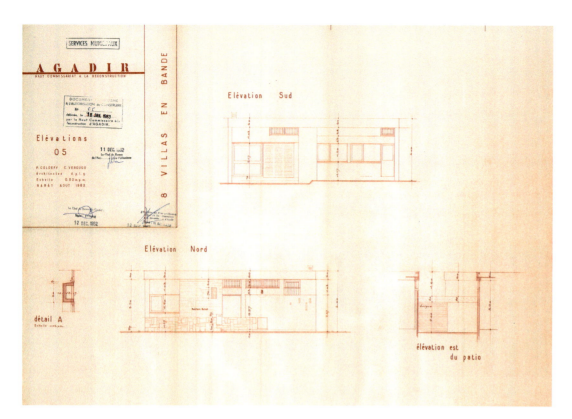

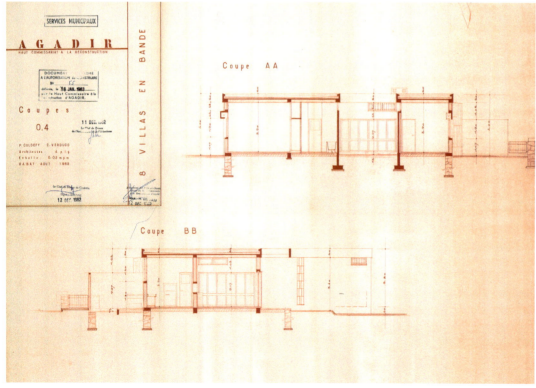

IMMEUBLE K2

ARCHITECT: Émile-Jean Duhon
YEAR: 1962–3 (opening of the construction site: 25 January 1963)
LOCATION: Centre Urbain
FLOOR AREA: 451 m²
CONSTRUCTION COST: 730,000 DM
COMMISSIONER: État Marocain

The four-storey residential Immeuble K2 (Building K2), with its commercial functions on the ground level, lies perpendicular to Avenue Hassan II and was designed by the French architect Émile-Jean Duhon in 1962. The Moroccan government commissioned it, and construction started in January 1963. Together with Immeuble K and the single-storey Immeuble Commerciale U1, Immeuble K2 forms a commercial and residential ensemble. These more hybrid building complexes of middle-rise housing typologies in combination with single-storey commercial buildings are frequently applied in the reconstruction of Agadir. The floor plans show very spacious dwellings that each have a rather large outdoor area, clearly indicating that these apartments were intended for large families from high-income groups. Sanitary functions, kitchens

and open-air *lavoirs* (washing rooms) are located at the rear of the building and have *mashrabiya*-like perforated walls, while a spacious living room and the majority of sleeping rooms are at the front with large windows and access to a loggia. Well-lit staircases lead to the various apartments and the communal roof. The architectural details reveal attention to the local climate, as the windows and the balconies are designed with large openings that allow cross ventilation. The building is divided into two structurally separated units by a double party wall due to seismic reasons. Confronted with the issue of density, the facade deals with privacy questions via the use of screens that prevent direct views from neighbouring buildings.

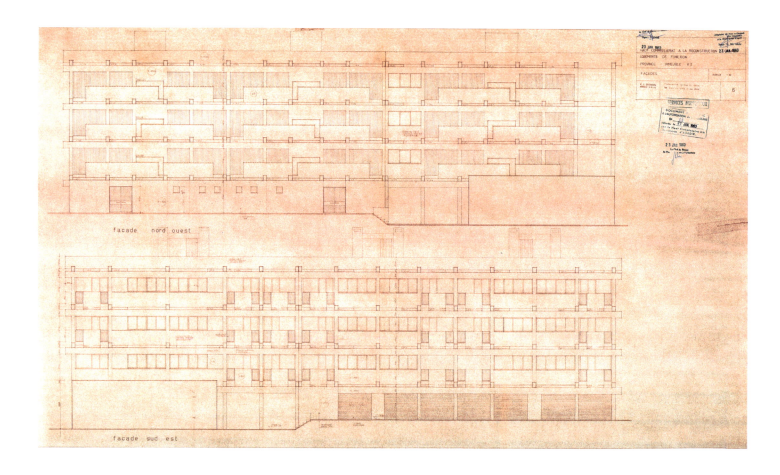

facade nord ouest

facade sud est

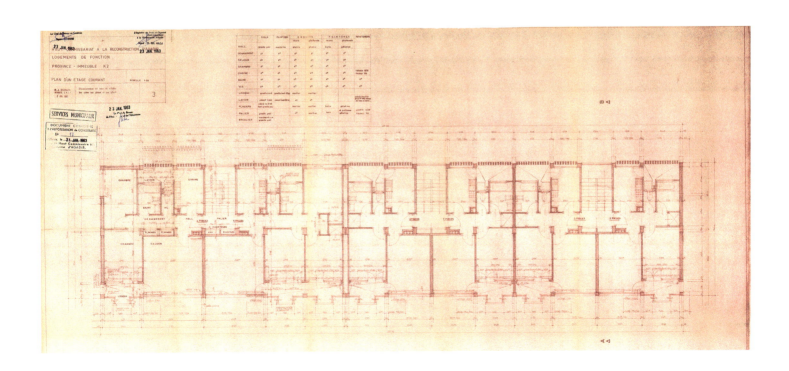

IMMEUBLE T1

ARCHITECT: Jean-François Zevaco
YEAR: 1962–3
LOCATION: Centre Urbain
FLOOR AREA: 1,650 m²
CONSTRUCTION COST: 409,000 DM
COMMISSIONER: État Marocain

The residential Immeuble T1 (Building T1) was designed by the Moroccan-born French architect Jean-François Zevaco in 1962 and built in 1963. Located in the Centre Urbain, Immeuble T1 is part of an urban ensemble consisting of other residential buildings such as Immeubles T2 and T3, the Villas en Bande and the Collège Souss Al Alima, which were all designed by Jean-François Zevaco. This urban ensemble features a spacious public green space around the school and many parking areas. The elongated three-storey-high Immeuble T1 is subdivided into four units, all of which are accessed by a staircase located between the units. These building units differ in size and in the compositions of their facades. Oriented towards the interior of the urban ensemble, three of the units have large square window openings, while one has smaller

horizontal rows of fenestration. The facade facing the parking is more enclosed and features perforated walls for the interior bathrooms and kitchens. Designed for administrative employees, the apartments feature well-designed and compact floor plans that vary from smaller one-bedroom flats to more spacious two-bedroom apartments.

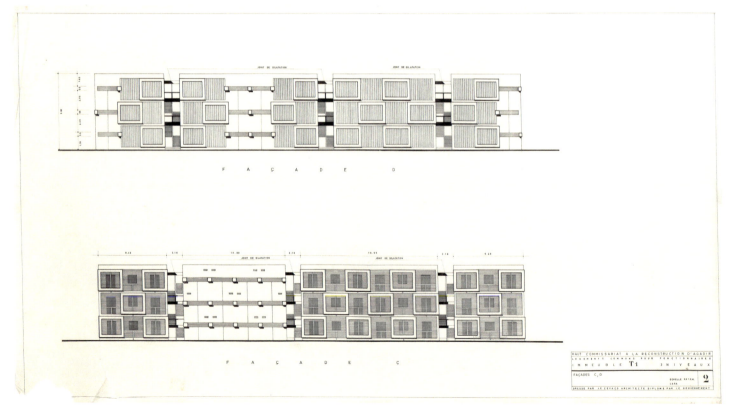

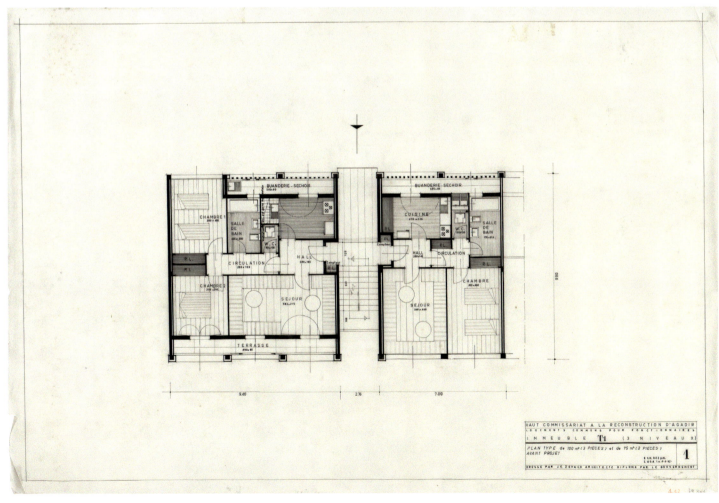

IMMEUBLE T2

ARCHITECT: Jean-François Zevaco
YEAR: 1962–4
LOCATION: Centre Urbain
FLOOR AREA: 1,900 m^2
CONSTRUCTION COST: 471,000 DM
COMMISSIONER: État Marocain

The residential Immeuble T2 (Building T2) was designed by the Moroccan-born French architect Jean-François Zevaco in 1962 and built in 1964. The two-storey apartment block is located in the Centre Urbain and is situated north of the urban ensemble consisting of the Collège Souss Al Alima, residential Immeubles T1 and T3 and the Villas en Bande – all conceived by Zevaco. Due to its location, parallel to Avenue Président Kennedy, Immeuble T2 frames the green campus of the Souss Al Alima school in the centre of the urban ensemble. The 95-m-long Immeuble T2 is divided into five units, each with four flats. Those on the ground floor are accessed directly from the outside, while the upper apartments are reached by a staircase. The spacious apartments have a continuous loggia on the south side and service balconies on the north side, connected to their kitchens. The compactly organised flats have a living room and two bedrooms, as well as a kitchen and a bathroom. The external appearance of the south facade of Immeuble T2 is characterised by distinctive rectangular concrete elements that cover the continuous loggia, together with a vertical semi-permeable structure. The rear facade also has covered openings, but is architecturally less elaborate.

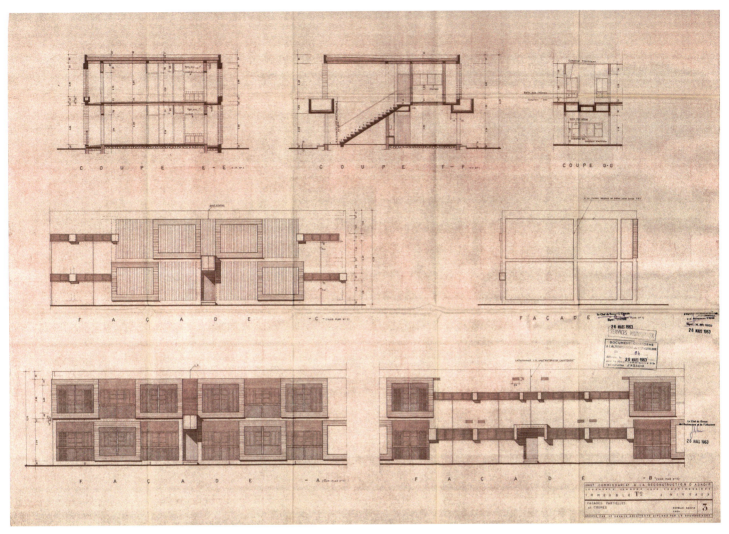

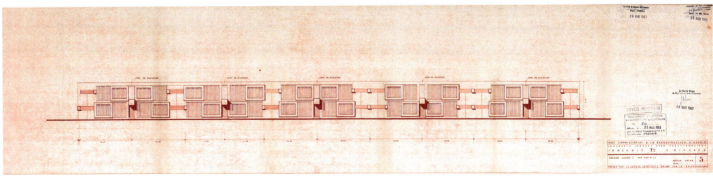

133

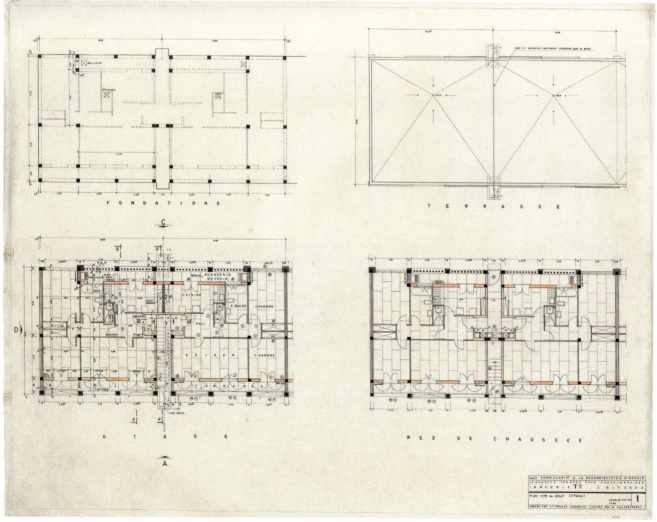

CENTRE RÄDDA BARNEN, CENTRE DE SANTÉ

ARCHITECT: Élie Azagury
YEAR: 1962–3
LOCATION: Centre Urbain
FLOOR AREA: –
CONSTRUCTION COST: 557,000 DM
COMMISSIONER: État Marocain, Ministère de la Santé Publique

The reconstruction of Agadir placed emphasis not only on housing, commercial and educational programmes but also on the accessibility of health facilities. For every 45,000 inhabitants, a Centre de Santé (Health Centre) was envisaged to provide access to specialised medical services. At the Rädda Barnen campus, which was commissioned by the Swedish foundation of the same name ('Rädda Barnen' translates as Save the Children), the Centre de Santé was complemented by three smaller houses and the Centre de l'Enfance (Childhood Centre) – all dedicated to the care of mothers and children. The campus is located between the Centre Urbain and the Nouveau Talborjt neighbourhood, facing the large public garden Ibn Zaïdoun. The health centre was designed by the Moroccan architect Élie Azagury

in 1962–3. It is organised around a central axis with waiting areas that are generously connected to green patios. At the periphery of the building are situated consultation rooms and offices that are directly related to the exterior. More general functions, such as a pharmacy and sterilisation rooms, are located at the end of the axis. The entrance area with reception desk at the start of the main axis is clearly recognisable through its sculptural character. The difference between public (higher) and semi-public (lower) functions is also accentuated in the room heights, as shown in the section. The language of sand-coloured *béton brut* beams and columns combined with white-rendered surfaces exemplifies the reconstruction architecture of Agadir.

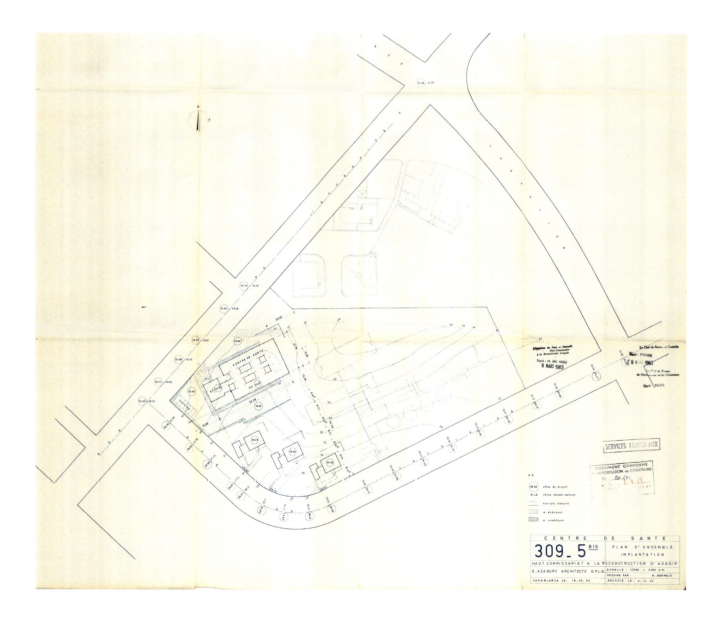

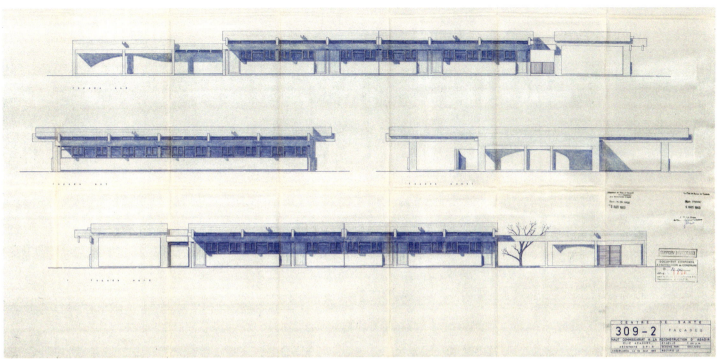

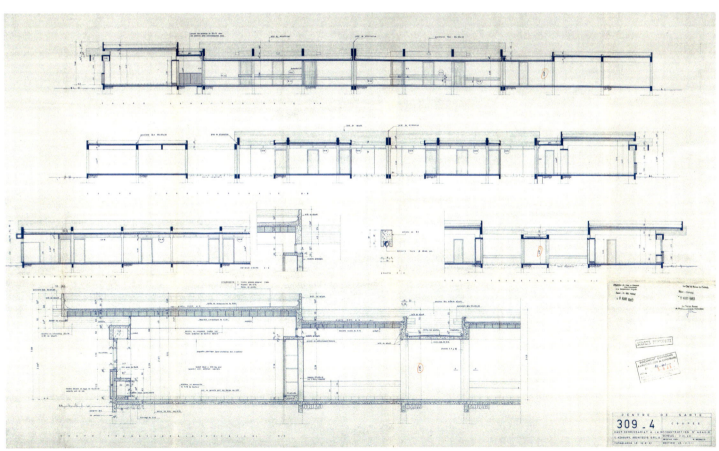

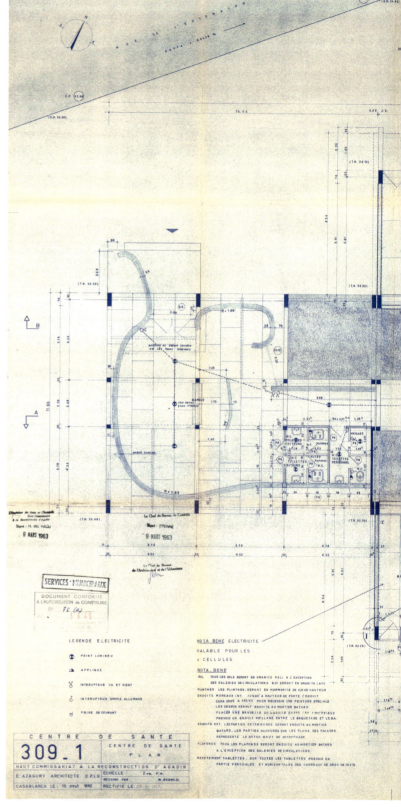

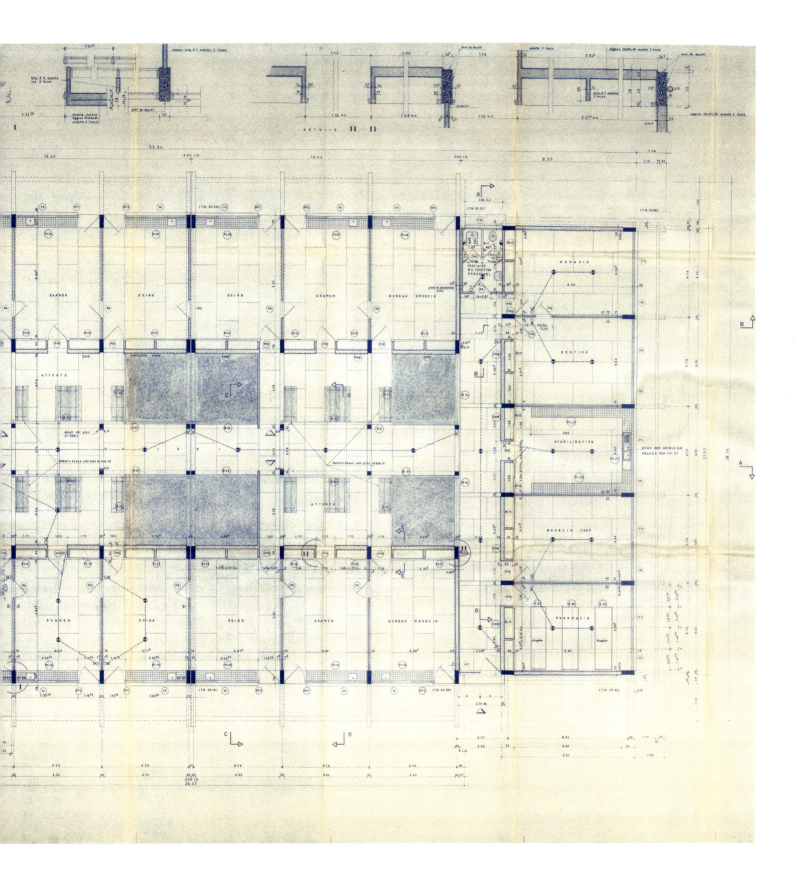

IMMEUBLE N

ARCHITECT: Émile-Jean Duhon
YEAR: 1962–3
LOCATION: Centre Urbain
FLOOR AREA: 545 m²
CONSTRUCTION COST: 495,000 DM
COMMISSIONER: État Marocain,
Ministère de l'Interieur

Immeuble N (Building N), also called Immeuble Résidentiel pour la Municipalité (Residential Building for the Municipality), was designed by the French architect Émile-Jean Duhon and realised in 1963. Together with the low-rise Immeuble M1–3 (today replaced by multistorey residential buildings), it complements the urban ensemble of the Hôtel de Ville and the Poste Principale. Accessed via Rue K, it served as a residential building for the employees of the municipality due to its immediate proximity to the most important administrative buildings. Unfortunately, only a few documents were found for Immeuble N, including a site plan and drawings of its facades. Hence, we know little about the floor plans and other aspects of its residential typology. What is clear, however, is that Immeuble N belongs to the everyday urban fabric of Agadir and has a less expressive architecture than other structures. The composition of its facades is less sophisticated than that of other, more prominent residential buildings in Agadir. The typical visible elements in *béton brut* are reduced to a minimum, and the window openings are distributed across the facade in a varying, rational rhythm.

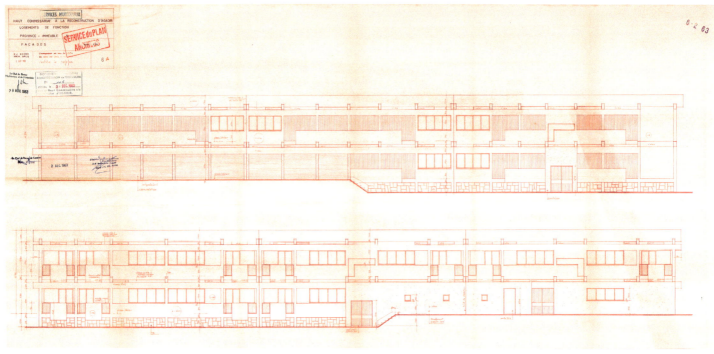

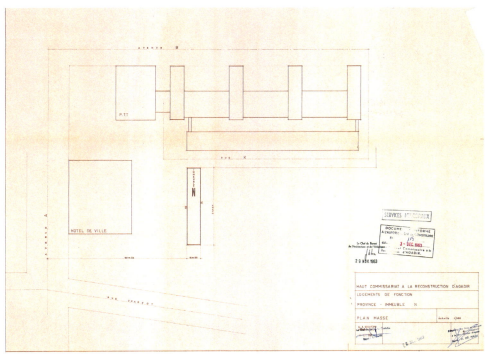

141

LOGEMENTS ET MAGASINS

ARCHITECT: Bureau de l'Urbanisme
YEAR: 1962–3
LOCATION: Quartier Industriel Sud
FLOOR AREA: 3,105 m²
CONSTRUCTION COST: 577,000 DM
COMMISSIONER: M. Ali B. M'Barek,
President de l'Association du Bloc 10

The Logements et Magasins (Housing and Shops) were designed by the Bureau de l'Urbanisme (Urban Planning Office) from 1962 to 1963. The thirty-two patio houses and four small commercial units were commissioned by M. Ali B. M'Barek, the president of the association of Block 10. From the archival documents, it can be identified that these plans were intended for the reconstruction of Blocks 10A and 10B located at the intersection of Rue de Marrakesh and Rue de Moulay Idriss in the Quartier Industriel Sud. The patio houses are organised on an eight-metre by eight-metre grid initially introduced by urban planner Michel Écochard prior to the earthquake. Compared with other patio houses, like the Villas en Bande in the Immeubles T1–T3 urban ensemble by Jean-François Zevaco, these patio houses were designed much

more modestly. Always grouped in a sub-unit of four houses, the single-storey dwellings are organised around a patio that is accessed either directly from the main road or through a smaller road internal to the block. The sanitary rooms, the kitchens and two other rooms all open onto the covered patio. These rational and sparsely equipped housing units stood on column foundations and their concrete structure was infilled with brickwork.

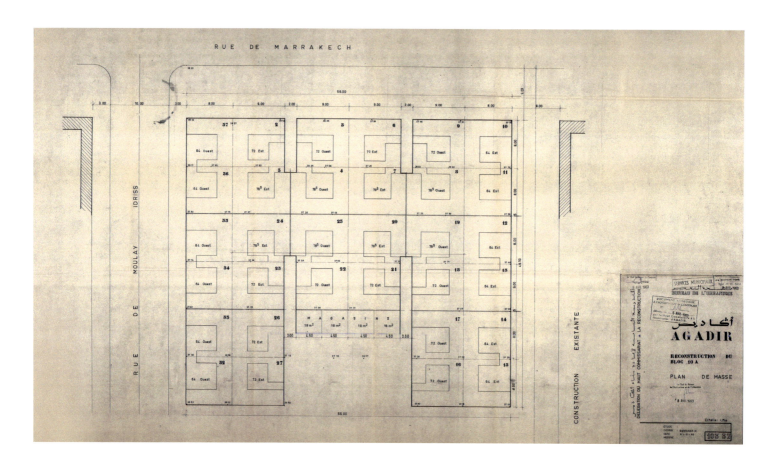

143

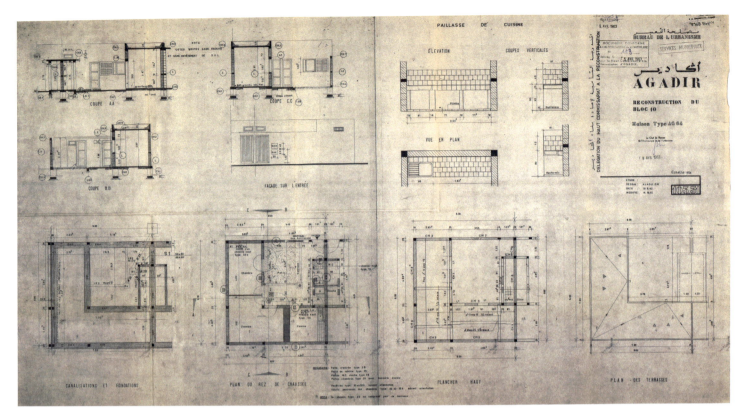

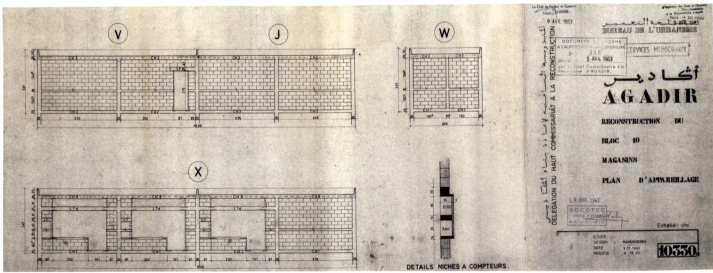

GROUPE SCOLAIRE N°1 DU NOUVEAU TALBORJT

ARCHITECT: Albert Planque, René Deneux
YEAR: 1963
LOCATION: Nouveau Talborjt
FLOOR AREA: 1,070 m^2
CONSTRUCTION COST: 770,000 DM
COMMISSIONER: État Marocain,
Ministère de l'Education Nationale

The Groupe Scolaire N°1 (School Group No. 1), also called École Taqadoum, was designed by the French architects Albert Planque and René Deneux in 1963. Located in the Nouveau Talborjt neighbourhood, the school buildings, together with a medical centre and the director's and caretaker's dwellings, form an urban ensemble on Boulevard Mohamed Cheikh Saadi. Unfortunately, only the plans of the dwellings were found in the archives. The two houses of the directors are slightly staggered, and each is equipped with a separate garage and a spacious garden. The two-storey dwelling units consist of a living room and kitchen on the ground floor with a terrace and three bedrooms, and a bathroom on the upper floor. The houses are rendered white and have an elementary architectural language. The caretaker's house is much smaller and has a more explicit external appearance. Located next to the school entrance and against a stone wall, the one-storey dwelling consists of a small living room, a kitchen, a bedroom and a tiny bathroom. Attached to the entrance wall lies an equally diminutive medical centre consisting of an examination room and a small waiting room.

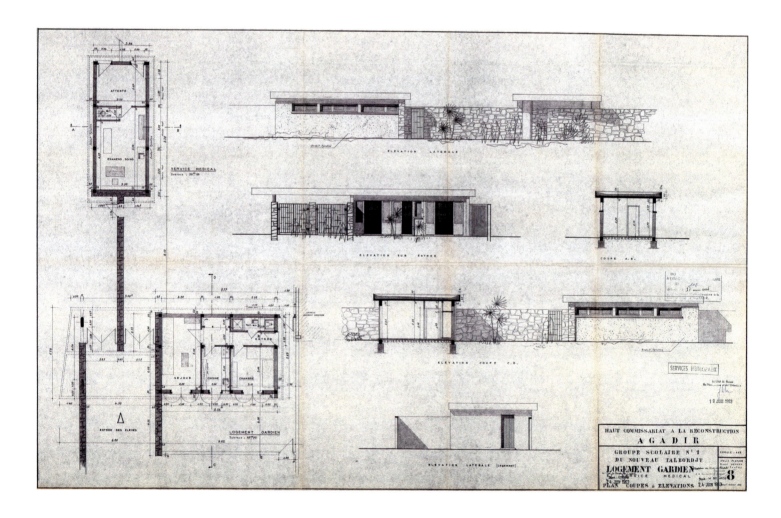

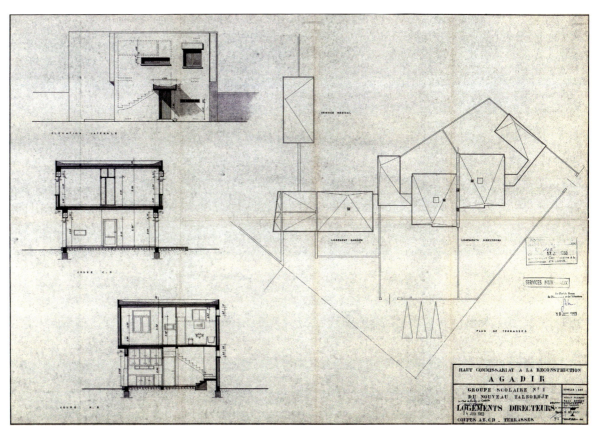

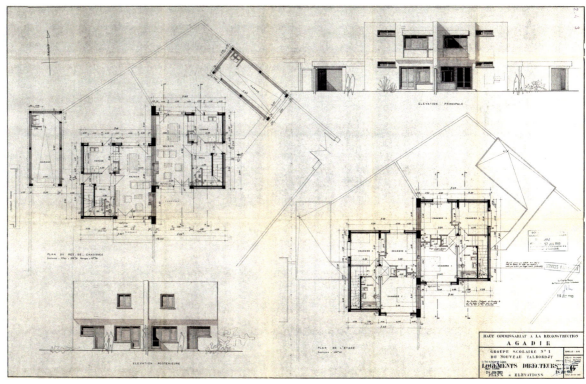

147

CENTRE COMMERCIAL

ARCHITECT: Patrice de Mazières
YEAR: 1960–3
LOCATION: Quartier Industriel Sud
FLOOR AREA: 2,600 m²
CONSTRUCTION COST: 528,000 DM
COMMISSIONER: État Marocain,
Ministère des Travaux Publics

The Centre Commercial (Commercial Centre), also called Petit Marché (Small Market), was designed in 1963 by the Moroccan-born French architect Patrice de Mazières. It was built as part of a larger urban ensemble called La Cité Hassani or the Cité Ouvrière d'Urgence (Emergency Workers' City) in the Quartier Industriel Sud (Industrial Neighbourhood South) together with the Mosquée Sénégal and the 500 logements designed by French architect Éliane Castelnau together with French architect Jean-Paul Ichter. The Centre Commercial is designed as a regular grid structure of concrete columns and beams that connects the mosque with surrounding functions such as the hammam and the car park, forming an L-shape that frames a public square. The juxtaposition of the cells of the grid constitutes the Small Market as well as a more extensive market hall. Two patios with trees and adjacent cafés and toilets are kept open in the grid. The market reconnects the surrounding streets with the square and with a set of passageways. The low-rise centre adapts to the topography with a stepped configuration. Its supporting structure is made of concrete and the walls are composed of bricks, giving the Centre Commercial its repetitive and rational appearance.

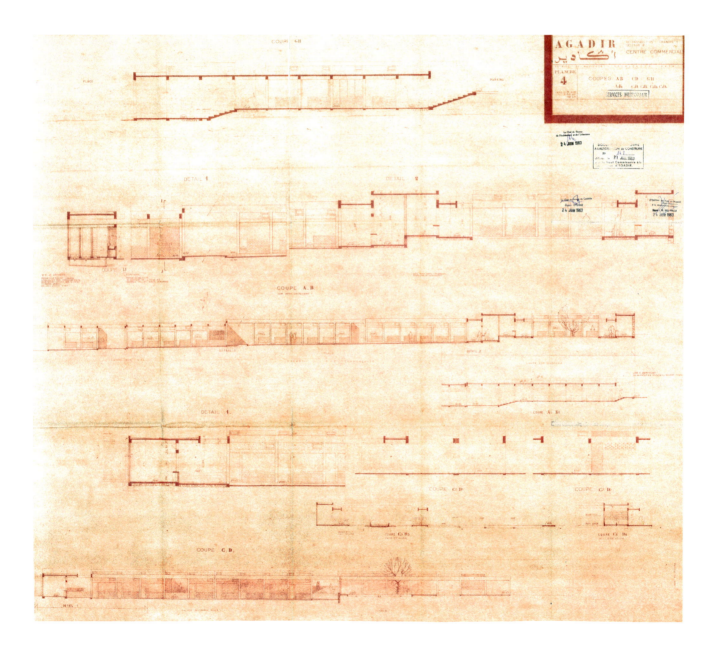

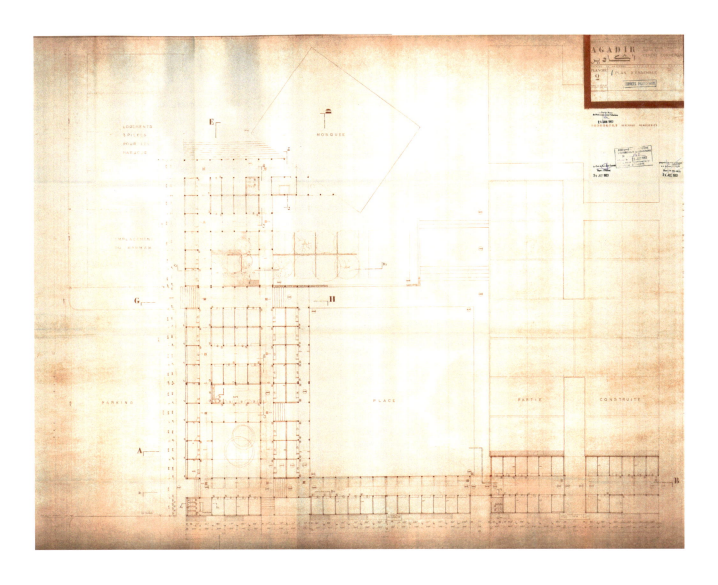

VILLAS À 3 PIECES

ARCHITECT: Abdeslem Faraoui, Patrice de Mazières
YEAR: 1963
LOCATION: Centre Urbain
FLOOR AREA: –
CONSTRUCTION COST: –
COMMISSIONER: État Marocain, Haut Commissariat
à la Reconstruction

Twenty Villas à 3 Pieces (Three-room Villas) were
designed by the Moroccan architect Abdeslem
Faraoui and the Moroccan-born French architect
Patrice de Mazières in 1963. According to the
archival records, the villas are situated in the Centre
Urbain. Compared with the Villas en Bande that
the two architects designed and built three years
later, there is very little information about the Villas à
3 Pieces. Their typology seems to accommodate
a luxurious urban style of individual housing with both
front and back gardens, a small service courtyard
and a parking space. The very spacious single-storey
villas are entered along a wall that connects the
building entrance to the central hall of the house.
From there, the kitchen, living room, two bedrooms
with a bathroom and toilet are accessed. The
main roof structure of the villas is constructed in a
sand-coloured *béton brut*. Immediately below,
there is a continuous row of horizontal windows that
provides the rooms with light and offers cross
ventilation. The external walls are primarily without
windows and white-rendered. The concrete support
structure stands on column foundations and is
completed with perforated walls that allow for rear
ventilation of the facade.

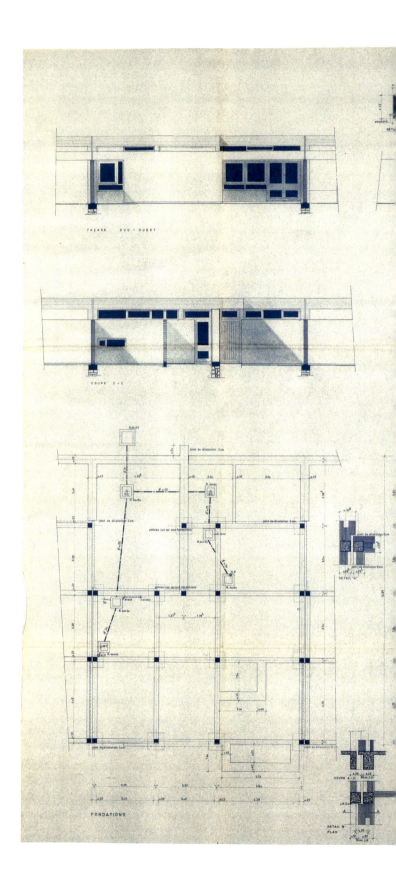

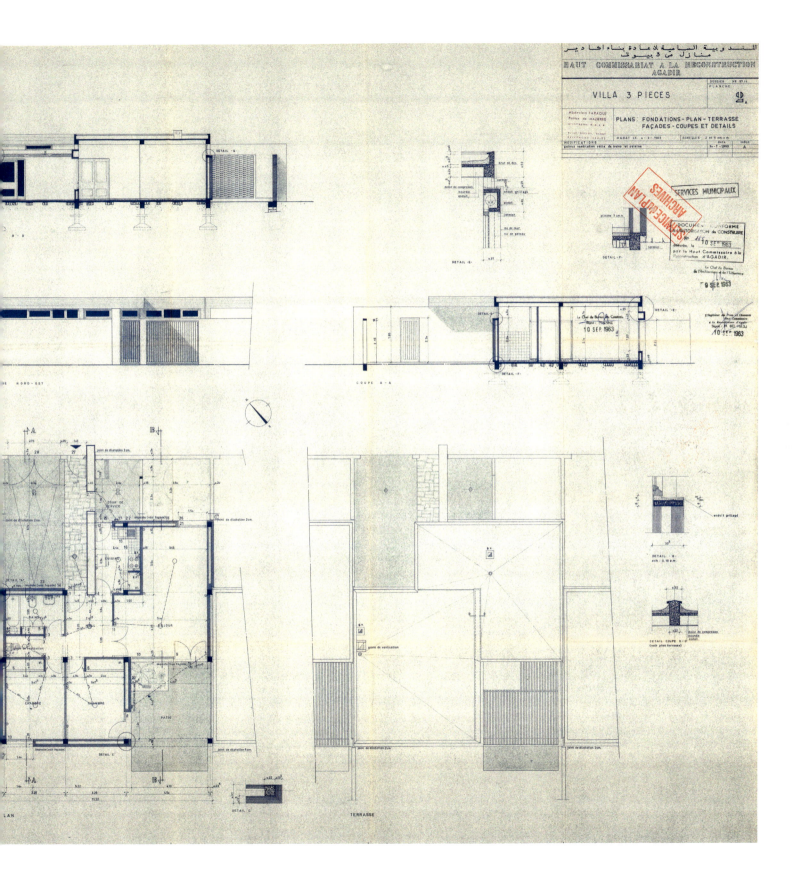

VILLAS EN BANDE

ARCHITECT: Jean-François Zevaco
YEAR: 1963–4
LOCATION: Centre Urbain
FLOOR AREA: 5,200 m²
CONSTRUCTION COST: 528,000 DM
COMMISSIONER: État Marocain,
Haut Commissariat à la Reconstruction

The Villas en Bande (Terraced Villas) were designed by Moroccan-born French architect Jean-François Zevaco in 1962 and built in 1964. They are situated in the western part of the Centre Urbain along Avenue des Forces Armées Royales and Avenue Président Kennedy. Together with Immeubles T1–T3 and the Collège Souss Al Alima, also conceived by Zevaco, the seventeen Villas en Bande form an urban ensemble. According to the architect, the terraced villas were 'economical in terms of their footprint, the houses were also economical to build, easy to maintain and perfectly suited to the lifestyle of an urban Muslim middle class population'. The dwellings consisted of two different typologies. Seven Type A villas were built with three habitable rooms, a kitchen and a bathroom, and ten Type B villas were built with four habitable rooms,

a kitchen and a bathroom. For reasons of economy, they form two compact blocks. Block 1 consisted of four Type A and six Type B villas, and Block 2 comprised three Type A and four Type B villas. All were equipped with several patios and spacious gardens, which ensured the privacy of the residents. To avoid the disadvantage of some villas being well oriented while others were unfavourably positioned, each room in each villa was double-oriented. Architect Jean-François Zevaco won the Aga Khan Award for Architecture in 1980 for these Villas en Bande.

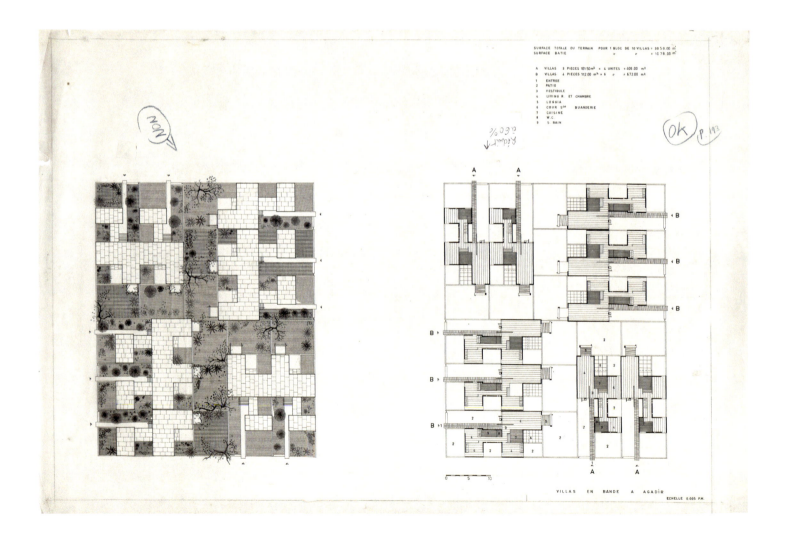

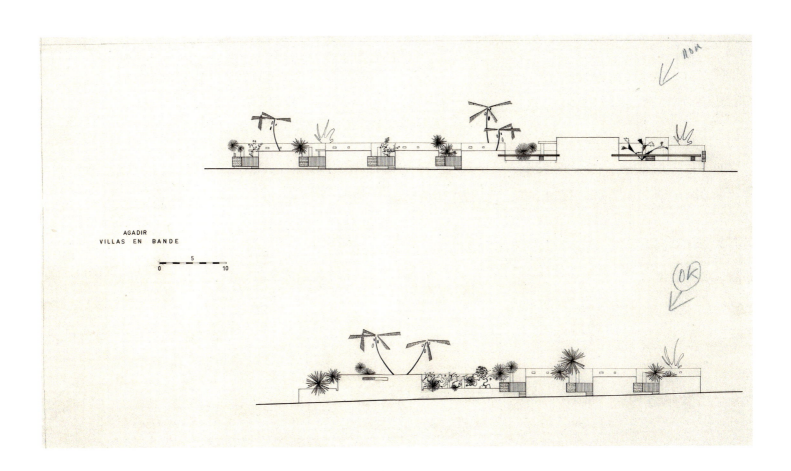

AGADIR
VILLAS EN BANDE

0   5   10

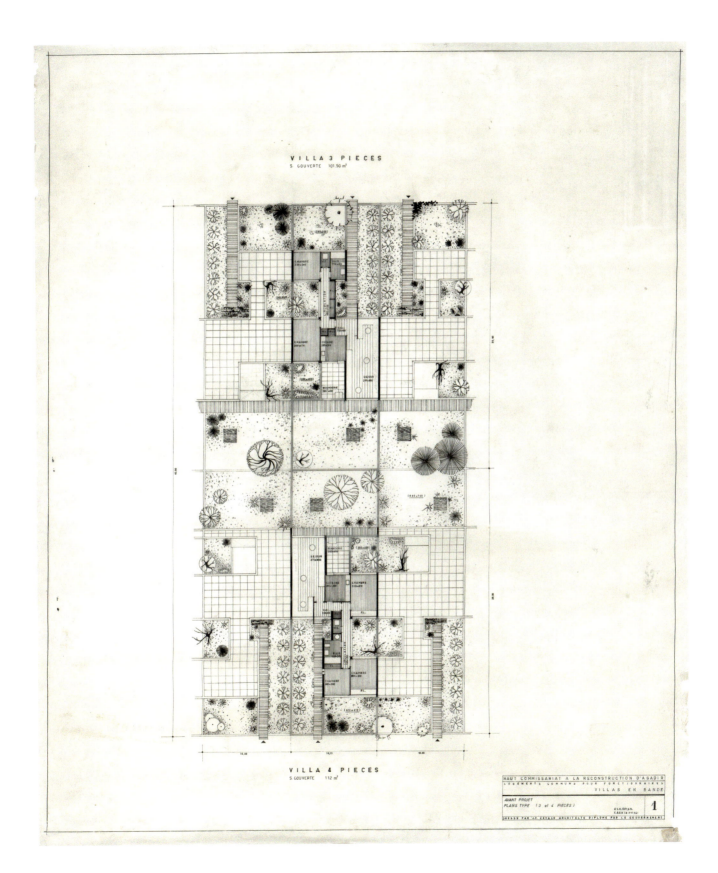

VILLA 3 PIECES

S. GOUVERTE   101.50 m²

VILLA 4 PIECES

S. GOUVERTE   112 m²

HAUT COMMISSARIAT A LA RECONSTRUCTION D'AGADIR
LOGEMENTS COMMUNS POUR FONCTIONNAIRES
VILLAS EN BANDE

AVANT PROJET
PLANS TYPE (3 et 4 PIECES)

ECH.0,01 p.m.
CASA Le 17-61

1

DRESSE PAR Jr ZEVACO ARCHITECTE DIPLOME PAR LE GOUVERNEMENT

IMMEUBLES O1 AND O2

ARCHITECT: Abdeslem Faraoui, Patrice de Mazières
YEAR: 1962–3
Location: Centre Urbain
FLOOR AREA: 1,090m^2
CONSTRUCTION COST: 1,600,000 DM
COMMISSIONER: État Marocain

The residential Immeubles O1 and O2 (Buildings O1 and O2) were designed by the Moroccan architect Abdeslem Faraoui and the Moroccan-born French architect Patrice de Mazières in 1963. They are positioned perpendicular to Avenue du Prince Moulay Abdallah next to Immeuble D. Both buildings stand on a massive plinth that has a wall facing the street and frames the space between the five-storey Immeubles O1 and O2. The communal area on this plinth takes the form of a lush green courtyard and a parking area. The floor plans of the two buildings feature spacious apartments with continuous loggias to the south. Staircases and kitchens with access to small loggias are situated on the north side. This interior organisation is reflected in the design

of the facades: structural elements such as beams are in sand-coloured *béton brut*, while walls and balustrades are in white render. Furthermore, the north facade features only small horizontal window openings while the south facade is characterised by open and continuous loggias with balustrades that are interspersed with closed elements. This system of closed north-oriented facades and more open south-oriented ones allows Immeubles O1 and O2 to stand in close proximity while nonetheless regulating the privacy of their inhabitants.

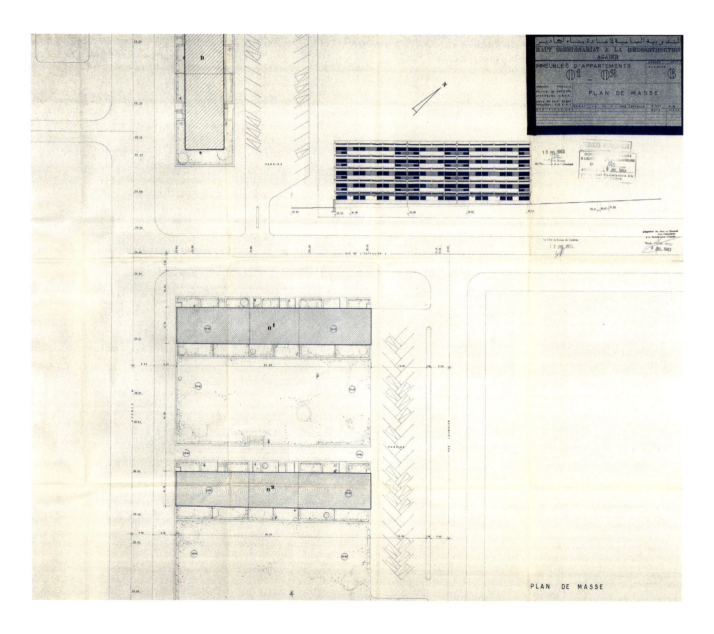

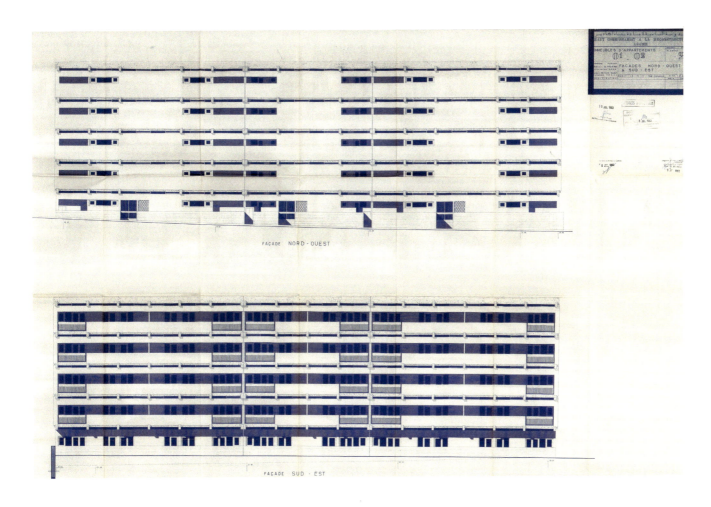

FACADE NORD-OUEST

FACADE SUD-EST

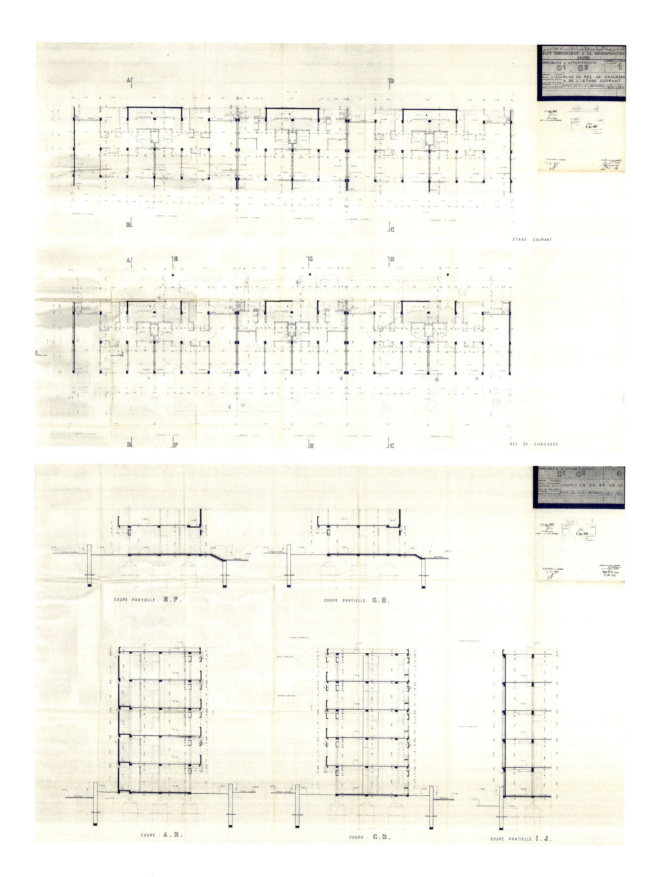

ETAGE COURANT

REZ - DE - CHAUSSEE

COUPE PARTIELLE : E . F .

COUPE PARTIELLE : G . H .

COUPE : A . B .

COUPE : C . D .

COUPE PARTIELLE I . J .

LE PETIT MARCHÉ DE TALBORJT

ARCHITECT: Pierre Coldefy, Claude Verdugo
YEAR: 1963–4
LOCATION: Nouveau Talborjt
FLOOR AREA: 2,100 m²
CONSTRUCTION COST: 487,160 DM
COMMISSIONER: État Marocain,
Ministère de l'Interieur

The Petit Marché de Talborjt (Small Market of Talborjt) was designed by the French architect Pierre Coldefy and the Moroccan-born Spanish architect Claude Verdugo in 1963 and built in 1964. Located close to the lively Place Tamri in the Nouveau Talborjt neighbourhood, it is a local market that provides fresh food as well as other products for everyday use. Three distinctive buildings – called Blocks A, B and C – form the ensemble of the Petit Marché de Talborjt. The two-storey Block A extends the street and the public square. It has a distinctive cantilevered roof construction in *béton brut* and a base in natural stone. It comprises larger shops with an open floor plan on the ground floor and storage rooms above. Block B and part of Block C are capped by vaulted roofs and mainly provide

the market with storage spaces and smaller shops. Block C houses a large loading dock for goods. It accommodates sanitary facilities on the ground floor and office spaces on the upper floor, accessed via a prominent spiral staircase.

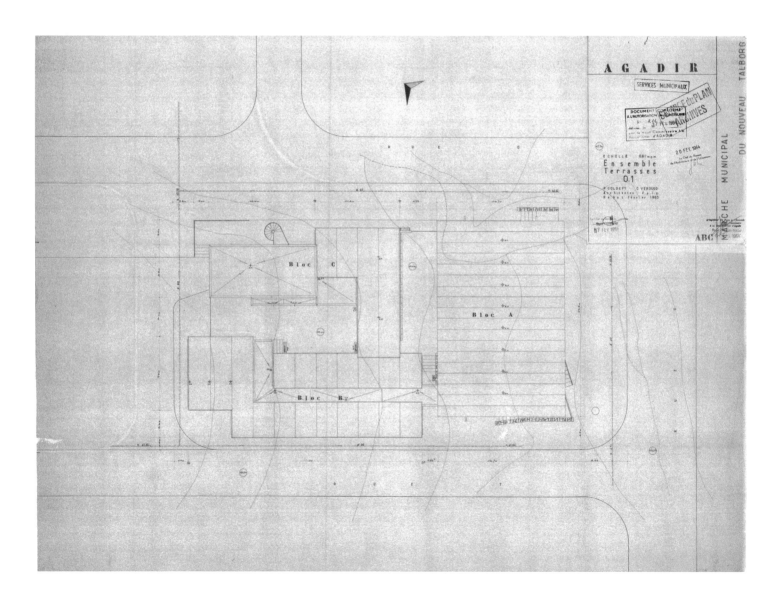

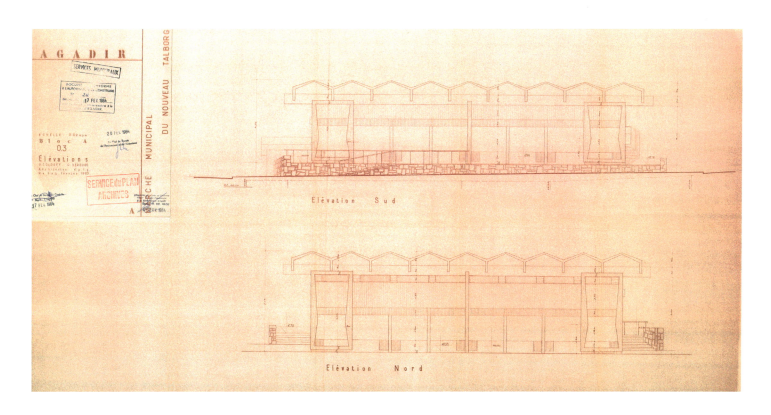

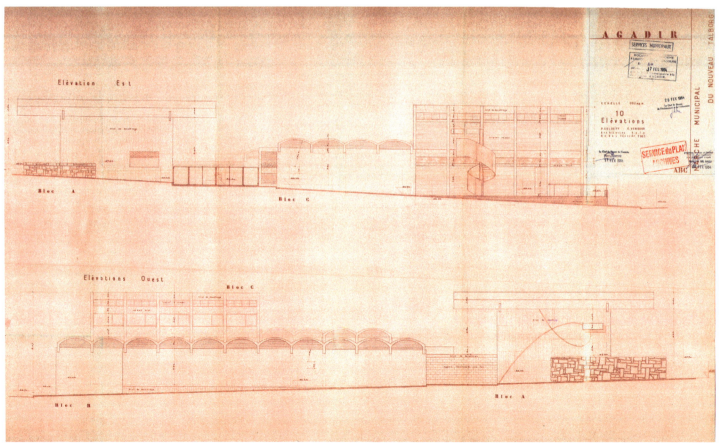

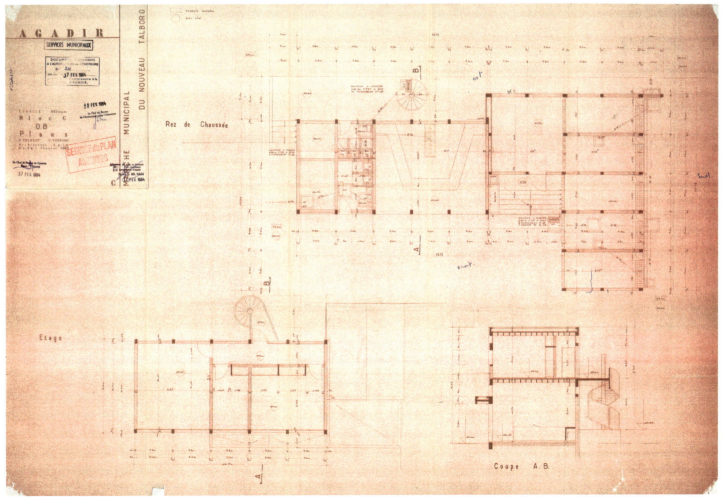

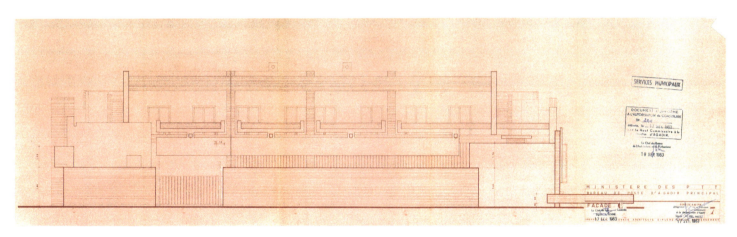

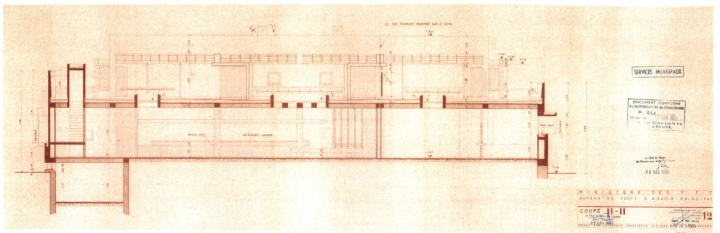

COLLÈGE SOUSS AL ALIMA

ARCHITECT: Jean-François Zevaco
YEAR: 1962–4
LOCATION: Centre Urbain
FLOOR AREA: 1,972 m²
CONSTRUCTION COST: 975,000 DM
COMMISSIONER: État Marocain,
Ministère de l'Éducation Nationale

The Collège Souss Al Alima (Souss Al Alima school), originally called Groupe Scolaire du Centre Urbain (school group of the Centre Urbain) was designed by Moroccan-born French architect Jean-François Zevaco and built in 1964. It is part of the urban ensemble consisting of Immeubles T1–T3 and the Villas en Bande – all also conceived by Zevaco. The school is located on a green public campus and is accessed via the small Rue de l'O.U.A to the south of the ensemble. Architecturally, the plan of the school takes the shape of a butterfly. It consists of four two-storey units, each with eight classrooms, and a centrally located canteen. The school's architecture is characterised by two large platforms that, on the one hand, provide a covered forecourt for access to the lower classrooms and, on the other hand, are reached laterally via stairs and thus provide access to the classrooms on the upper floors. In addition, standing perpendicular to the complex to the north are the caretakers' quarters and, to the south, the sanitary rooms. The school was developed with great attention to detail, which is reflected in the intermediate spaces that mediate between inside and outside but also in the recessed window openings that allow the classrooms to open to the exterior while providing shade.

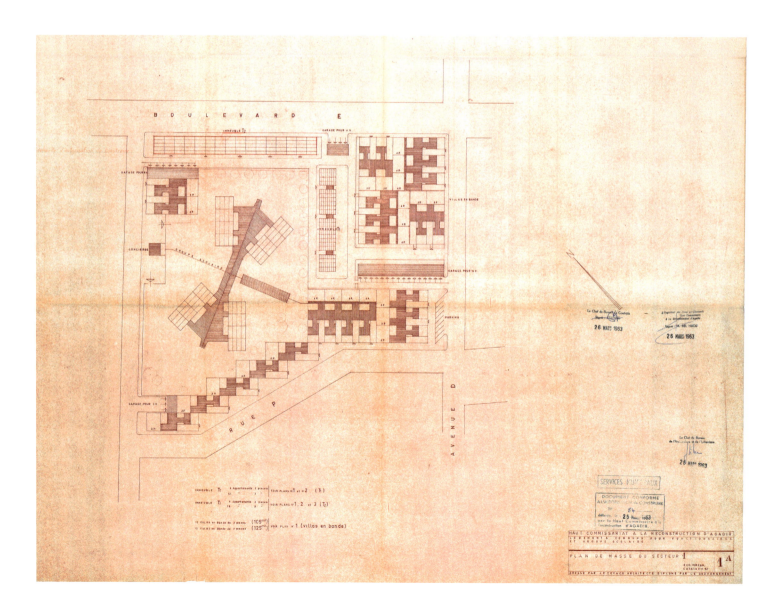

TRIBUNAL ADMINISTRATIF

ARCHITECT: Élie Azagury
YEAR: 1963–4
LOCATION: Centre Urbain
FLOOR AREA: –
CONSTRUCTION COST: –
COMMISSIONER: État Marocain,
Ministère de la Justice

The Tribunal Administratif (Administrative Court), also known as Tribunal du Sadad, was designed by the Moroccan architect Élie Azagury in 1963 and built in 1964. The building is located in the Centre Urbain, in the immediate vicinity of the Cité Administrative along Boulevard Hassan II. It faces a smaller public square along the boulevard. The monumental architecture of the Tribunal Administratif, in *béton brut* with white-rendered elements, is closely interwoven with the landscape around it. On the ground floor, the courthouse consists of a conglomeration of different buildings with various functions – such as an entrance building, premises for a caretaker and office spaces – which are located around a garden and connected via covered galleries. A large part of the ground floor consists of the open Salle des Pas Perdus (Hall of Lost Causes), a spacious and open public lobby in the middle of the garden that is shaded by the courtrooms above. From the Salle des Pas Perdus, the three courtrooms on the first floor are accessed by a generous monumental public staircase in *béton brut*. A parallel system of staircases (without access to the ground floor) offers access to the basement, where the incarcerated are detained and the archives are located.

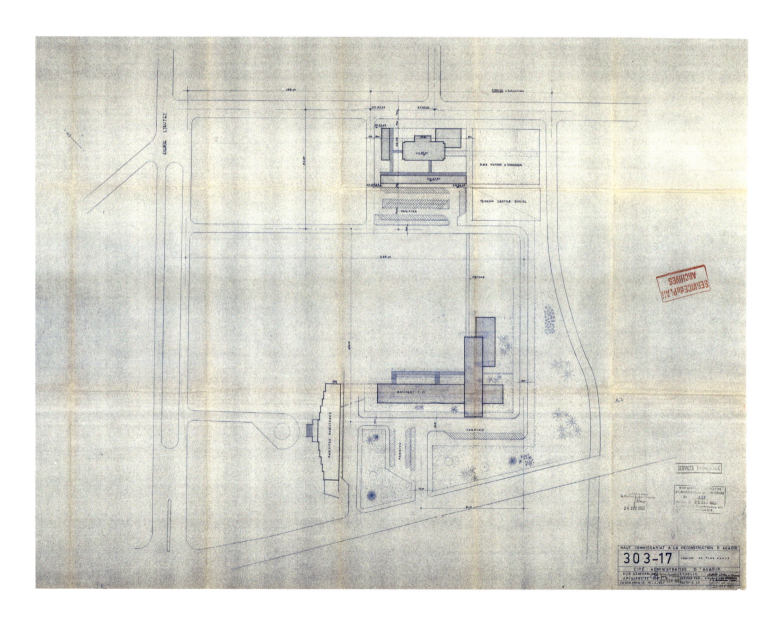

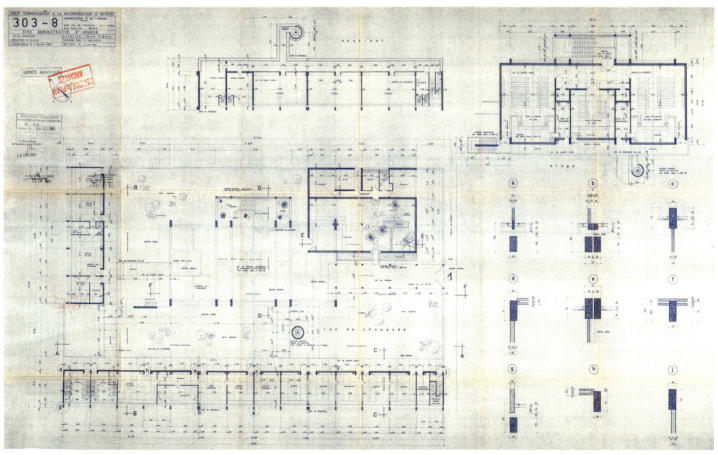

179

CENTRE RÄDDA BARNEN, CENTRE DE L'ENFANCE

ARCHITECT: Élie Azagury
YEAR: 1963
LOCATION: Centre Urbain
FLOOR AREA: 1,600 m²
CONSTRUCTION COST: 600,000 DM
COMMISSIONER: Societé de bienfaissance Suédoise
Rädda Barnen

The second entity at the Rädda Barnen campus is the Centre de l'Enfance (Childhood Centre), designed by Moroccan architect Élie Azagury. It is an ensemble of four different, single storey buildings that are related through a common pathway system. The main central path, connected to Rue Lavoisier, navigates the topographical differences and offers access to the Centre de l'Enfance as well as the Centre de Santé located in the west of the campus. Typologically, the two centres differ from each other. The childhood centre's four single-storey buildings, with their different dimensions, each take on a separate function. The main building to the north, known as Hygiène Scolaire (School Hygiene), houses offices, changing rooms and radiology rooms. The Garderie d'Enfants (Childcare Centre) to

the east is housed in the second-largest building. Connected with a canopy to the Garderie, we find the kitchen building with its very expressive concrete roofscapes – the so-called 'lanterns', which provide air circulation. Next to the main pathway, we find the Salle des Conférences et des Projections (Conference and Projection Room). The architectural language of the Centre de l'Enfance is comparable with that of the Centre de Santé. The structural elements are made of *béton brut* and support the roofs of the buildings with their distinctive cantilevered double beams, while the walls in between are in white render.

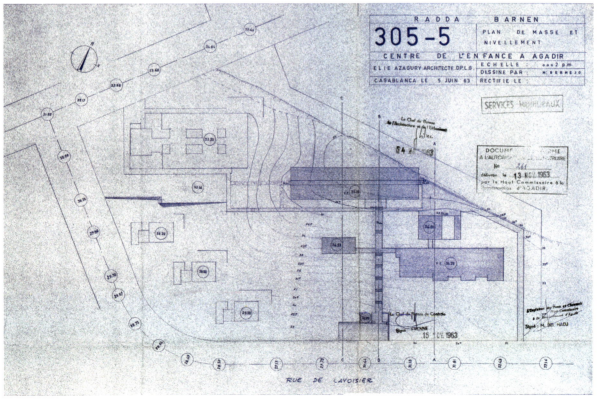

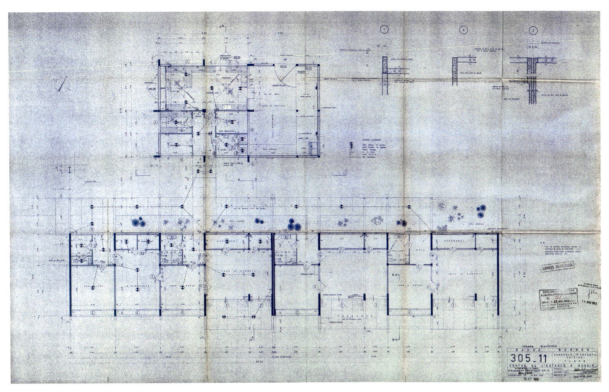

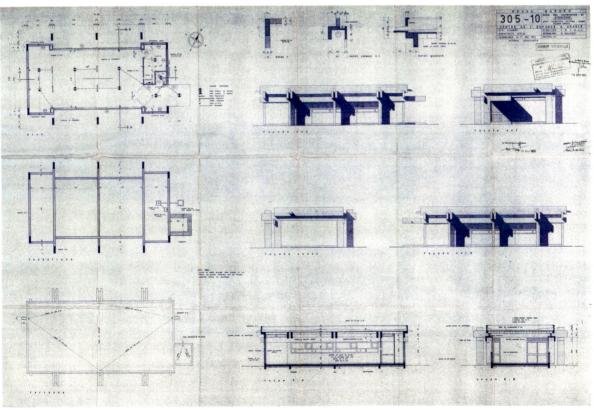

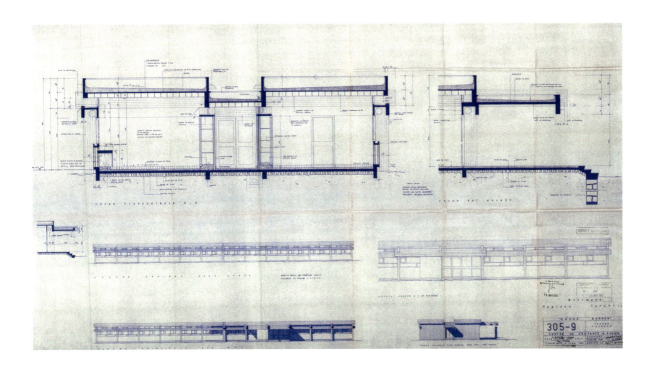

183

CITÉ SUISSE

ARCHITECT: Albert U. Froelich
YEAR: 1963–5
LOCATION: Secteur Résidentiel
FLOOR AREA: 4,361 m²
CONSTRUCTION COST: 1,631,000 DM
COMMISSIONER: Société Suisse de Radiodiffusion et Télévision

The Cité Suisse (Swiss Neighbourhood) was designed by the Morocco-based Swiss architect Albert U. Froelich in 1963 and built in 1965. It was financed by aid funds from Switzerland and the Swiss Red Cross. The neighbourhood is located between Rue du Koweit, Rue du Caire, Rue Mokhtar Soussi and Rue d'Alger in the Secteur Résidentiel of Agadir. It consists of fifty-six three-room houses, six central commercial entities and a Maison des Jeunes (Youth Centre) located southwest of the Cité Suisse in combination with a sports field. The individual houses are clustered in small groups of staggered units that are carefully positioned in the landscape and surrounded by gardens. They all have vaulted roofs, which define the characteristic exterior appearance of the neighbourhood. The units are designed to be earthquake-proof, built with a steel frame with walls and roofs constructed with light materials made of porous concrete. The single-storey residential units are equipped with two bedrooms, a living room, a kitchen, a hall and a bathroom. A corridor connects all the rooms with the garden. Houses, shops and the youth club are connected by a system of roads and pedestrian paths, and form a close-knit urban ensemble within the wider urban fabric of Agadir.

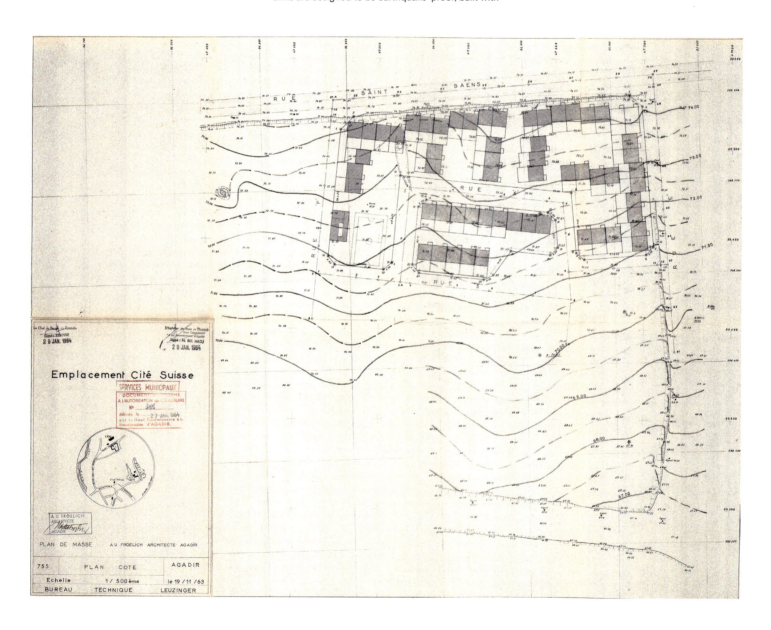

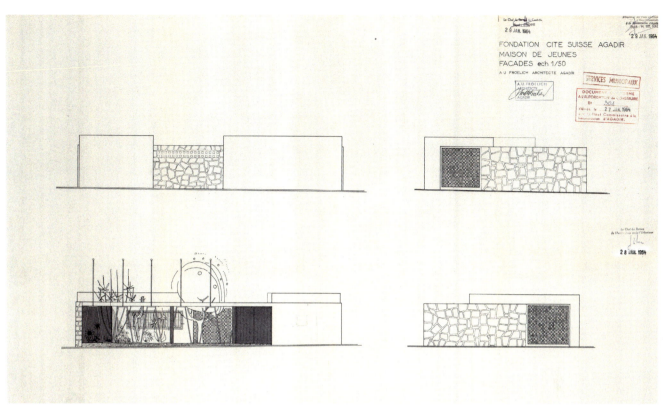

FONDATION CITE SUISSE AGADIR
MAISON DE JEUNES
FACADES ech 1/50

A U FROELICH ARCHITECTE AGADIR

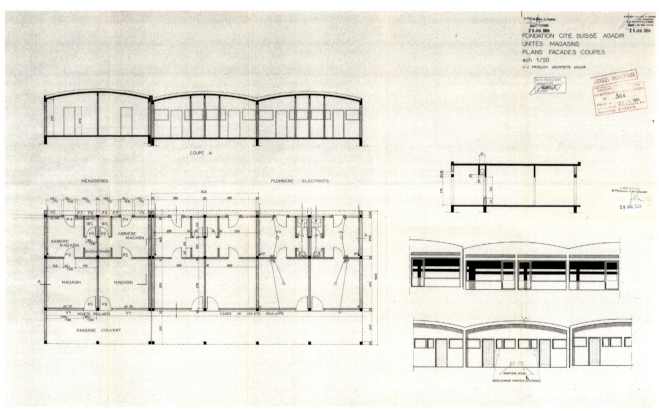

FONDATION CITE SUISSE AGADIR
UNITES MAGASINS
PLANS FACADES COUPES
ech 1/50

A U FROELICH ARCHITECTE AGADIR

COUPE A

MENUISERIES   PLOMBERIE · ELECTRICITE

ARRIERE MAGASIN   ARRIERE MAGASIN

MAGASIN   MAGASIN

VOLETS ROULANTS   CAGES DE VOLETS ROULANTS

PASSAGE COUVERT

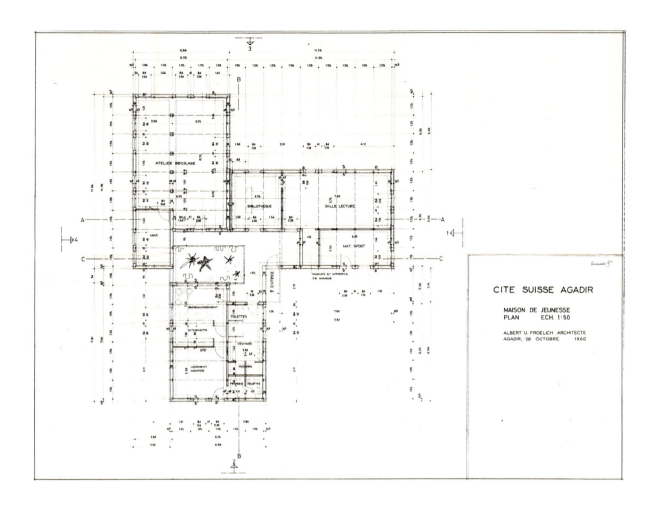

CITE SUISSE AGADIR

MAISON DE JEUNESSE
PLAN   ECH. 1:50

ALBERT U. FROELICH ARCHITECTE
AGADIR, 28 OCTOBRE   1960

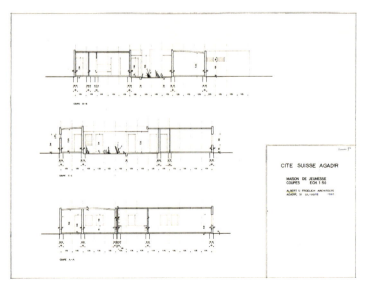

CITE SUISSE AGADIR

MAISON DE JEUNESSE
COUPES   ECH 1:50

ALBERT U. FROELICH ARCHITECTE
AGADIR, 31 OCTOBRE   1960

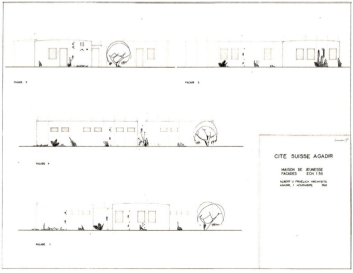

CITE SUISSE AGADIR

MAISON DE JEUNESSE
FACADES   ECH 1:50

ALBERT U. FROELICH ARCHITECTE
AGADIR, 1 NOVEMBRE   1960

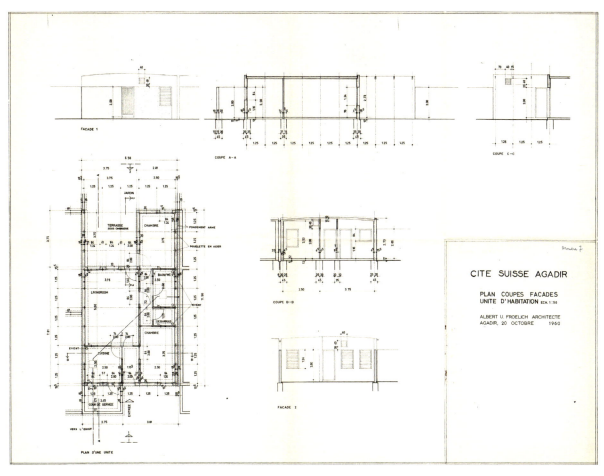

CITE SUISSE AGADIR

PLAN COUPES FACADES
UNITE D'HABITATION ECH.1:50

ALBERT U. FROELICH ARCHITECTE
AGADIR, 20 OCTOBRE 1960

BÂTIMENT LOGEMENT

ARCHITECT: Hans-Joachim Lenz
YEAR: 1964–5
LOCATION: Nouveau Talborjt
FLOOR AREA: –
CONSTRUCTION COST: –
COMMISSIONER: –

The Bâtiment Logement (Housing Building) was designed by the German architect Hans-Joachim Lenz and was built in 1965. The residential building was intended as one of the components for the reconstruction of the Nouveau Talborjt neighbourhood. The dense two-storey conglomeration consists of ten connected units that together form an urban block. The ground floor features commercial functions and residential units, while the upper floor is furnished with dwellings only. Each unit is also equipped with a patio. Compared with the residential architecture and typology of Agadir's Centre Urbain, this type of building echoes a much more traditional way of living. It is designed to combine housing, commerce and working spaces, as was often the case in more traditional Moroccan settlements. With only small window openings to the street, its facades appear more closed than those on other residential projects for the reconstruction of Agadir. However, large window openings towards the patios allow light to enter the dwellings. The patios, surrounded by a single- or two-storey wall, are always directly accessible from the street and concentrate the living spaces around them.

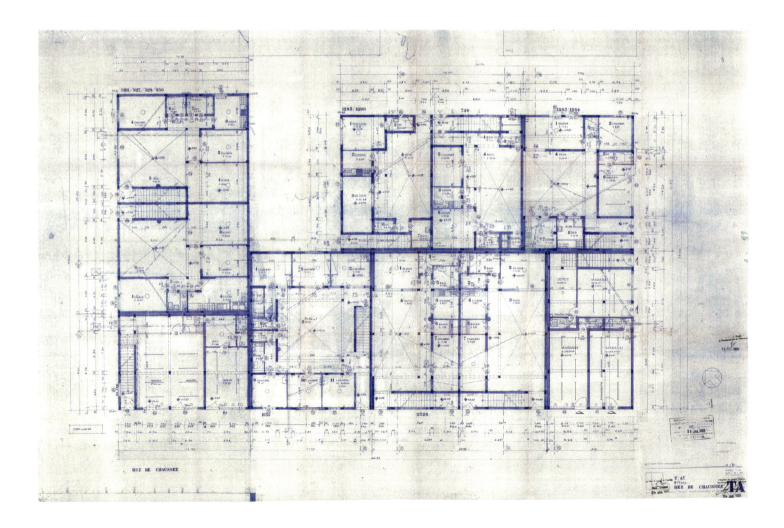

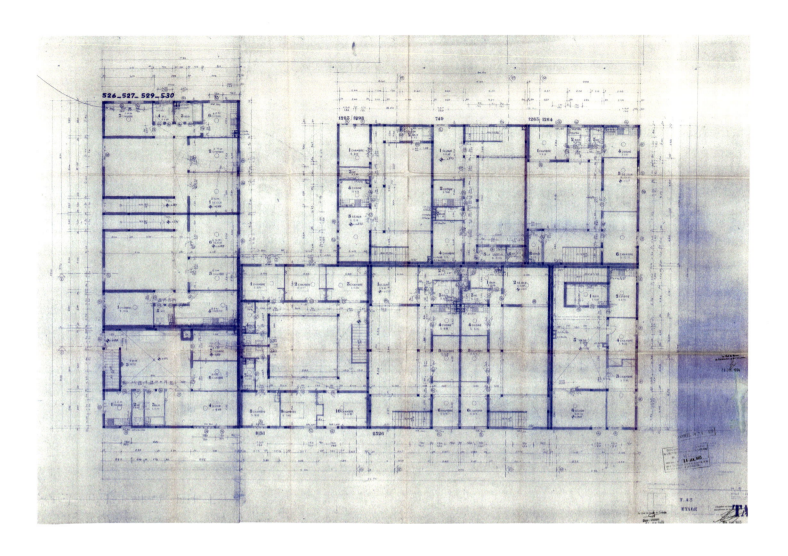

526_527_529_530

189

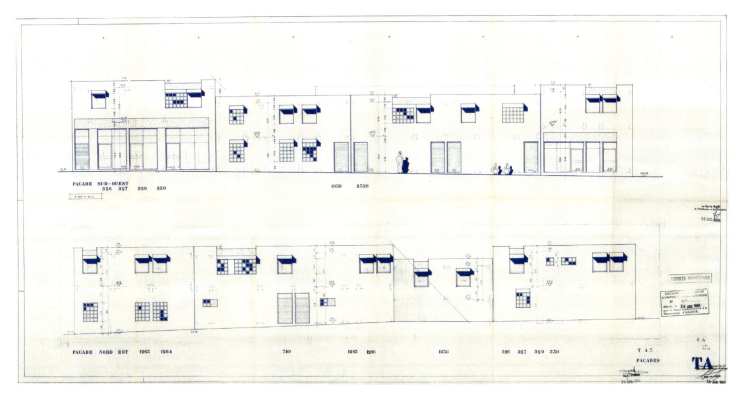

FACADE SUD-OUEST
326 327 329 550

1858 2526

FACADE NORD EST 1265 1264

749

1295 2296

1858

326 327 329 550

T A 5
FACADES

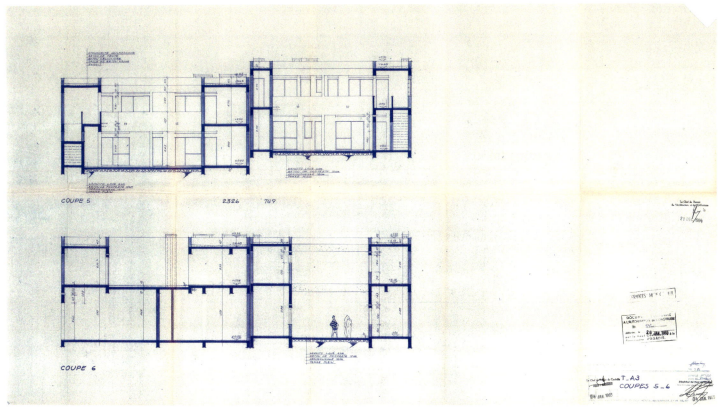

COUPE 5

2326 749

COUPE 6

T_A3
COUPES 5_6

CITÉ ADMINISTRATIVE

ARCHITECT: Élie Azagury
YEAR: 1964–6
LOCATION: Centre Urbain
FLOOR AREA: –
CONSTRUCTION COST: –
COMMISSIONER: État Marocain,
Ministère des Travaux Publics

The Cité Administrative (Administrative Centre) was designed by the Moroccan architect Élie Azagury in 1964 and finished in 1966. It is located south-west of the Centre Urbain of Agadir, between Boulevard Hassan II and Avenue Mohammed V. The Cité Administrative was designed to group together all the main administrative buildings of Agadir, complementing the Hôtel de Ville. The offices of several municipal and provincial administrations – such as Public Works, the Department of Mining and Trade, and the Ministries of Finance and of Agriculture – are organised around a publicly accessible green landscape that respects the site's natural topography. The various buildings are connected by a system of equally accessible, covered galleries that are positioned in the landscape and cross the administrative centre from east to west and from north to south. At the edges of the Cité Administrative, this system of shaded public galleries connects to the surrounding streets. All the office buildings are constructed in materials typical of the reconstruction of Agadir: sand-coloured *béton brut* structural elements and white-rendered facades. They vary from single-storey to five-storey in height. The combination of well-organised building volumes, shaded galleries and green public spaces offers a unique public experience to the citizens of Agadir.

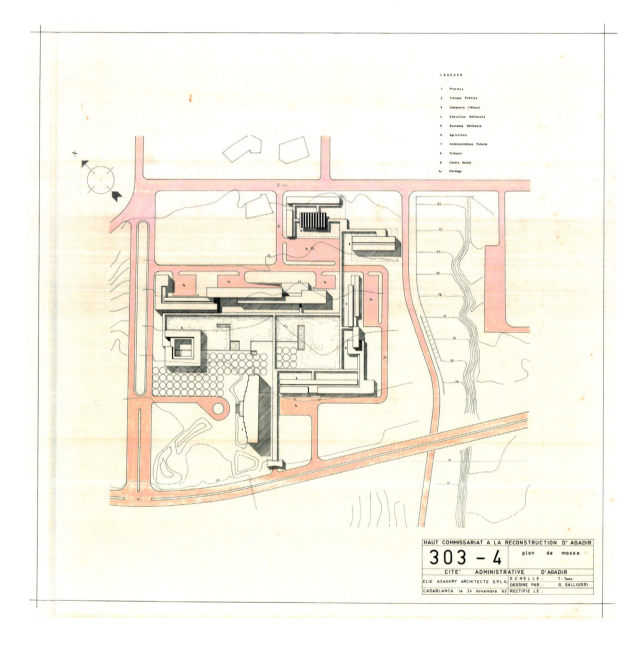

195

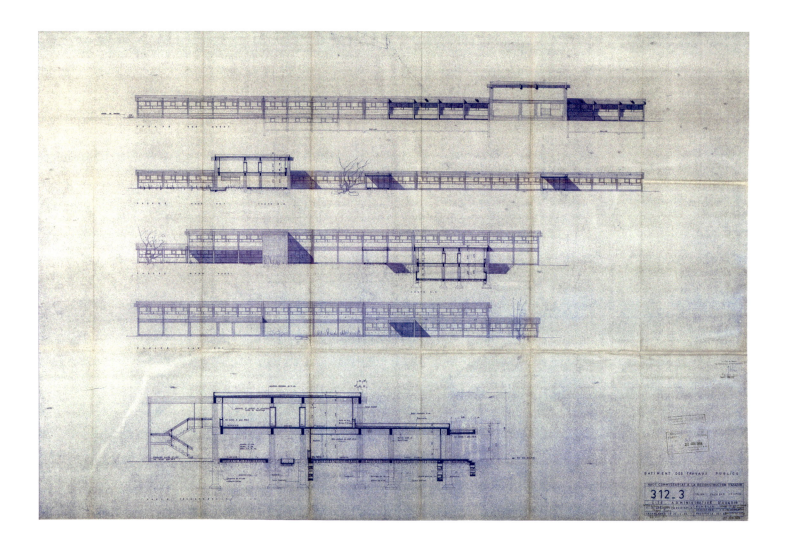

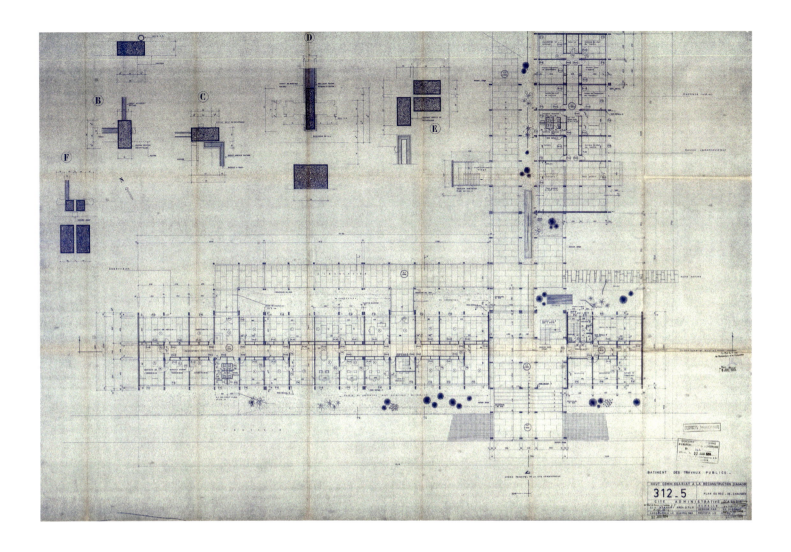

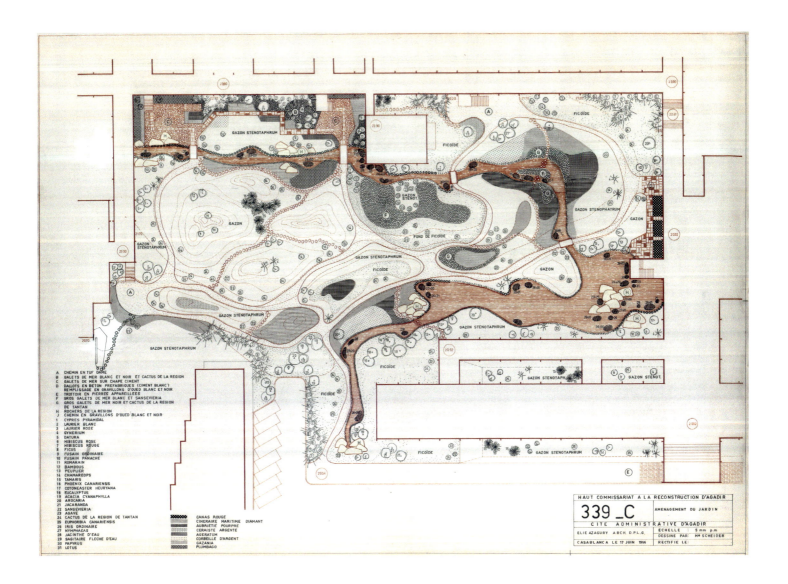

A CHEMIN EN TUF DAME
B GALETS DE MER BLANC ET NOIR ET CACTUS DE LA RÉGION
C GALETS DE MER SUR CHAPE CIMENT
D DALLOTS EN BÉTON PRÉFABRIQUÉS (CIMENT BLANC)
REMPLISSAGE EN GRAVILLONS D'OUED BLANC ET NOIR
E TROTTOIR EN PIERRES APPAREILLÉES
F GROS GALETS DE MER BLANC ET SANSEVIERIA
G GROS GALETS DE MER NOIR ET CACTUS DE LA RÉGION
DE TANTAN
H ROCHERS DE LA RÉGION
J CHEMIN EN GRAVILLONS D'OUED BLANC ET NOIR
1 CYPRÈS PYRAMIDAL
2 LAURIER BLANC
3 LAURIER ROSE
4 GYNERIUM
5 DATURA
6 HIBISCUS ROSE
7 HIBISCUS ROUGE
8 FICUS
9 FUSAIN ORDINAIRE
10 FUSAIN PANACHÉ
11 ROMARAIN
12 BAMBOUS
13 PEUPLIER
14 CHAMAREOPS
15 TAMARIS
16 PHOENIX CANARIENSIS
17 COTONEASTER HEURYANA
18 EUCALYPTUS
20 AROCARIA
21 JACARANDA
22 SANSEVIERIA
23 AGAVE
24 CACTUS DE LA RÉGION DE TANTAN
25 EUPHORBIA CANARIENSIS
26 IRIS ORDINAIRE
27 NYMPHAEAS
28 JACINTHE D'EAU
29 SAGITAIRE FLECHE D'EAU
30 PAPYRUS
31 LOTUS

CANAS ROUGE
CINÉRAIRE MARITIME DIAMANT
AUBRIÉTIE POURPRE
CERAISTE ARGENTE
AGERATUM
CORBEILLE D'ARGENT
GAZANIA
PLUMBAGO

HAUT COMMISSARIAT A LA RECONSTRUCTION D'AGADIR

339 _C   AMENAGEMENT DU JARDIN

CITE ADMINISTRATIVE D'AGADIR

ELIE AZAGURY ARCH. D.P.L.G.   ECHELLE : 5 mm p.m
DESSINE PAR Mr SCHEIDER
CASABLANCA LE 17 JUIN 1966   RECTIFIE LE :

199

HÔTEL ROYAL

ARCHITECT: Hans-Joachim Lenz, E. Leoncavallo,
Albert U. Froelich
YEAR: 1964
LOCATION: Secteur Touristique et Balnéaire
FLOOR AREA: 520 m²
CONSTRUCTION COST: 805,000 DM
COMMISSIONER: Hadj Abderrahmane Iraâ

The Hôtel Royal (Royal Hotel) was co-designed by
the German architect Hans-Joachim Lenz and
the Italian architect E. Leoncavallo in 1964 and built
in the Secteur Touristique et Balnéaire (Coastal
and Touristic Sector) of Agadir. It stands on an
elevated plateau in the centre of the sector in the
immediate vicinity of the Hôtel Kasbah and the
Hôtel Mabrouk. The four-storey Hôtel Royal is thus
located on a prime site in the centre of the upper
part of the tourist and seaside area, and lies perpendicular to both the ocean and Avenue Mohammed
V. Approximately thirty-three rooms had a panoramic
view of the ocean thanks to this location and the
fact that all rooms were equipped with a balcony set
at forty-five degrees to the central corridor. This
internal organisation of the Hôtel Royal characterises
the building's external appearance. The public
areas (hall, bar, restaurant) extend beyond the main
body of the building on the ground floor. In 1968,
an exterior pool, forty-one bungalows, a villa and a
second entrance were added by the Swiss-born
Agadir-based architect Albert U. Froelich as an extension of the hotel complex.

CASERNE DES POMPIERS

ARCHITECT: Jean-François Zevaco
YEAR: 1963
LOCATION: Quartier Industriel Sud
FLOOR AREA: 3,013 m²
CONSTRUCTION COST: –
COMMISSIONER: État Marocain,
Ministère de l'Interieur

The Caserne des Pompiers et Tour d'Exercice (Fire Station and Exercise Tower) were designed by the Moroccan-born French architect Jean-François Zevaco in 1963. Located at the junction of Rue du 18 Novembre and Avenue du Prince Moulay Abdallah in the Quartier Industriel Sud, the complex forms an important focal point and marks the entrance to the Centre Urbain of Agadir. Intended as a monument symbolising the modernity and power of the city, the Caserne des Pompiers is characterised by its unique circular shape that is intersected by a long wall to form the entrance and by its distinctive and monumental exercise tower. An additional four-storey building is superimposed on the circular wall of the Caserne. A swimming pool is located perpendicular to the wall that defines the entrance area. All components of the Caserne des Pompiers are realised in sand-coloured concrete with various finishes. The circular vehicle hall is of *béton brut* with a visible vertical-shuttering pattern. The exercise tower of rough ribbed concrete elements and the four-storey building are composed in the typical interplay between sand-coloured *béton brut* and white-rendered walls. The exercise tower is equipped with clocks on all four sides, and was originally adorned with a crown.

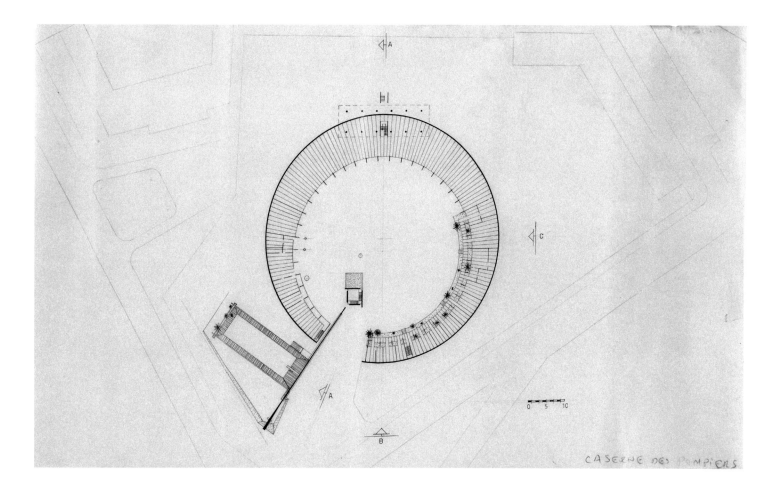

CASERNE DES POMPIERS

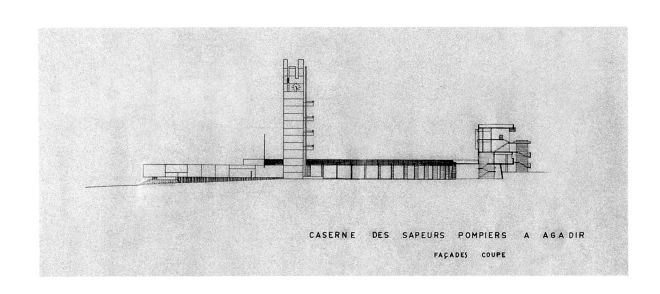

CASERNE DES SAPEURS POMPIERS A AGADIR

FAÇADES COUPE

205

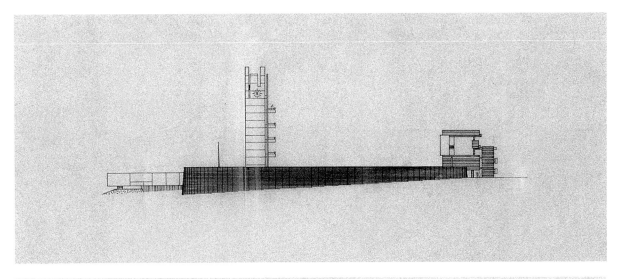

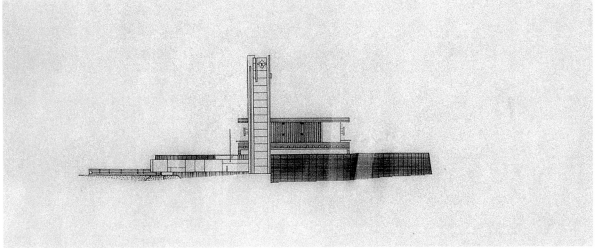

CINÉMA SAHARA

ARCHITECT: Alain Le Goaster
YEAR: 1965–6
LOCATION: Nouveau Talborjt
FLOOR AREA: –
CONSTRUCTION COST: –
COMMISSIONER: M. Yahida Idder

The Cinéma Sahara (Sahara Cinema) was designed in 1965 by the French architect Alain Le Goaster and named after an existing cinema in Ancien Talborjt built in 1954 and destroyed in the earthquake of 1960. Located on Place Tamri, the new Cinéma Sahara – together with Le Petit Marché de Talborjt, designed by the Moroccan-born Spanish architect Claude Verdugo and French architect Pierre Coldefy, and the nearby bus station – contributes to the creation of a diverse and lively public life in Nouveau Talborjt. According to the testimonies of residents, the crowded environment around the bus station ensured that the Cinéma Sahara was well frequented by travellers waiting for their buses. It consists of one spacious cinema hall, which is accessed via a single-storey volume located on the long side of

the building. The load-bearing structure, made of sand-coloured *béton brut*, is visible from the exterior. The building is subdivided into four sections of varying heights and widths that follow the internal organisation of the cinema hall. Together with the external spiral staircase, this feature defines the building's characteristic appearance. Since 2012, however, the cinema has been closed and opens its doors only for exceptional occasions such as the screening of televised football matches.

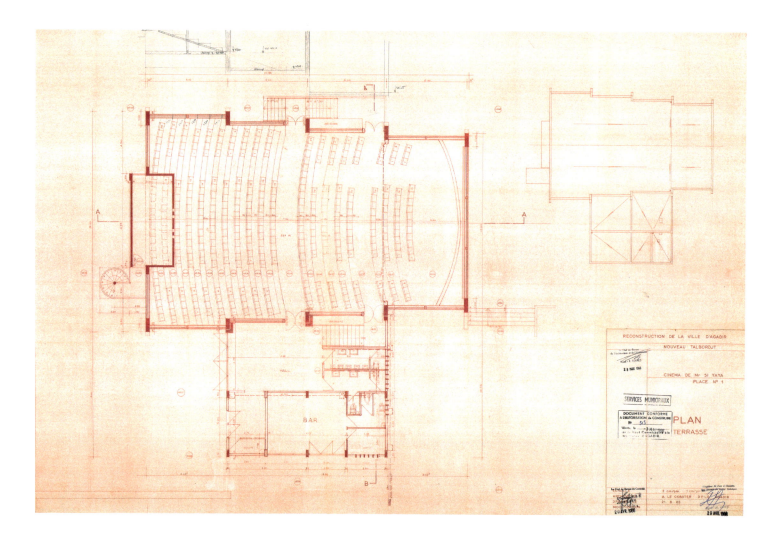

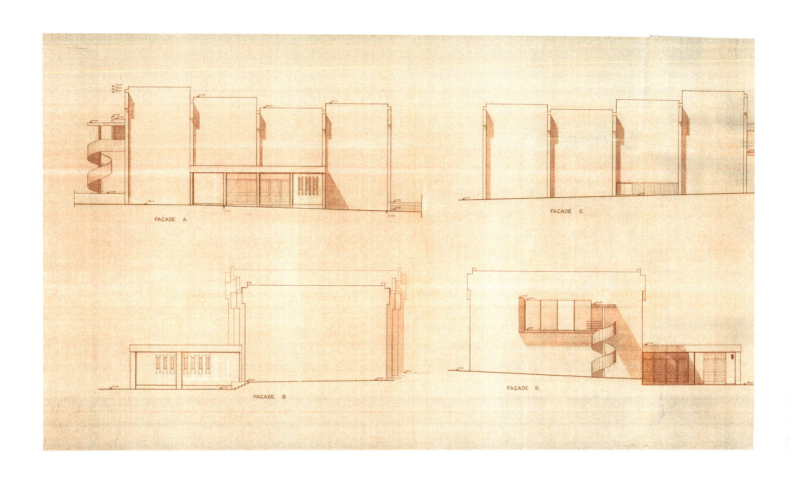

FAÇADE   A

FAÇADE   C

FAÇADE   B

FAÇADE   D

HÔTEL DE VILLE

ARCHITECT: Émile-Jean Duhon
YEAR: 1964–6
LOCATION: Centre Urbain
FLOOR AREA: 1,981 m²
CONSTRUCTION COST: 2,000,000 DM
COMMISSIONER: État Marocain,
Ministère de l'Interieur

The Hôtel de Ville (Town Hall), designed by the French architect Émile-Jean Duhon and built in 1966, is located, together with the Poste Principale, on the Place Hôtel de Ville – one of the three main public squares of the Centre Urbain in Agadir. From this square, the Hôtel de Ville is reached through a wide entrance in the form of a large concrete grid and a concrete canopy, which provides access to the main hall and a visual connection with the building's interior courtyard. Standing on a massive concrete plinth facing the street, the monumentality of the town hall is amplified. A large courtyard with plants and a water basin forms the centre of the plan, with all the administrative rooms arranged around it. The four facades of the Hôtel de Ville differ from one another and respond differently to the public spaces around the building. Various architectural elements, such as *brise-soleils* (sun shades), offer different degrees of openness and depth to the facades and thus create a multiplicity of relationships with the city. According to architect Émile-Jean Duhon, the somewhat monumental architecture of the Hôtel de Ville is reminiscent of a communal Moroccan granary – referring to the origin of the name of the city of Agadir, which translates as 'collective fortified granary'.

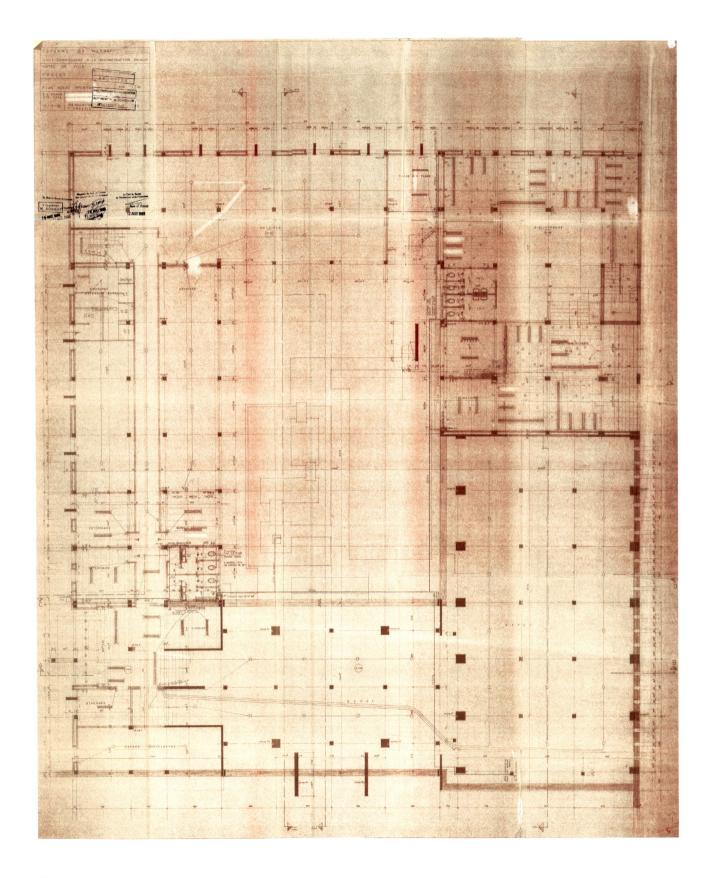

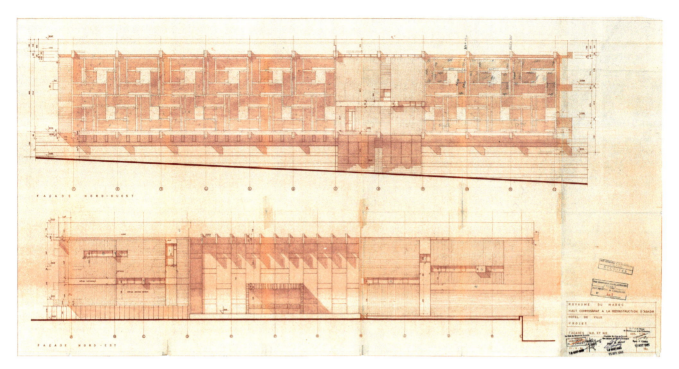

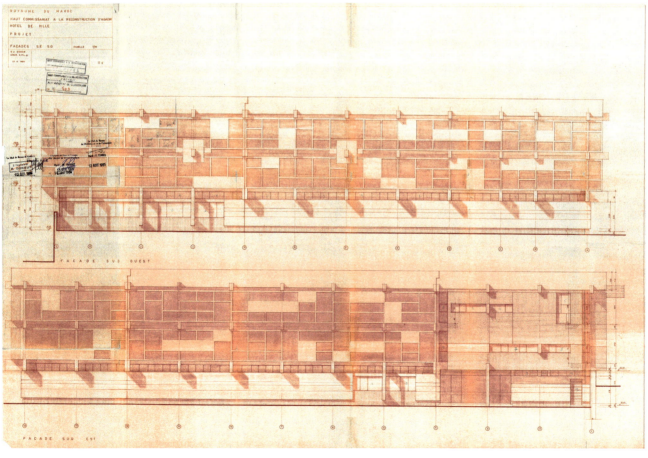

215

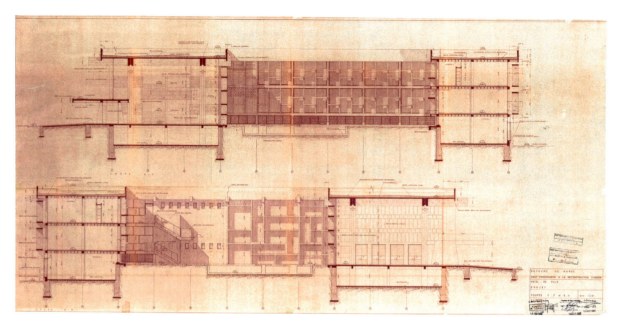

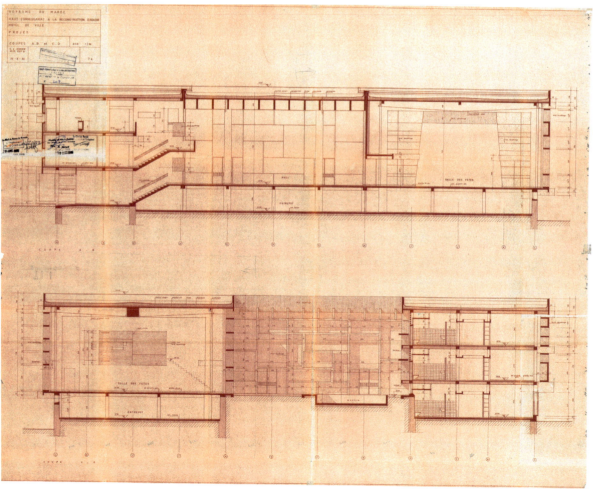

IMMEUBLE A

ARCHITECT: Louis Riou, Henri Tastemain
YEAR: 1964–6
LOCATION: Centre Urbain
FLOOR AREA: –
CONSTRUCTION COST: –
COMMISSIONER: État Marocain

Immeuble A (Building A) and the adjacent Place Hassan II were designed by the French architects Louis Riou and Henri Tastemain in 1966. The 183-m-long commercial and residential building is located in the Centre Urbain, in the immediate vicinity of the Poste Principale and the Hôtel de Ville, and was built on the old riverbed of the Waddi Tanaout. Due to its position on Place Hassan II and its porous ground floor, Immeuble A plays a major role as both the 'urban heart' and the 'spine' of the reconstruction of the city of Agadir. The building is a connector in the urban fabric, linking the central Avenue du Sidi Mohammed with the perpendicular Avenue du Prince Moulay Abdallah. This connective function of Immeuble A is reinforced by architectural elements such as a large ramp linking Place Hassan II with the public gallery of Immeuble A. In addition, the covered commercial passages and porticoes on its ground floor expand the public functions to the surrounding avenues, and thus clearly affirm the commercial character of Place Hassan II. Immeuble A is composed of two commercial levels, one level of offices and two levels of housing. Architecturally, a great deal of emphasis was placed on the composition of the facade. The over-dimensioned tectonic elements of its elevations are said to represent the stability of the reconstruction of Agadir. The interplay of distinctive vertical features made of *béton brut* banded with white-rendered horizontal elements characterises the building's architectural appearance.

BÂTIMENTS ÉCONOMIE NATIONALE

ARCHITECT: Élie Azagury
YEAR: 1964–6
LOCATION: Centre Urbain
FLOOR AREA: –
CONSTRUCTION COST: –
COMMISSIONER: État Marocain,
Ministère des Finances

The two structures known as the Bâtiments Économie Nationale (National Economy Buildings) that form part of the Cité Administrative located in the Centre Urbain were built in 1966 to the designs of the Moroccan architect Élie Azagury. The long, two-storey administrative block with offices and the four-storey residential building are connected via bridges to the covered gallery system that covers the entire administrative centre. Together with the Bâtiment de l'Agriculture (Agriculture Building), the two Bâtiments Économie Nationale form an entity at the western entrance of the Cité Administrative. The long administrative building has a lengthy central corridor with offices along it. It is accessed from the street via an exterior staircase. The composition of its facade reflects the internal structure, with continuous elements of sand-coloured *béton brut*

that emphasise the horizontality of the building. The four-storey residential block is also accessed via a bridge that connects to the covered gallery system of the Cité. Its small ground-floor apartment is entered through a garden-like area that also opens onto the staircase to the upper floor, which houses more spacious three-bedroom apartments. The facade's composition is again articulated with striking vertical elements. However, the parts made of *béton brut* are more restrained and the closed, white-rendered surfaces are more pronounced than in the neighbouring buildings.

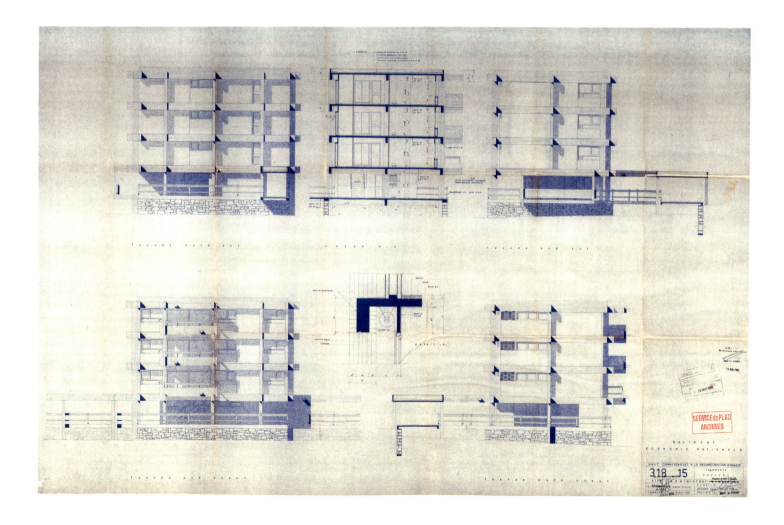

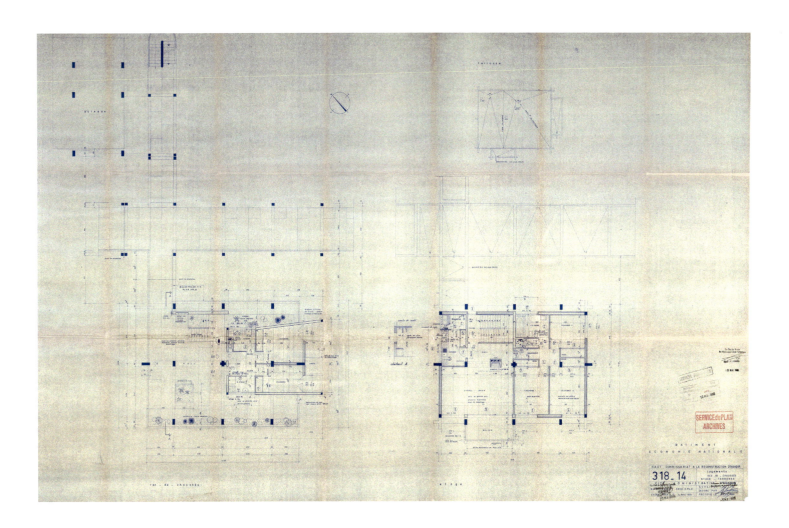

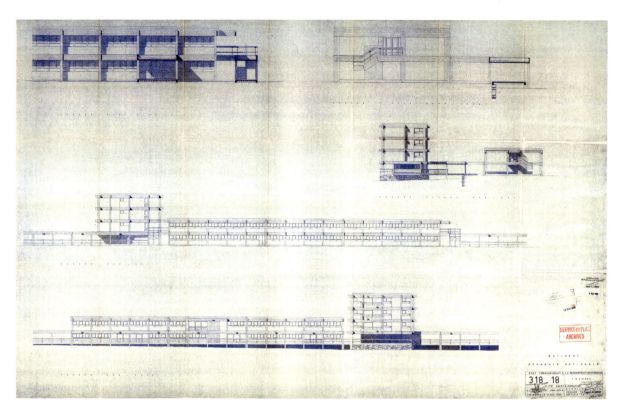

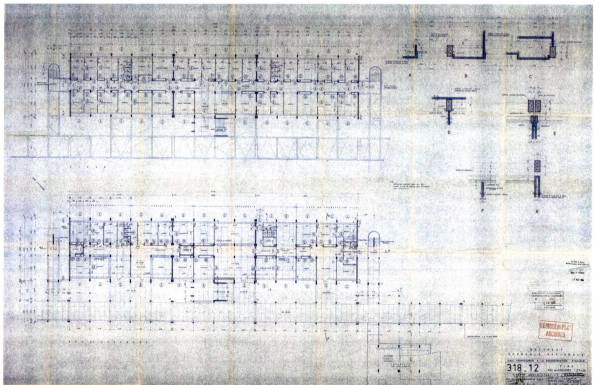

IMMEUBLE UNIPRIX

ARCHITECT: Alain Le Goaster
YEAR: 1964–6
LOCATION: Centre Urbain
FLOOR AREA: –
CONSTRUCTION COST: –
COMMISSIONER: Abdeslem Messaoudi

The commercial and residential Immeuble Uniprix (Uniprix Building), also called Immeuble B (Building B), was designed by the French architect Alain Le Goaster and completed in 1966. Bordering Hassan II Square, where Immeuble A is also located, the L-shaped two-storey building was initially designed to house a large commercial space on the ground floor and a restaurant and a hotel on the first floor. However, the floor plans from the archives suggest that, instead of a hotel, most probably apartments were built on the upper floor with large balconies facing both Avenue Hassan II and Place Hassan II. The floor plans feature generous layouts with large kitchens and two or three bedrooms each. Immeuble B, together with Immeuble A, plays an important role in framing the public space of Place Hassan II. Immeuble B also takes up the level

difference between Avenue Hassan II and Place Hassan II. The square is accessed on both sides of Immeuble B by a wide staircase. These stairs lead, on the west side, to a covered gallery bordering Place Hassan II that extends to Immeuble A and, on the east side, from Avenue Hassan II to the restaurant in Immeuble B. With its slightly raised roof, the restaurant forms an important visual element for the public space on Place Hassan II.

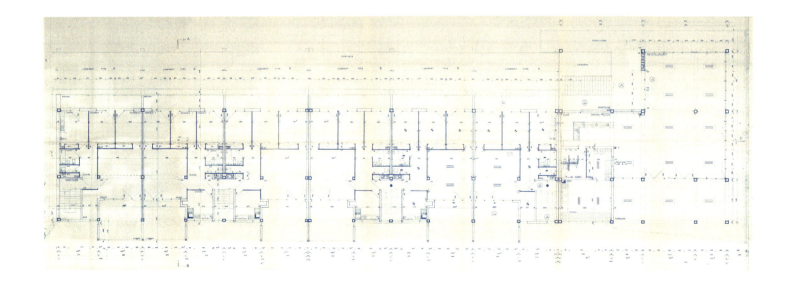

196 LOGEMENTS

ARCHITECT: Bureau de l'Urbanisme
YEAR: 1964–6
LOCATION: Nouveau Talborjt
FLOOR AREA: –
CONSTRUCTION COST: –
COMMISSIONER: Mohamed Ben M'Hand,
président of the Association des Sinistrés
des Îlots 2 et 4 A

The 196 Logements (196 Residential Units) planned on the initial Écochard-based grid are located north of Nouveau Talborjt. They are an extension of the Talborjt neighbourhood and situated in the immediate vicinity of an orphanage, a nursery and a school. Designed by the Bureau de l'Urbanisme (Office of Urban Planning) between 1964 and 1966, they represent only one of three envisaged *îlots* (plots) with residential units. They are part of an expansion of the city north of today's Boulevard Mohammed Cheikh Saadi and on Rue Zellaqa. This project adapted the so-called *Trame Écochard*: (Écochard Grid) an urban grid of eight metres by eight metres that French urban planner Michel Écochard developed as a basic module for constructing new neighbourhoods in Morocco. To rationalise the building process, the measures of the grid were adjusted so that they would allow for construction with concrete elements and cement bricks. While previously natural stones had been used, in this project an explicit choice was made of cement bricks. This would allow a faster building process, since the format of the bricks was unified and thus no selection was needed. The rooms and sanitary facilities of the houses are organised around a patio, accessed directly from the street. The simply equipped and single-storey units stand on column foundations.

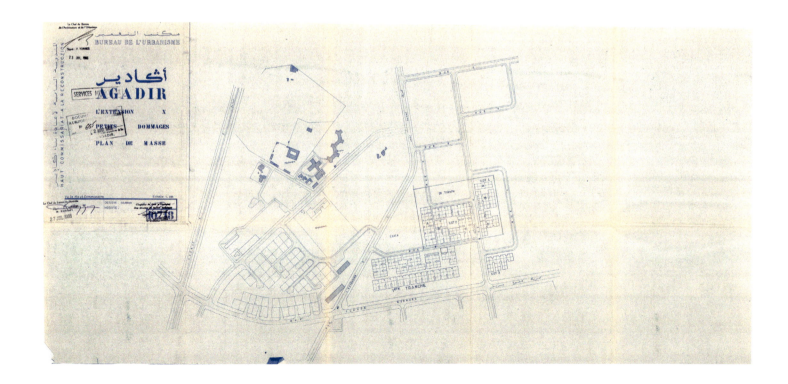

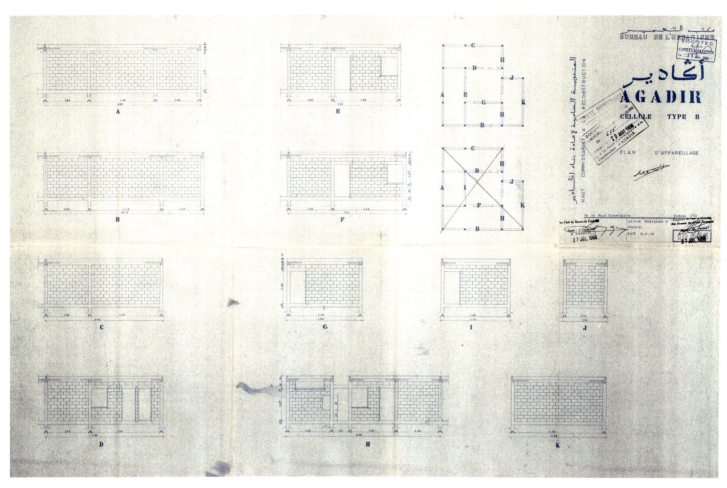

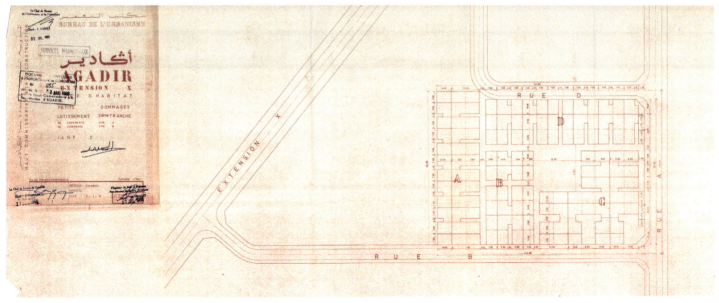

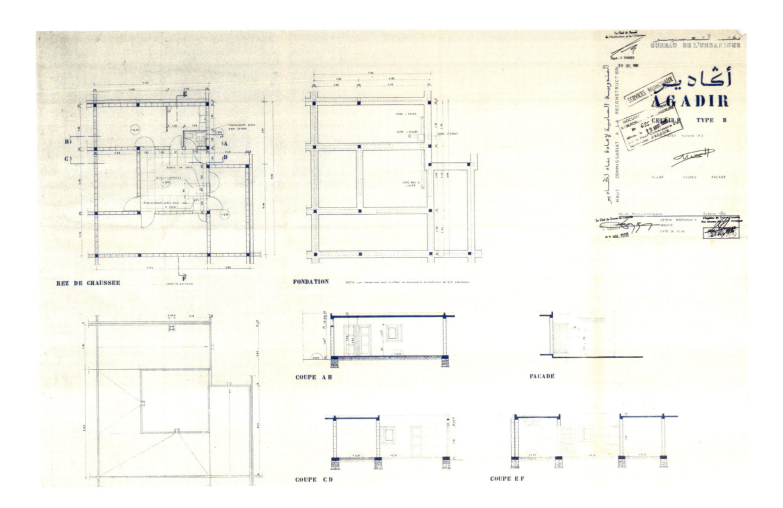

REZ DE CHAUSSEE

FONDATION

COUPE A B

FACADE

COUPE C D

COUPE E F

AGADIR

TYPE B

GRANDE MOSQUÉE

ARCHITECT: Hans-Joachim Lenz
YEAR: 1964–7 (inaugurated in 1969)
LOCATION: Centre Urbain
FLOOR AREA: –
CONSTRUCTION COST: –
COMMISSIONER: Ministère des Habous

The Grande Mosquée (Great Mosque) of Agadir was designed by the German architect Hans-Joachim Lenz from 1964 to 1967 and inaugurated in 1969 by King Hassan II. He gave the name of *Loubnane* (Lebanon) to the building in commemoration of the first Islamic summit held in Rabat that year. Located in the Centre Urbain, the Grande Mosquée is related to the surrounding buildings by a covered gallery-like structure. Its almost 30-m-high minaret culminates in three spheres of decreasing size, and a flagpole that is used to hoist a white flag to announce the second and third daily prayers and a black flag for Friday. While the minaret was executed in a uniform white render, the rest of the mosque displays the typical reconstruction architecture of Agadir with its interplay of sand-coloured *béton brut* and white-rendered surfaces. The interior of the Grande Mosquée is characterised by sets of columns that support square, box-like domes forming the ceiling of the building. Today, the building no longer appears in its original state as later exterior and interior decorations in the Moroccan–Andalusian style have been added over the years.

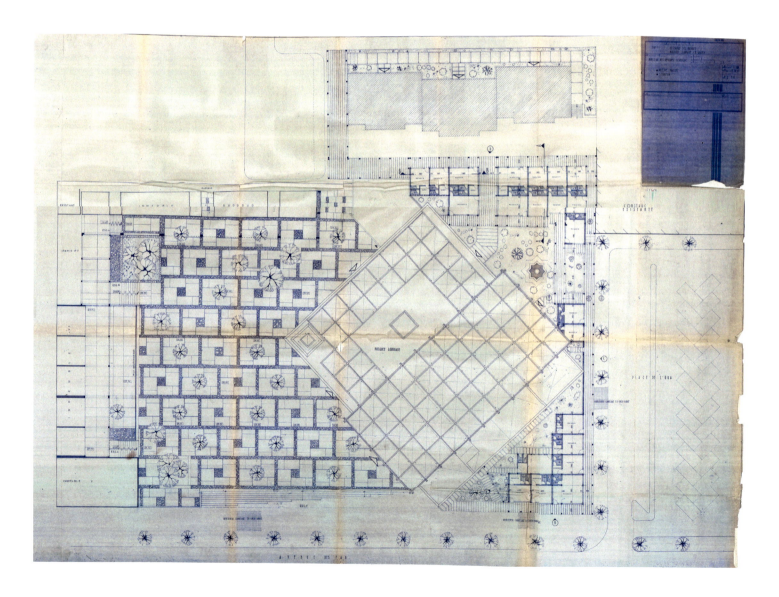

233

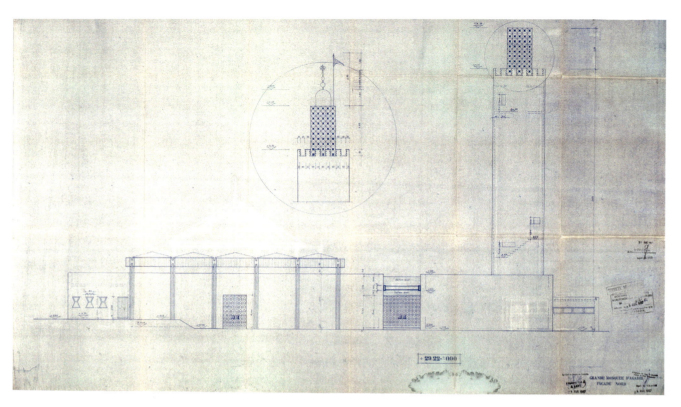

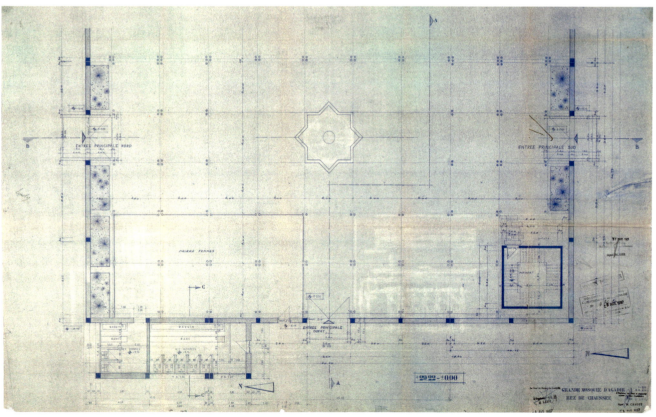

235

CINÉMA RIALTO

ARCHITECT: Alain Le Goaster
YEAR: 1965–6 (date of opening: 24 May 1967)
LOCATION: Centre Urbain
FLOOR AREA: –
CONSTRUCTION COST: –
COMMISSIONER: Le Rialto Company for Yahia ben Idder

The Cinéma Rialto (Rialto Cinema) was designed by the French architect Alain Le Goaster in 1965 and completed in 1967. It is located next to Place Hassan II, which is connected to the public space of Immeuble A, and is near the covered Marché Central designed by Moroccan-born Spanish architect Claude Verdugo. The new facility took the name of the old Rialto Cinema, which had been built in the Ville Nouvelle in the 1950s and destroyed by the earthquake. The cinema is surrounded by single-storey commercial buildings and large parking areas. A section through the building shows the continuity of the outdoor public realm into the public spaces inside it – a continuity that is accentuated by the prominent canopy over the entrance. The Cinéma Rialto contributes to the public spaces of the Centre Urbain, animating them and introducing leisurely functions. Its vaulted roof structure in sand-coloured concrete is discernible from the outside because of the contrast with the white render of the walls. It defines the general appearance of the cinema. Accessible from the front facade, a public foyer leads to the hall or the balcony via two staircases.

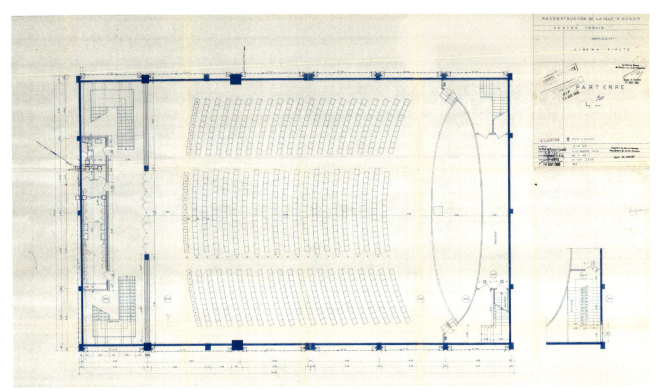

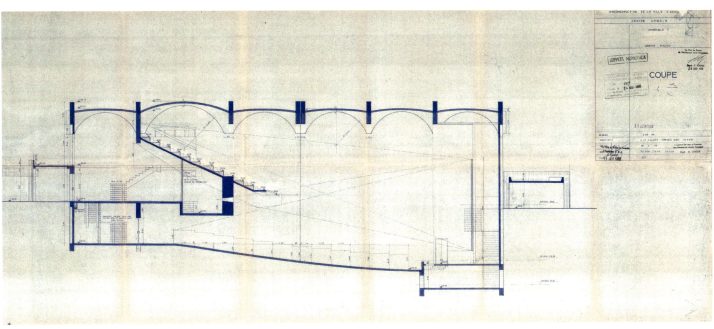

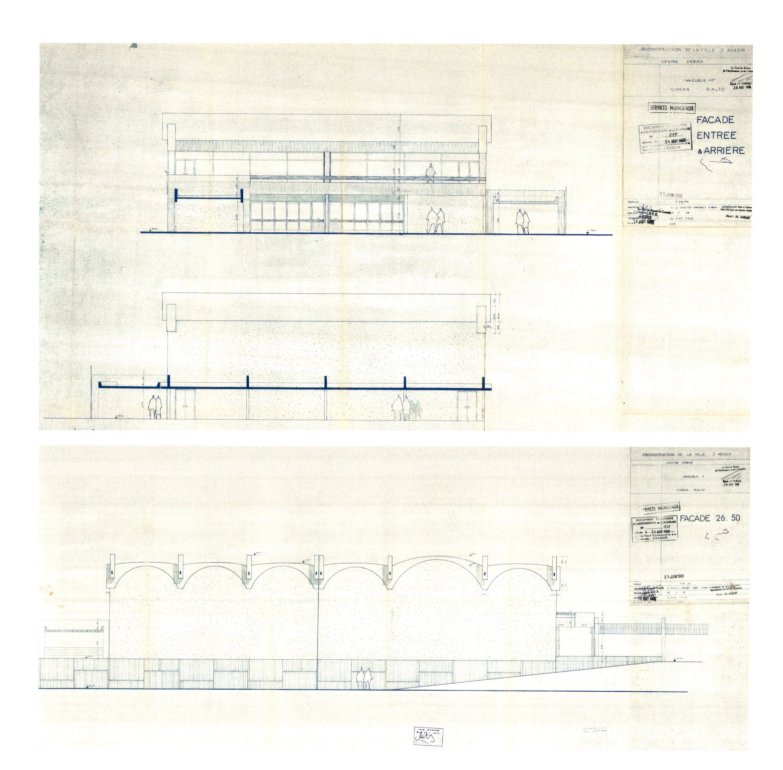

IMMEUBLE DE BANQUE J2

ARCHITECT: Albert U. Froelich, Alain Le Goaster
YEAR: 1964–7
LOCATION: Centre Urbain
FLOOR AREA: –
CONSTRUCTION COST: –
COMMISSIONER: M. Christian, heir representative
of Mr. Rocca Silvain

The Immeuble de Banque J2 (Bank Building J2), also called Immeuble Barutel-Rocca, comprises a combination of a large single-storey bank building and a three-storey slab with housing. It is located at the crossroads of Boulevard Hassan II and Avenue des Forces Armées Royales. The two parts of Immeubles Barutel-Rocca were designed by the Swiss-born Agadir-based architect Albert U. Froelich and the French architect Alain Le Goaster in 1964 and most probably built in 1967. Unfortunately, not all of its plans were found in the archives, so only the single-storey portion of the bank can be shown in the plan. What we can read from the plans, however, is that the hybrid function of Immeuble Barutel-Rocca is reflected in the architectural design of the two parts of the complex. The commercial plinth is open throughout and is characterised by large shop windows along the important Avenue des Forces Armées Royales. The residential building has generous balconies facing the street and large, square windows on the rear facade facing a calmer courtyard.

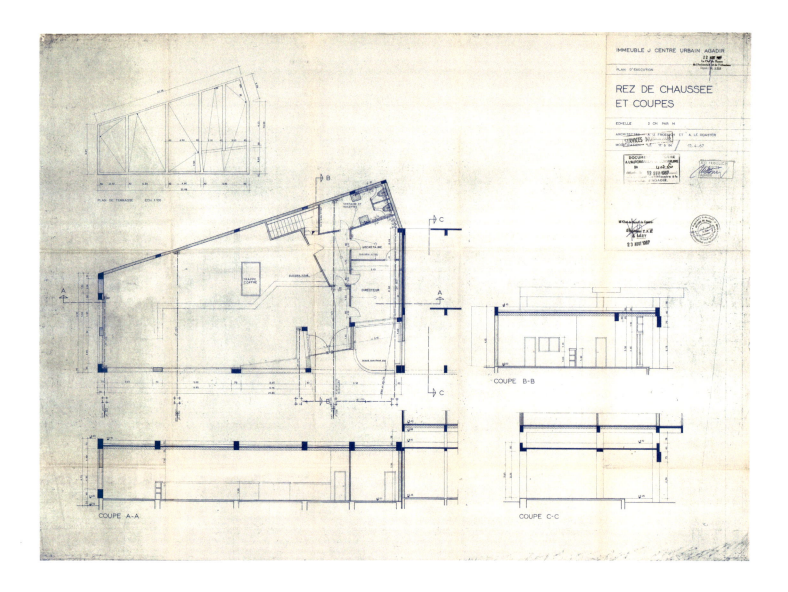

IMMEUBLE   J2/2   BANQUE
CENTRE   URBAIN   AGADIR
PLAN   FACADES
ECH   1:50

A.U   FROELICH   ARCHITECTE

AGADIR   LE...

SERVICES MUNICIPAUX

DOCUMENT CONFORME
A L'AUTORISATION de CONSTRUIRE

FAÇADE   SUR   AV   DES   FAR

SUR   AV   HASSAN   II

IMMEUBLE DE LOGEMENTS À 3 NIVEAUX

ARCHITECT: Albert U. Froelich
YEAR: 1968–70
LOCATION: Centre Urbain
FLOOR AREA: –
CONSTRUCTION COST: –
COMMISSIONER: M. Le Caid Gouad Bouchta

Immeuble de Logements à 3 Niveaux (Three-Storey Residential Building), commissioned by M. Le Caid Gouad Bouchta, was designed by the Swiss-born Agadir-based architect Albert U. Froelich in 1968 and built in 1970 in the Centre Urbain. It features a square floor plan with a large patio, around which a restaurant is located on the ground floor, and nineteen small studio apartments. These studios are each equipped with one bedroom and a small kitchen and bathroom. Their sparse design and immediate proximity to the main administrative buildings in the Centre Urbain indicate that this building primarily provided short-term accommodation for Agadir's administrative staff. Despite their simple layout, all studios on the upper two floors are equipped with balconies of different depths and widths. The sand-coloured structural elements in *béton brut* combined with white-rendered surfaces contribute to the general urban architecture of Agadir. Today, the Immeuble de Logements à 3 Niveaux is a hotel called Résidence Tislit.

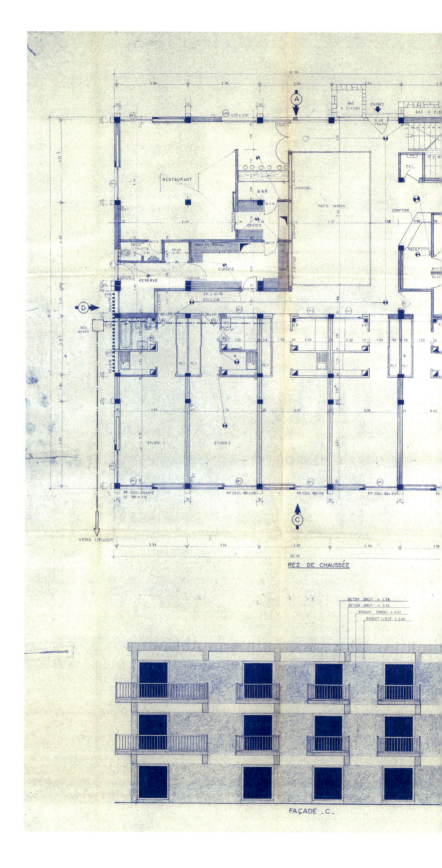

REZ DE CHAUSSÉE

FAÇADE _C_

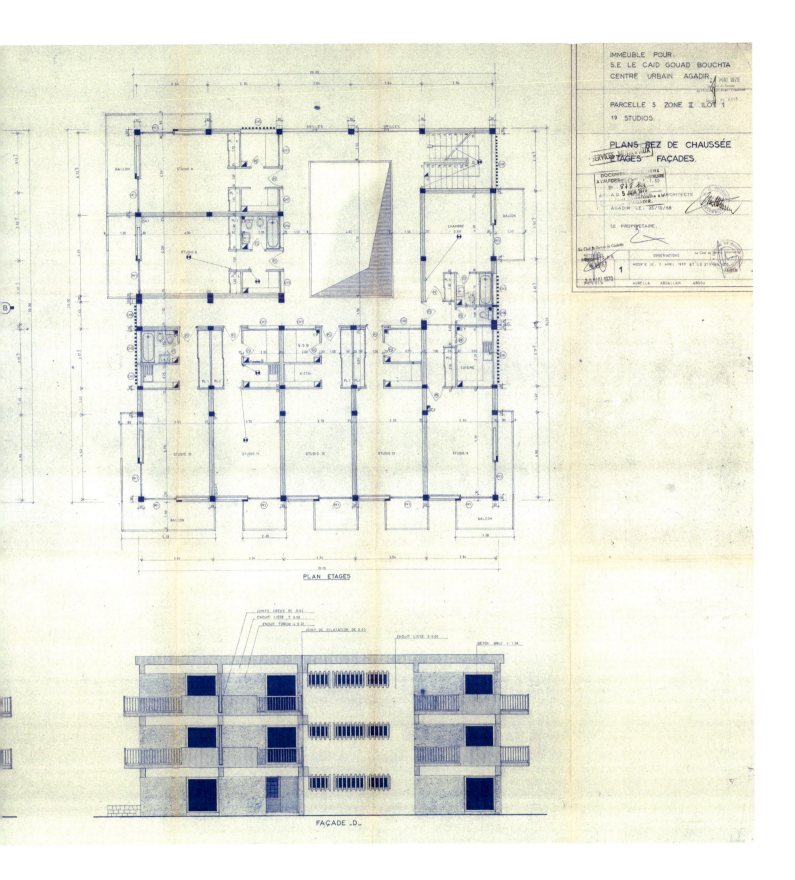

PLAN ETAGES

FAÇADE _D_

TRANSLATIONS

THE RECONSTRUCTION

Lahsen Roussafi

When did reconstruction actually begin?

Reconstruction really fully took off in 1961–1962. The emergency settlement already existed. People had left the prefabricated campground.

Did the Haut Commissariat à la Reconstruction d'Agadir (High Committee for the Reconstruction of Agadir) collaborate with the international aid organisations?

The Haut Commissariat's office had been put in place and announced in the government newspaper. There were a lot of reactions. It had to choose between the Americans and the Europeans. The Americans wanted to get the commission. The Moroccan King Mohammed V chose the Europeans who already knew Morocco. The Americans wanted to build in the American style, too expensively. The Americans were dropped and France was chosen. The engineers and Moroccan architects were trained in France and understood each other.

Other nationalities were involved. The Swiss were already present among the first responders and they supervised the Cité Suisse (Swiss Neighbourhood) right up to the end, according to their own taste. Others among the first responders stayed in Agadir for the rest of their lives. They are buried at Yachech. I am thinking of architects like Hans Leuzinger, Albert U. Froelich, who stayed. They worked with the city government until their deaths.

It's interesting that there had been a first phase when all the countries sent their aid, then a second phase of reconstruction when only a few of them were involved.

The Americans already had several military bases in the country, and so they were the first to bring help. The greatest aid came from the American bases in Kenitra and Casablanca.

What role did the architects play and how were they chosen?

Young Moroccan architects were called to help. Several of the big Moroccan architects gave their advice. Moroccan architects trained in France called in architects they knew, and the big Moroccan architects agreed that the French should come, also the young Moroccans trained in Rabat.

Mourad Ben Embarek coordinated these architects, and selected them; they worked as a team. Sharing the work was important. The motto was 'Work together'. Each evening, they consulted with one another.

There were also other specialists. There was Mr. Danny, a landscape architect, who is still living in Tangier. He is old but I paid him a visit. He had a German workshop at the time but at least 80 per cent of its members were French. Israel participated in the construction of the big Hôpital Hassan II (Hassan II Hospital). I'm still searching for a plaque to put in place which says 'Eretz Israel'.

Who else played a role in the reconstruction of Agadir?

After our vacation, we, the youth of Agadir, worked as volunteers for free in the municipal services. We worked on the census and also on the *livrets* (family record books). At the time we didn't use family names. Only first names. You were 'Ait' – that is, part of a family. The name of my high school was Ait Hadj Lahsen. There were a lot of people called 'Ait' but after the 1960 earthquake we stopped using this system of naming. When family record books were made, everybody said their name was 'Ait'. People had to be told that using that pronoun was no longer possible. Because it wasn't a name at all, you had to choose your name. Names were proposed for people to put in their family record books. They chose one, the name was accepted, the book was made.

What role did the various local administrations play?

The Haut Commissariat, with its many branches, was the most important administrative entity because it had lots of experts, city planners, architects and so on. They were the actors who actually accomplished the reconstruction. Special standards were adopted for managing the architects and engineers. The Société de Contrôle Technique et d'Expertise de la Construction (Company for Technical Control and Construction Expertise, SOCOTEC) was the body in charge of ensuring that those standards were met. It wasn't part of the Haut Commissariat, because it was created separately, but was nevertheless connected to it.

Building codes are usually understood to be restrictive, but the buildings that went up in Agadir look very innovative. How was that possible?

It was a challenge. The buildings that went up were indeed truly innovative so the codes can't have been too restrictive. It was a matter for the architects to deal with. The opportunities were there for them to take advantage of. The climate is very good. There is always plenty of sunshine and warmth, which allowed a number of openings to be made in the buildings. It wasn't necessary to use electric light during the day. The architects had taken account of that.

Then a problem became apparent. The destroyed areas and the new buildings had nothing in common with each other. Previously, specifically southern Moroccan-style buildings of good quality had been constructed, like at Talborjt. Then another 'look' appeared with the modern style being rapidly adopted. At first, this was accepted because the modern buildings were protected against earthquakes. Later on, people realised that these weren't at all the Moroccan houses they had hoped for. What they had wanted was a shelter that was secure, where you could sleep peacefully if there was another earthquake. Modern architecture was accepted because it was seen to be secure. But, with the passage of time, people saw there were other ways of achieving this end.

What was the role of local builders? Are there any documents or other kinds of evidence about the people who built the city?

No; their names were not recorded, unfortunately. Many people from the area worked here. They were local. Sometimes they were known, like the people of Agadir, but the names of the majority of the people remain unknown. They left no paper trail.

What was the specific role of the Haut Commissariat à la Reconstruction d'Agadir?

The Haut Commissariat coordinated everything. The builders did nothing on their own. The functionaries of the Haut Commissariat represented the authorities in Rabat and in the city government. They had a lot of power. They hired people for the projects and, together with the relevant ministries, they distributed the work. But they didn't construct the buildings themselves.

The Haut Commissariat was an intermediary with a lot of power over all the actors. The experts within the Haut Commissariat were present in the city and made their decisions on site. For example, in the Ville Nouvelle (New City) a decision was made to destroy reparable buildings to make way for a road. The Haut Commissariat experts had the power to decide whether to expropriate the land and move its owners wherever they wished.

How did the people of Agadir react? Did they protest against the edicts of the Haut Commissariat à la Reconstruction d'Agadir?

There were no visible reactions or protests. The city's inhabitants had confidence in the way the reconstruction was organised. At first, this was because they had worked previously with French engineers and architects. France, through the French Consulate, followed the work closely. There are thousands of documents in the French Consulate that provide evidence of the quality control exerted by the French authorities.

Another reason why the Haut Commissariat's decisions weren't contested is that there was a clear juridical structure. Local people couldn't do anything. They were subject to decrees. The kasbah, Talborjt, as well as the 7,000 residents of my village Yachech – they were all expropriated by decree. These zones were declared 'unconstructable'. That means all the buildings in these zones were expropriated, even if they were still in good condition.

Where did the expropriated people have to live?

Expropriated people were offered land to build on elsewhere in the city. This offer was accompanied by the obligation to build within twenty-four months. Citizens didn't have any other choice but to accept this offer. If they refused, no alternative was offered.

They had to build following the rules of the Haut Commissariat. Experts indicated the ground on which they were to build. You were given 50 per cent of the value your house had at the moment of construction. So, the houses were not evaluated according to the standards of 1960 but to those pertaining to when the building was first built. The land was given for free. The owner had to pay 50 per cent of the cost of construction.

Where did people find the means to build their houses?

The Banque Populaire played a very specific role in this context, being at once a money-lender and the developer which was building houses for the citizens of Agadir. So, the bank was building the housing right up to the point where it gave you the key. In other cases, however, the bank simply loaned the money so the citizens themselves could build. You had to repay the loan within fifteen years.

How did the Moroccan government finance the reconstruction of the city?

The Moroccan government raised taxes on a highly prized product: sugar. From 1960, Moroccans had to pay more for their sugar. It had cost two DM (Moroccan Dirhams) and now rose to three. All Moroccans consume sugar. For Moroccans there are two principal elements in their diet: sugary tea and bread. It was a very well-thought-out tax.

Moroccan citizens were not opposed to the rising cost of sugar. They were proud to have contributed to the reconstruction of Agadir through buying their daily sugar. They were proud and happy. It was a well-targeted act. They said 'We rebuilt Agadir' with great pride.

Furthermore, Moroccan King Hassan II addressed wealthy citizens, initially those from the south of Morocco, and invited them to build some houses. The rich were targeted. By order of the king. He told them to build new buildings but also offered them all the necessities: builders were put at their disposal; the Haut Commissariat gave them the plans for free. The role of wealthy people was limited mainly to financing construction. It is what is called self-financed construction.

What role did the Haut Commissariat à la Reconstruction d'Agadir play after the buildings went up?

At first, the Haut Commissariat remained responsible for all public buildings, but after a few years this responsibility was transferred to the city government. In addition to public buildings, schools and housing were managed by the Haut Commissariat. Also, apartment buildings were passed on to the municipality.

From the 1980s, the municipality adopted a distinctive approach. Because it didn't have the means to maintain apartments, it began to sell them off. Instead of paying rent, people (like those in retirement who couldn't move elsewhere) were encouraged to buy their homes. After fixing a sale price, the apartment was sold. The municipality could thus benefit from immediate access to revenue, and receive a higher yield than came from renting the apartments. What began as a public initiative shortly became a private one.

ON SQUARES, STAIRS, PATHS, PLINTHS, TREES AND SHADE IN AGADIR'S RECON-STRUCTED CENTRE

Hans Teerds

Under the blazing sun, any shade is welcome. Nevertheless, one can find hardly any shade at Place Hôtel de Ville, one of the central public spaces in Agadir. The surrounding buildings are low compared with the size of the square – or placed at a distance, detached from the space by more or less busy roads. Also, the palm trees lined up neatly on one side of it, with their open crowns and tall bare trunks, hardly cast any shade on the square. Only somewhere at the back – at a place where the construction of the square seems to have stopped and the orthogonal pattern of the pavement dissolves, where the formal image of the square becomes an informal setting, between the post office and the town hall – does one find a large tree that provides ample shade. It is rightly there, under this tree, that a few people stand, talk and meet while the space is otherwise virtually empty. The palm trees in a planting bed of grass and flowers, which of course need daily care in these conditions, nevertheless do lend a touch of tropical softness in a stone desert.

But moreover, together with the prestigious pavement with straight lines and right angles, the palm trees articulate the square as the centre of local administration. With their loftiness and their strict pattern, they are like soldiers forming an honorary guard – lined up in front of the entrance to the town hall (Fig. 1).

A civic square of the size of Place Hôtel de Ville is a rather unique feature of cities in North Africa. After all, the historic centres of, for instance, Casablanca and Marrakesh or Algiers and Tunis are characterised by density, alleys, narrow streets and small public spaces. This unique square is testament to the attempts to turn Agadir into a modern city after the devasting earthquake of 29 February 1960. 'This program will make of Agadir a modern and active city,' Crown Prince Moulay Hassan, who had been entrusted with the task of reconstruction, stated a few months after the earthquake, 'endowed with all the equipment necessary for life today: broad

Fig. 1
Place Hôtel de Ville
with, on the left, the
Poste Principale and
the Hôtel de Ville at
the far end.
Figs. 2 & 3
The initial drawings
and sketches show how
buildings and public
spaces are intertwined.

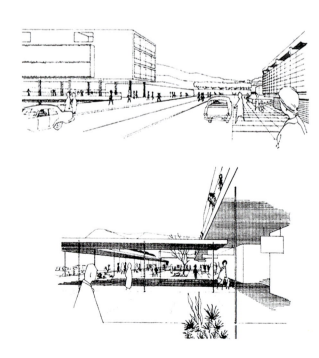

avenues, pleasant gardens, abundant light, mosque, schools, administration, etc.'[1] For the royal family of Morocco, the reconstruction was understood at once as an act of independence from France, the former coloniser, and proof of the modernity of the country.[2] This ambition, of course, was ambiguous from the beginning. After all, modernism, at that time, was undeniably bound to dominant Western perspectives – and thus to the colonial past of the country. The Moroccan-born architects who were assigned by the royal family to design the reconstruction plan, including Jean-François Zevaco and Mourad Ben Embarek, had been trained in France and, in their work in other cities in Morocco, had already brought Western modernity to the country. Their plan for Agadir indeed followed modernist principles: residential, governmental and commercial buildings are distributed to specific locations in the urban territory, clustered according to their function. Each building was designed as a separate architectural object, and carefully placed in an open morphology. This open setting consists of 'broad avenues and pleasant gardens', offering 'abundant light' to the city centre as the crown prince had announced. In addition, a series of intensively designed squares, of which Place Hôtel de Ville is one, offer a break with the traditional urban patterns. The 'fortified city' – Agadir in the local language, Berber, means 'wall', 'enclosure' – became a wall-less city.[3]

The modernist principles that were applied to the new Agadir have often been criticised along predictable lines: being unable to 'make a city' or to 'represent local culture', 'zoning leads to fragmentation' and, of course, the 'blurring of public space'.[4] Although these criticisms rightly point to contested aspects of urbanity in a modernist approach to the city, there is more to discover in Agadir's urban centre. The figure-ground plan may be 'modern', but to reduce the reconstruction plan to this black-and-white diagram is a serious and dangerous reduction of the diversity in buildings and spaces that Agadir offers.

Moreover, this narrow view overlooks the manifold ways in which the conditions of the location – such as topography, geography and climate – have helped to determine the placement of the buildings. The relationship between local conditions, buildings and public structures as well as considerations of function, zoning and materiality have shaped the 'immeasurable space' – the open space or 'ground' of modernist planning – into a diversity of public spaces that somehow can be seen as an attempt to rethink and reconsider the traditional Moroccan morphology while also attempting to move forward. Already from the initial drawings and sketches, one can see how buildings and public spaces merge, when spaces such as squares and courts, alleys and boulevards, shortcuts and plazas form a continuous public space and are thought of together with the buildings that provided enclosure, openness, covered and internal streets, canopies, ramps and stairs (Figs. 2 & 3).

In this chapter, I explore and analyse the public spaces and public buildings of Agadir's city centre. Somehow, the plan has its roots in the colonial past of the country. As Nasser Rabat, the Aga Kahn Professor of Islamic Architecture at MIT, argues, it was the colonial regimes that, in many Arab countries, introduced 'new forms of public space, [like] the plaza or the square'.[5] My exploration, however, also makes clear the way in which this modern plan is grounded in this particular location and is also to be seen as an attempt to rethink and reconsider traditional Moroccan public spaces. To develop this perspective, I use the work of Françoise Navez-Bouchanine who, in her article 'Public Spaces in Moroccan Cities', emphasises the need to go beyond the accepted notion of public space as it is dominated mostly by a Western perspective. This Western view, she argues, is hardly sensitive to the nuances of public practices in Morocco. Contemporary Moroccan public spaces are the result of 'patterns of social appropriation whose dynamic demands a double reading, accounting both for cultural foundations and social transformations'.[6] Even though Navez-Bouchanine presents in her article a reading of public spaces that is based on observations in densely populated Moroccan urban districts, where appropriation of space takes place extensively, this call for a close reading also offers a lens through which to understand the public spaces in less-densely populated districts like Agadir's city centre. To understand public space in this context is to go beyond material and formal characteristics and to look for its informal qualities. I already touched upon this aspect in the very first paragraph, when I entered Place Hôtel de Ville: it was in the corner, between post office and town hall, on that spot where the formal pavement dissolved, under this single tree that provided ample shade, that people gathered, talked, met.

This is not to say that architectural qualities do not matter with regard to Moroccan public spaces. Navez-Bouchanine, after all, stresses not only the very moment of appropriation but also the inherent possibilities of appropriation through the material qualities of the spaces. The objective of this chapter, then, is to explore the 'immeasurable spaces' of the modern centre of Agadir together with its public, civic and commercial buildings in order to understand its publicness and discuss its spatial and architectural richness and quality, which sometimes is apparent but today is often obscured by processes of decay.[7]

THE URBAN PLAN AND ITS PUBLIC STRUCTURE

Place Hôtel de Ville is located halfway down Avenue du Prince Moulay Abdallah, the so-called 'spine' or 'backbone' of the reconstruction plan for the centre of Agadir. This linear street stretches from the residential area and the fire station in the south-east to the Grande Mosquée (Great Mosque) in the north-west of the centre. Even though Avenue du Prince Moulay Abdallah is understood as the spine of the plan, it is not the largest or the busiest street in the centre of Agadir. It is thus considered since it is centrally located in what, in the first drawings of the reconstruction plan, is designated as the central zone, mediating between the upper and lower parts of the centre. These initial drawings show how two large traffic roads, which connect the port and coast with the hinterland, are understood as the boundaries of the centre. The largest road, drawn as a highway, curves along the foot of the Atlas Mountains range towards the hinterland. The other road partly follows the coastline, creating a zone for beach tourism and sports detached from the urban centre. At the edges and in the middle, three green zones meet the central zone, connecting the centre to the mountain range and the hinterland as well as to the beach. These zones make use of the existing differences in the topography of the location. The central green zone is located in a former ravine that was filled with the debris of the collapsed buildings in order to unite the different parts of the centre.[8] It offers the most direct connection between the urban core and the beach. Alongside this former canyon, a space has been left open. In some of the original drawings it is mentioned as the location of a bus station, but other drawings leave it open and assign it as a space for events. It might be understood as a so-called *maydan*, which in other Arab cities offers room for military parades, equestrian exercises and sometimes for commercial markets.[9] North-west of the centre, a central park is drawn, the Jardin Ibn Zaidoun, which connects the urban centre with the more distant residential areas.

The urban centre of Agadir stretches in a straight line from north-west to south-east, more or less following the topography of the landscape. These local conditions offered a slightly different orientation to the urban centre than parts of the larger territory such as, for instance, the mountain range and the coastal zone. The previously mentioned Avenue du Prince Moulay Abdallah, the so-called

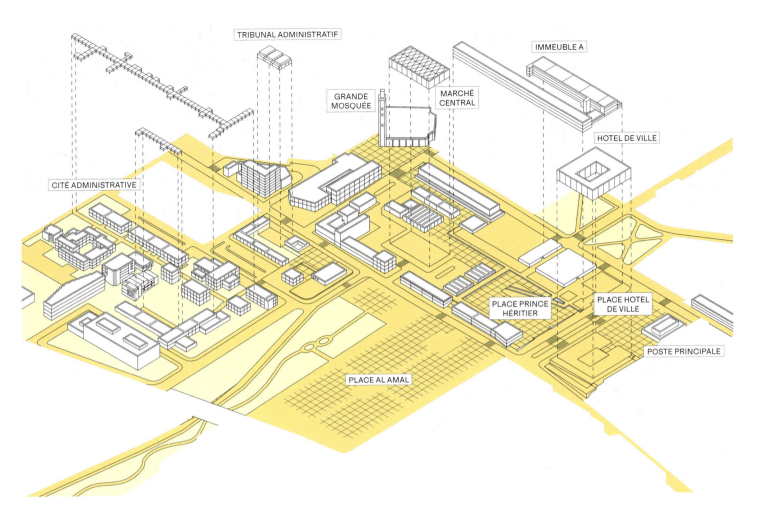

TRIBUNAL ADMINISTRATIF

IMMEUBLE A

GRANDE MOSQUÉE

MARCHÉ CENTRAL

HOTEL DE VILLE

CITÉ ADMINISTRATIVE

PLACE PRINCE HÉRITIER

PLACE HOTEL DE VILLE

POSTE PRINCIPALE

PLACE AL AMAL

Fig. 4
The public space, consisting of very different squares and gardens, alleys and pathways which together form a continuous figure.
Fig. 5
The Grande Mosquée as seen from the shopping area.

ON SQUARES, STAIRS, PATHS, PLINTHS, TREES AND SHADE IN AGADIR'S RECONSTRUCTED CENTRE

spine, is at the centre of Agadir's urban core. The edges of the urban centre are defined by two roads, Avenue Président Kennedy to the north-east and Avenue Hassan II to the south-west, which also follow the direction of the zone although they bend every now and then according to the curves of the topography. Together with Avenue du Prince Moulay Abdallah and a few streets perpendicular to it, they form an erratic grid that has its centre of gravity around Place Hôtel de Ville, the heart of the local administration, and the adjacent Place Prince Héritier Agadir, the space for local services and commerce. The buildings in this central zone follow the direction of the spine – most of them in a parallel formation, like Immeuble A (Building A, by French architects Henri Tastemain and Louis Riou, 1964) and Immeuble D (Building D, by Moroccan architect Abdeslem Faraoui and Moroccan-born French architect Patrice de Mazières, 1963), but sometimes perpendicular to it, like Immeubles O1 and O2 (Buildings O1 and O2, by Abdeslem Faraoui and Patrice de Mazières, 1963). All buildings are placed separately into the space according to modernist principles of urban planning. The public space cannot be seen as simply the residual area between the buildings and roads. Moreover, it cuts through the buildings and roads, following its own trajectory, and by doing so it offers a fine-grained pattern of connected squares, paths, green spaces, bridges, raised alleyways, gates, stairs, courtyards and ramps (Fig. 4).

RELIGIOUS SPACE

In the Islamic city, Nasser Rabat argues, the mosque is 'the equivalent of the agora in the ancient Greek city and the public square in the medieval Western city'.[10] Such a central role is not assigned to the mosque in Agadir, however. It does not figure as a centrepiece of the new plan, nor does it dominate the structure of public spaces even though it is located at the very end of the urban spine.

This peripheral location in the urban plan seems to underline the tension with religion within the modern approach to the city. Moreover – with its concrete, flat roof and its lack of a dome – the mosque is not designed as a building that dominates the plan. Only its minaret offers a tall element to the city – but even this tower is not placed exactly on axis with the spine, and thus does not offer a landmark to the urban plan either.[11] This location, between prominence and periphery, is sometimes understood as the result of a modernist bias against religion and its central role in Arab public life. But this is, to me, a superficial reading of the architecture and location of the mosque in Agadir, as well as the unique place organised around it. The mosque deviates from the basic direction of the urban plan as it is oriented almost exactly to the east, in the direction of Mecca. It thus creates an angle of about 45 degrees with the surrounding urban pattern, and thereby provides a series of unique (public) spaces around itself.

I would argue that the Grande Mosquée and its immediate surroundings testify to another approach to the urban territory, wherein neither religious nor cultural, administrative, governmental or commercial buildings dominate the space. This mosque reveals an everyday understanding of religion – one that already was part and parcel of, for instance, the urban-development plans of French urban-planner Michel Écochard for the city of Casablanca. In his plans for new neighbourhoods, religious buildings were, from the very start, embedded in the local structures and thus were understood on the level of the domestic and neighbourhood structures. Moreover, in Agadir, the mosque actually was an undeniable part of the reconstruction plan from its initial proposals. The crown prince, after all, not only specified its green tiles but, moreover, declared that he could not imagine a plan without a mosque.

GRANDE MOSQUÉE, HANS-JOACHIM LENZ, 1969

As stated, the mosque makes no attempt to dominate the space. One corner of the building marks the end of Avenue du Prince Moulay Abdallah. The tall minaret is not built in this prominent location, but is placed at the westernmost corner of the site. On this side, the building offers shade to the adjacent square with a couple of arches (which are a later addition) and some small entrances. A few palm trees mark the border of the other side of this square. The commercial buildings on this side are located at least one level down due to the sloping topography in this place and, since they only consist of a single storey, one can overlook them. The space thus opens up in the direction of the beach; however, the ocean actually cannot be seen by the pedestrians. The main entrance to the mosque is located on the other side of the building, where a particular court is created a few steps down from the 'regular' public space that follows the topography at this point up the slope. A circular washing basin dominates this forecourt, whereas the entrance to the mosque itself is rather humble.

The mosque building is organised around a large congregational room, today decorated in a classical architectural style. Photographs of its initial state show a space dominated by specifically designed columns and high roof beams. Usually in mosque architecture, this central space is articulated by a large, single dome. The most prominent feature of this mosque, however, is its Brutalist roof work, in which squared beams bear a series of little domes. The roof is supported by concrete columns, all of which are divided into four knotted, round pillars. Daylight enters from the sides, high up in the space where the side walls do not quite reach up to the roof beams, as well as through the adjacent court, which today is decorated with green tiles. Similar green tiles have also been used to ornament the minaret – but, again, this is of a later date. Images of the mosque soon after its construction show a pristine, white-plastered and straightforward building with a shallow-pitched concrete pitched roof hovering above the congregational spaces. Only the minaret, with its tiles, boasts a roofscape. The crown prince, it is said, was quite specific about the architecture of the mosque: it had to have the characteristic green tiles (Fig. 5).[12] Currently, however, the building has been reconfigured to look even more like a traditional mosque: it has been extended with columns, galleries and cornices in traditional forms and ornamentation. The minaret today is decorated by carved plasterwork and its top with so-called *zellij* tilework in shades of green and maroon.

CIVIC SPACE

PLACE HÔTEL DE VILLE (TOWN HALL SQUARE)

Of the formal public spaces in the urban centre of Agadir, Place Hôtel de Ville, which I described in the very first paragraphs of this chapter, was certainly intended as the most central square of the city. On two sides, it is bordered by busy streets, residential buildings and another square that is one level down; the other two sides accommodate two separate buildings: a town hall and a post office. The placing of these buildings on the square follows modernist principles of architectural and urban design – purposely stressing the fluidity, rather than the enclosure, of space.

In her reflections, Navez-Bouchanine stresses three different spectrums in the character of Moroccan public spaces: from a situation in which users know each other to places of anonymity; from a social mixture to a generalized one; and, finally, from restricted and codified spaces to generalised polyvalence.[13] It is immediately clear from the line of palm trees and its formal pavement that Place Hôtel de Ville can be understood as 'restricted' and 'codified' in her interpretation. Avenue du

Fig. 6
Place Hôtel de Ville: in the foreground is Avenue du Prince Moulay Abdallah and its crossing with Avenue du Sidi Mohammed, which descends at a slight slope.

Fig. 7
Front facade of the Poste Principale, with the flowerbeds and stairs in front of it mediating between the square and the building.

Prince Moulay Abdallah, on the other hand, is clearly characterised by a general polyvalence in which, as Navez-Bouchanine states, 'the unexpected plays a distinct role'.[14] The diversity of users and the appropriation of the space for street vending creates conflicting situations and unexpected events (or accidents). The contrast with the square could not be greater. The rectangular space, dominated by its stone pavement, expresses its formal character (Fig. 6). Despite the green borders on the side of the post office and Place Prince Héritier Agadir, it feels hard and untouchable. Towards the side of the post office, another design occupies the plane of the square. It consists of an expressive ensemble of ramps and lazy stairs; green borders; concrete elements on which one can sit; and overlapping concrete slabs – and, as such, creates a smooth connection between the post office and the square, forming an extension of the Brutalist architecture of the building. The square literally functions as a stage for the two aforementioned buildings, all the more so due to the topography of this part of the city. The streets and its surroundings descend towards the sea, while the flat square is kept on the same level. It thus increasingly towers above its surroundings. The increasing difference in height is first mediated by steps and stairs, but on the side of the town hall it is marked by sturdy retaining walls, which form at once a pedestal and bastion for this building.

POSTE PRINCIPALE (MAIN POST OFFICE), JEAN-FRANÇOIS ZEVACO, 1965

The post office, the Poste Principale, designed by Moroccan-born French architect Jean-François Zevaco in 1965, might be the best-known building of the reconstruction of the urban centre of Agadir. It is a rather low building compared with the size of the square and the heights of the adjacent city hall and apartment building to its rear. The building's main function is located on a single floor, but hidden at the rear is a second floor on which some apartments for employees of the post office are situated.[15] On the side of the square, this floor is barely visible (Fig 7). The apartments also have their roof terrace on this side, which is hidden from public view by the upper part of the impressive, carefully designed Brutalist facade. This elevation is marked by large concrete slabs, which alternate with stucco elements, narrow window openings and protruding beams to, together, form a balanced composition. The facade tilts forward a little, which reinforces the impression of massiveness and stability, sturdiness and steadiness. The narrow window openings between the concrete facade sections, marked with protruding beams, give the facade an expressive appearance. It has also been given a small height accent to left and right: on the left, via a flagpole on a narrow cantilever; on the right, a modest concrete tower – no more than an upright solid concrete slab. The main entrance is marked with a concrete canopy and a glazed screen that stands a little further back. Together, these form a portal through which to cross the massive and thick boundary of the facade: a space on its own; an in-between that offers a smooth crossing of the border between inside and outside, between the sharp light of the square and the much darker interior space of the foyer. The foyer is finished with wooden furniture: a desk row and fixed tables at which mail can be written or banking matters handled. The narrow facade openings bring in some daylight, while the thickness of the facade keeps direct sunlight out.

The side elevations are also expressive, a balanced mix of stucco and concrete elements, and on the north-east side an impressive fence hides the window openings. The rear elevation, situated on the street, is characterised by a collection-and-dispatch yard, with some additional parking lots for the employees and inhabitants of the previously mentioned apartments, which can be accessed from here.

HÔTEL DE VILLE (TOWN HALL),
ÉMILE-JEAN DUHON, 1966

The Hôtel de Ville is a straightforward building, with a main entrance on the square and a rear entrance in the basement, one level down. The building is two storeys high above this basement, which is hidden behind bastion-like retaining walls that are, however, very conspicuous from the surrounding streets since the square sits on a higher level, with the surrounding streets sloping down around it. A rather heavy concrete cornice offers a continuous element on each of its four facades while, below, sizeable concrete frames in front of large windows alternate with more closed concrete elements, which are articulated by beams, and with smaller windows. The aforementioned concrete frames – which together create a varied and playful pattern of open and closed, rectangular and L-shaped elements – provide shade for the offices and protection from direct sunlight (Fig. 8).

The main entrance combines a two-storey-high transparent section in the building's front facade, which opens it up to the square, with a rhythm of beams that support the cornice and a concrete portico with an expressive canopy – all of which offers an extended threshold between the inside and outside of the building. This is clearly the formal entrance to the town hall. It leads towards an equally formal two-storey lobby with broad stairs and balconies that access the various floors, with offices for the mayor and the administrative staff, but it does not offer direct access to the more public functions of the town hall like the desks for the request of formal documents and permits. For these functions, one has to enter the building via the basement – where the counters of the diverse sections of the administration are located, while waiting areas are provided in the corridors. However, besides the large transparent facade addressing the square, the lobby also opens up towards a lush, green court. In this courtyard, which is full of trees and plants, concrete elements simultaneously form basins for ponds, paths

cutting through the greenery and seating elements. The court clearly offers a marvellous and shady oasis in the midst of a concrete environment.

COMMERCIAL SPACE

PLACE PRINCE
HÉRITIER AGADIR

Adjacent to the Hôtel de Ville, a few steps down, one finds Place Prince Héritier Agadir, which was meant to be the commercial heart of the city. Due to topographic circumstances, it is located about one level lower than the previously discussed administrative core. The square is dominated by a huge ramp, which bridges over a shallow rectangular pond and connects the square with the Avenue du Prince Moulay Abdallah through the ensemble of buildings comprising Immeuble A. The square is circumscribed by three buildings – one of them the aforementioned Immeuble A, which is the highest of the three (Fig. 9). On the side adjacent to the Place Hôtel de Ville, a road, stairs and a retaining wall bridge the difference in height. The building to the south-east side has two storeys: a commercial plinth, which today is occupied by a supermarket, and apartments with large balconies facing the square on the first floor. The roofscape of these apartments rises slightly towards the side of the town hall, thereby articulating the transition from the commercial to the administrative core of the city. The north-eastern part of the square is bordered by another two-storey building, with commercial functions on its ground floor. The top floor was previously meant to be used as a hotel. The pavement of the square is similar to that of the Place Hôtel de Ville: a pattern of lines and rectangles formed by stones of differing colour. One border, with some trees, offers some greenery to the space – from there, a small seating element with, at its heart, a water canal runs in the direction of

Fig. 8
Front facade of the
Hôtel de Ville. The court
is visible through the
entrance hall.
Fig. 9
Place Prince Héritier
Agadir with the
ramp to the public path
on the second floor
of building Immeuble A.

Fig. 10
The two-storey-high
plinth of Immeuble A
gives room to shops and
coffee houses. Those
located on the second
level can be reach
by a public path, which
functions as a canopy
for the lower level.
Fig. 11
At the northern side of
Immeuble A, the public
path connects to a
shopping area, where
the market, the cinema
and shops together
echo the structure of
a kasbah.

the hotel. It creates a zone between the square and the commercial plinth of the building.

In Navez-Bouchanine's terms, one can describe this space as rather 'restricted' and 'codified', in a similar way to the previously discussed square in the administrative centre. As the pattern of the pavement is similar to the one in that square, it is clear that it is meant as a joint – even though the one is intended as the formal square and the other as its commercial counterpart. However, due to the very different edges of this space – with their shops, cafés, terraces, the shady zones under the ramp and Immeuble A, and the stairs – it certainly feels more informal, less empty. Shop owners and waiters here clearly know many of their clients, and thus it also avoids any atmosphere of anonymity. Cafés and their terraces, which here occupy the public spaces, play a particularly important role in Moroccan public life. Navez-Bouchanine specifically stresses those further away from the private sphere as places where youths can distance themselves from their family milieu.[16] This is particularly the case for the female clientele of the cafés, she states. Said Graiouid, in turn, in his reflection on Moroccan cafés, confirms this observation. Even though cafés are mainly male-dominated, they represent – particularly for women – places of a radical break, neutral ground: sites of association and solidarity.[17]

It might be the case that Place Prince Héritier Agadir has been functioning as such a place of distancing and as neutral ground. It can still be occupied by residents of the city, particularly at moments when events are organised on the square. However, it seems that the daily attraction of this public space has been taken over by the promenade along the beach, with its tourist attractions, its cafés and clubs – or by the cafés and fast-food restaurants along Avenue Président Kennedy.

THE PUBLIC PLINTH. IMMEUBLE A (BUILDING A), LOUIS RIOU, HENRI TASTEMAIN, 1964

The most prominent building along the square is the apartment complex to the north-east: a series of elongated buildings, amongst them Immeuble A.[18] The latter is the highest building: it consists of a two-storey-high plinth and, on top of that, seemingly detached from this base (as if forming an enormous beam in itself), three storeys of apartments. The elongation of the building is articulated by the closed parapets of the balconies that stretch along its facade as well as through the rhythm of concrete beam ends, which in places connect with one another across the facade. This provides each 'nave' of the building with a visual accent, and also delivers some depth and variation to the facade. The plinth is articulated by its prominent concrete structures, which appear to offer a 'table' for the three levels above (Fig. 10). The beam structure visible here is rotated perpendicular to that seen in the previously mentioned apartment block. This makes the structure of the building clearly visible; it also offers an extra accent to its elongated form. The ground floor of Immeuble A directly borders the square, although the pond in the square creates some distance between the commercial activities like shops, cafés and restaurants and events organised in the space. On the first floor, a large internal street, open but covered, runs through the building, connecting the commercial market – a modern variation on the souk, with a pronounced roofscape – the cinema and some other shops located behind the hotel building with Place Hôtel de Ville. It is through these two storeys that the building also mediates between the square and the spine, Avenue du Prince Moulay Abdallah: since this internal street is always shady, it functions as a retreat from the harsh square. A huge ramp, which is distinct from the building and also placed at a slight angle to it, connects the square with this higher level as well as with a pedestrian route that connects

Fig. 12
Garden of the Cité Administrative surrounded by the governmental buildings. On the left side, behind these buildings, the Tribunal is visible.

Fig. 13
The two courtrooms are elevated, which creates an open-air but covered space below them, providing a pleasant climate to this space, where visitors to the trials gather before they can enter the rooms.

the Avenue with the square through the building. This ramp is very prominent, and effectively dominates the square. It offers a balcony, from which one can overlook the space.

At the height of the originally planned hotel, a second raised path joins the buildings. Stairs connect this path to the square, where every now and then bridges connect it to the internal street and its commerce underneath the building. Here, a similar canal element to that which can be found on the square is used to mark the distinction between path and shopping area. This continuous path connects the square with a commercial area, behind the hotel, where the complex of Immeuble A opens up and affords room for an intimate square and pedestrian paths with further shops. This space presents a stark contrast to the large square on the other side of the building and even seem to suggest the figure of the medina, where little alleys and open space cut through a dense building mass. Amongst the small shops there also is a cinema, with a great vaulted roof, as well as a covered market for fresh foods, which can be reached by a bridge (Fig. 11).

This commercial core of Agadir offers a range of different public spaces. The diversity of public spaces ranges from the large square, which offers room for events but which is also rather prescriptive and codified, towards the internal street; the plinth of Immeuble A; the medina-like configuration, with its small shops and alleys, behind Immeuble A; and the covered market – which, all together, offer many more informal commercial and social spaces than the large square does. These interior and exterior spaces, which provide both enclosure and shade, are clearly characterised by the general polyvalence that Navez-Bouchanine describes as being highly characteristic of Moroccan public spaces.[19] In this part of the city, one might conclude, the reconstruction plan for Agadir not only reassesses, rethinks and reimagines the place

of commerce in the modern city but also takes up the traditional typologies of public space and fits them into the modernist urban plan.

GOVERNMENTAL SPACE

The south-western corner of Place Prince Héritier Agadir and the commercial area around it connects to the regional administrative centre. This part of the city has a much greener expression than the local administrative core and the commercial heart of Agadir. It is connected to the park, part of the city's main green infrastructure, which borders the centre and connects its commercial spaces with the beach via a natural slope that runs underneath the large road. In his original plan for this part of the city, Moroccan architect Élie Azagury foresaw a compound-like structure – an area separated from the hustle and bustle of the city, not by a wall but through its design as a unique green landscape wherein the administrative buildings were separately placed. A covered pedestrian bridge connects all the buildings here. The area is surrounded by roads, which give access to parking zones at its edges. From these parking areas (as well as from the commercial centre of the city), one can enter the pedestrian path and reach the administrative buildings (Fig. 12). Only the part of this plan lying between the administrative offices was built as intended. The plan for the Tribunal Administratif (Administrative Court) is slightly changed, since it is detached from the overall plan and not connected to the constructed path. Nevertheless, the architecture of the facades is similar to those of most of the regional government buildings, with expressive concrete beams and columns framing large windows that are set back to provide shading of the glass. Despite the fact that the plan to create a large green campus, wherein all buildings are connected to one another and to the surrounding city by the covered path, has not been executed completely, this area still retains an architectural unity.

TRIBUNAL ADMINISTRATIF
ÉLIE AZAGURY, 1963

The Tribunal Administratif offers another profound and unprecedented public space to the urban fabric of Agadir. This courthouse is organised around an impressive courtyard, which is fenced off from the public space. The courtyard arranges the buildings with, on the side of Avenue Hassan II, the two courtrooms and, on the other side, the offices of employees and the lawyers, advocates and judges on duty. The space also functions as a waiting place for visitors to the public trials. This courtyard is very pleasant – particularly as it provides shade and cross ventilation, which are very welcome in the challenging climate of the city. Moreover, the architecture of the building, together with the lush garden that characterises its courtyard, offer different places where one can enjoy the shade to such an extent that it has shaped the way in which the programme of the courts is organised around this space. The two courtrooms are elevated, which creates an open-air but covered space below them. Shade and cross ventilation create a pleasant space underneath, where benches offer visitors a seat. The courtrooms are supported by concrete columns, while large beams above the rooms articulate the roofscape. This Brutalist idiom fits within the architecture of the other regional government offices. The courtyard is, on its south-western and north-western sides, enclosed by two single-storey buildings wherein the offices for the magistrates and attorneys are located. Their facade at the side of the parking area, which is located between the governmental buildings and the courthouse, has the typical Brutalist architectural appearance that has also been employed by Élie Azagury in his design for the governmental buildings: emphatic concrete columns and beams, with large window-frames between

them but set back. On the side of the courtyard, these low buildings are articulated by a concrete canopy, supported on a series of concrete columns. Together, these features offer a tranquil space, a modern form of an arcade, with benches in front of the offices and a view onto the garden. Once again, shading and cross ventilation create comfortable conditions for visitors to and employees of the court (Fig. 13).

The entrance to the building is marked by a large canopy, hovering over the wall on the aforementioned little square that connects the commercial core of Agadir with the complex of regional ministry offices. Under the extensive canopy, two large gates can be opened so that entrance to the garden is possible by car. Vehicles can drive up to the point at which the courtrooms hover over the garden – the place where both judges and suspects can enter the building via two separate concourses. The courtrooms themselves; the stairs towards the rooms; and the different, separated corridors that surround these rooms are all sufficiently enclosed but also have openings to the garden. The breeze can cool these spaces, while canopies prevent the sun from shining fully on the facade or even reaching the interior.

The public also enters the garden from the side of the square, but by a separate gate. Here, a small gateway gives access to a corridor in front of the offices under the previously mentioned canopy. There are several shaded areas and seating elements in the garden and under the courtrooms, allowing the public to wait comfortably before entering. Entry is organised at the back of the courtrooms, where stairs allow entry to a rather small foyer in front of the rooms. Around the courtrooms, a small corridor gives access to the other side where judges and suspects enter. On this side, in the midst of the garden, a concrete, enclosed, circular staircase offers direct access to this small corridor for suspects.

Fig. 14
The Cité Administrative
was designed as a
compound-like struc-
ture, where the
administrative buildings
are places within a
unique green landscape.

Fig. 15
A covered pedestrian path connects the city with the administrative buildings, parking lots and green spaces. Because of the shade, it is much used by visitors waiting for their appointment as well as vendors selling their goods.

Fig. 16
The public space of Agadir forms a continuous figure, consisting of a wide range of interconnecting spaces, infrastructures and objects: stairs and ramps, bridges and paths, alleys and interior streets, covered pathways, interior public spaces.

The building has an expressive architectural appearance. The columns and beams that support the courtrooms and its roof are articulated, while the facades of these rooms remain rather anonymous. Columns and beams also feature prominently in the offices around the garden. A trabeated concrete grid structure articulates both the facades and the canopy, and is continued in the design of the garden. Within this grid, the office facades have their infill. The grid also characterises the building's outward appearance, towards the car park between the Tribunal and the offices of the regional ministries.

CITÉ ADMINISTRATIVE (ADMINISTRATIVE CENTRE), ÉLIE AZAGURY, 1963

A large section of the centre of Agadir is reserved for premises of the regional ministries. These offices are placed together in what might be understood as a compound, although its perimeter is not walled. The ministry buildings are placed separately in a green, rough and inaccessible landscape, full of trees and existing rocks (Fig. 14). The initial drawing of a part of this area indicates that it had been planned as a 'show garden'. The site is bordered on all sides by roads, from which parking areas can be accessed. From these car parks, a pedestrian path can be reached. This 'boardwalk', which is raised as well as covered, has the shape of an 'L'. It stretches the length of the site, with a perpendicular section to the south-east side where it connects – down a few stairs, due to the topography – with the square facing the Tribunal Administratif building. The path is constructed on an orthogonal five-by-five-metre grid, with the columns that support its roof placed outside it – turning it into a colonnade. A wooden handrail prevents visitors from falling off this 'boardwalk', the ceiling of which is rather low. Every now and then, bridges and staircases give access to building entrances and parking areas. The surrounding buildings – ranging from two to four storeys in height – follow a similar architectural structure, with a columnar structure on the outside and small window openings whose wooden shutters prevent sunlight from entering. Only the highest building is somewhat different, with an expressive, rounded facade and a partly transparent horizontal structure of shutters above its windows. For those buildings that are close to the public path, staircases to the second storey are regularly placed outside them and connected to the pedestrian path.

Navez-Bouchanine argues that, apart from the three spectrums of public spaces, there are, of course, also spaces that are simply apart from these categorisations. The raised path between the administrative buildings is in a way clearly codified, clearly conceived as infrastructure. But since it offers shade, and since there are always people waiting in front of the offices, the path and its connecting bridges also function as a vibrant threshold space. It is the perfect place for employees to meet one another; for visitors, while waiting their turn or wandering around between appointments. It even, sometimes, becomes a place of vending – informally, drinks are offered or shoes are polished. However, one also can argue that this space is so specific that it escapes the general logic of public spaces. As Navez-Bouchanine states of such places, '[o]ne notes that despite a specialization imparted on them by the physical terms of their conception, they are enriched through use and become increasingly polyvalent as they are appropriated'.[20]

It is, of course, not only the shade-giving roof that turns this path into a unique public space. The atmosphere is also set by the garden. The architecture of concrete columns and the roofscape mediate between space and landscape, shade and sun, infrastructure and place. This element, intended chiefly as a connection between buildings, has proven to be an innovative and properly modern public space (Fig. 15).

EPILOGUE – A DIVERSIFIED PUBLIC STRUCTURE

The new reconstruction plan, informed by the novel building regulations that were formulated in the Normes Agadir 1960 after the earthquake, together with the carefully designed buildings, courts, gardens and squares, offered a diversified public space to the citizens of the city. These spaces were envisaged as offering room for a variety of different activities, properly distributed over the territory according to the modern doctrine of zoning. The city plan made a clear distinction between, for example, zones meant for religious practices and those with a civic, commercial or governmental function. Within these zones, the plan provided a diversity of spaces, which all have their particular qualities, atmospheres, forms and typologies and which are strongly articulated by the public buildings and apartment blocks bordering them. In particular, within the commercial zone of the centre, the design offers manifold spaces that collectively echo the diversity of traditional Moroccan cities. Besides the large public space, which is rather prescriptive, this zone also offers polyvalent structures like the internal street in the plinth of Immeuble A and the shopping area behind this building, where narrow streets and small squares together with little shops, a cinema and a covered garden provide a contemporary echo of the old medina. This pedestrian public space in Agadir indeed offers a secondary structure adjacent to the city's infrastructural street grid, and its large boulevards and squares. This continuous public, pedestrian space often literally cuts through the buildings, connecting a range of spaces. These different zones, despite their particular characters, are not treated as separate and inwardly organised areas. Moreover, the public spaces are interconnected and together form a continuous and integral public structure that unites the urban core of Agadir into a single but diverse structure. However, the plan offered not only a range of public and private spaces but also less formal interconnecting spaces, infrastructure and objects: stairs and ramps, bridges and paths, alleys and interior streets, covered pathways, interior public spaces. One of the main qualities of this differentiated public space, moreover, is the differences in height caused by its topography and articulated by stairs, ramps, retaining walls and bridges. Such figures are often threshold spaces, between two different 'zones' in the urban core: spaces of overview and interaction.

The design of these spaces, their size and capacity, and their interconnectedness show how public life was imagined. The public would occupy the central squares and wander through the green zones towards the beach and back. They would frequent the cafés and the cinema, and do their daily shopping in the market. There would be festivities on the boulevard along the beach, as well as on the *maydan*. Citizens and tourists together would enjoy free time on the beach, on the terraces of Place Prince Héritier Agadir and at the cinema behind Immeuble A. Public life, in other words, is imagined here along the lines of centralised modern squares and modernistic functions that, according to Nasser Rabbat, were introduced in colonial times, as well as around the everyday and local appropriations and businesses that Navez-Bouchanine urged as the very heart of Moroccan public space.

Roughly sixty years after its completion, the centre of Agadir does not seem to fulfil this joint image. Public life in the city has seeped away to the suburban centres, to the shopping malls in the outskirts and to the touristic beach zone – all of which seem to be detached from the urban centre.[21] Formal festivals still attract people to the main squares, but these are rare occasions. The cinema is closed, shops are empty and even the market hall is only half occupied by trading stalls. Only at the edges of the formal public spaces, on their fringes and in their shadows, can one still find the hustle and bustle of public life that Navez-Bouchanine

describes, where inhabitants and business-
people claim and defend their territories in
informal ways. Under the harsh sun, any shade
is welcome, as I wrote at the beginning
of this chapter. Truly so: it is where canopies,
roofs and trees, on the edges of the formal
spaces, offer a cool place and a fine breeze,
creating a polyvalent hiding place even in
this rather empty urban centre, that this public
life still unfolds (Fig. 16).

1
Quoted in Segalla, Spencer D., *Empire and Catastrophe: Decolonization and Environmental Disaster in North Africa and Mediterranean France Since 1954*, Lincoln NE: University of Nebraska Press, 2020, p. 134.
2
The crown prince insisted on modernist principles for the reconstruction plan. As king, however, he turned to traditional Moroccan architecture for his building projects. See Roberson, Jennifer, 'The Changing Face of Morocco under King Hassan II', *Mediterranean Studies*, vol. 22, no. 1 (2014), p. 66.
3
Orlando, Valérie K., 'Mean Streets, Bad Boys, Drugs and Rock 'n' Roll, Morocco's Urban Legends of the 21st Century', *South Central Review*, vol. 28, no. 1 (2011), p. 67.
4
Segalla, *Empire and Catastrophe*, p. 145.
5
Rabat, Nasser, 'The Arab Revolution Takes Back the Public Space', *Critical Inquiry*, vol. 39, no. 1 (2012), pp. 202, 203.
6
Navez-Bouchanine, Françoise, 'Public Spaces in Moroccan Cities', in Tom Avermaete, Serhat Karakayali and Marion von Osten (eds), *Colonial Modern. Aesthetics of the Past, Rebellions for the future*, London: Black Dog Publishing, 2010, p. 213.
7
See the chapter 'Agadir's Shifted Centralities' by Janina Gosseye and Hans Teerds in this publication.
8
According to the urban designer Pierre Mas, 'This operation permitted the unification of the site of the new city, making disappear a geological accident troublesome for its development.' Quoted in Segalla, *Empire and Catastrophe*, p. 158.
9
Nasser Rabat writes in his reflection on public spaces in Arab cities that the *maydan* can hardly be seen as a civic space: 'Although the *maydan* sometimes doubled as an open-air marketplace or was even appropriated by the populace for public protest, it was always the privileged space of the rulers and was never considered a civic space, one that is related to the city and its citizens.' Rabat, 'The Arab Revolution', pp. 202–3.
10
Ibid., p. 199.
11
As Spencer Segalla notes, 'there were no towering buildings to dominate the urban space: no clock tower, no royal palace, no grande mosque'. Segalla, *Empire and Catastrophe*, p. 162.

12
Roberson, 'The Changing Face of Morocco', p. 66. See also Segalla, who suggests that Le Corbusier gave back the assignment because of the insistence of Prince Moulay Hassan on green tiles for the mosque: Segalla, *Empire and Catastrophe*, p. 132.
13
Navez-Bouchanine, 'Public Spaces in Moroccan Cities', p. 216.
14
Ibid., p. 216.
15
See also the chapter on housing in the reconstruction plan, 'Housing Figures: Social and Spatial A-Synchronicities', by Irina Davidovici in this publication.
16
Navez-Bouchanine, 'Public Spaces in Moroccan Cities', p. 217.
17
Graiouid, Said, 'A Place on the Terrace: Café Culture and the Public Sphere in Morocco', *Journal of North African Studies*, vol. 4, no. 12 (2007), p. 234.
18
I focus here on the public plinth of Immeuble A. For the residential programme, see the chapter 'Housing Figures: Social and Spatial A-Synchronicities' by Irina Davidovici in this volume.
19
Navez-Bouchanine, 'Public Spaces in Moroccan Cities', p. 216.
20
Ibid.
21
See the chapter 'Agadir's Shifted Centralities' by Janina Gosseye and Hans Teerds in this volume.

REORGANISING AGADIR, RECONSTRUCTING THE NEIGHBOURHOOD

Janina Gosseye

Prior to the earthquake of 29 February 1960, Agadir consisted of several distinct urban areas, some of which had developed over centuries while others had only emerged in the first half of the twentieth century (Fig.1). By 1960, when the tremor struck, large parts of the city fabric were already quite modern, even if some areas retained their traditional character. Agadir's kasbah, also known as Agadir Oufella,[1] was in the latter category. Perched up in the mountains to the north of the city, above the port of Agadir, the origins of the kasbah dated back to the sixteenth century, to the reign of Mohamed Cheikh Saadi, the first sultan of the Saadi dynasty of Morocco. He planned it as a fortified settlement for defence against the Portuguese, who had occupied the area of Founti – located between the kasbah and the port. From the 1950s, the kasbah faced depopulation as inhabitants relocated to other, more modern (or modernising) areas of Agadir such as Founti, a former fishers' village that had begun modernising at

that time. As noted in the book *Memoires d'Agadir au XXe Siècle*, 'Founti seems to be continuing its ascent towards modernity. Multi-storey constructions are built in the modern style, but with a Moroccan cachet.'[2]

Apart from Founti, Ancien Talborjt, the Ville Nouvelle, the industrial areas to the south-east and Agadir's coastline had all begun urbanising and modernising in the first half of the twentieth century.[3] Ancien Talborjt and its adjacent Plateau Administratif, which were located to the immediate south-east of the kasbah, underwent a rapid urbanisation process from the mid-1940s when a large number of modern buildings were constructed in the area as well as several new public squares – such as Place Talborjt. Agadir's Ville Nouvelle had also become a vibrant neighbourhood by 1960. From the 1920s, successive plans had been developed for this area by the Service de l'Urbanisme (Department of Urbanism) of the

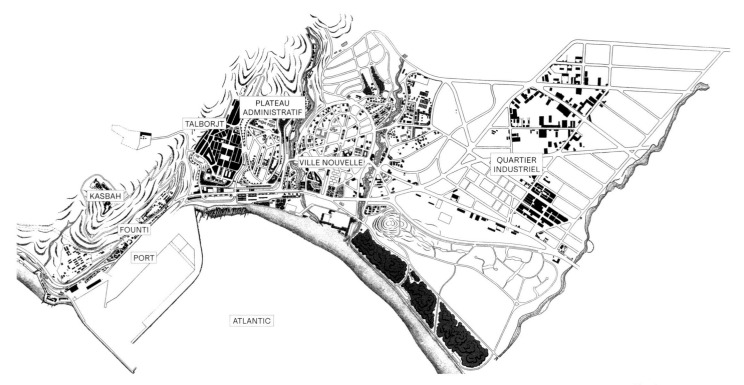

KASBAH

FOUNTI

PORT

TALBORJT

PLATEAU
ADMINISTRATIF

VILLE NOUVELLE

QUARTIER
INDUSTRIEL

ATLANTIC

Fig. 1
Urban neighbourhoods
of Agadir, prior to
the 1960 earthquake.

French Protectorate in Morocco under the direction first of Henri Prost and then Michel Écochard, who led the department from 1946 to 1952.[4] The result was an entirely new urban neighbourhood – designed especially for Europeans – with grand, geometrically organised boulevards.[5] Finally, to the south-east lay a large industrial zone that had urbanised rapidly in the years following the Second World War when, faced with continuing population growth, the authorities had decided to build another ('indigenous') district in the vicinity of the existing slaughter-houses.[6] By 1960, the western part of this industrial zone had become an important economic centre of Agadir – particularly, the area around Boulevard Jules Cambon, which was described in *Memoires d'Agadir au XXe Siècle* as 'one of the most prestigious avenues of the city, all the more so because it was the only road linking the north of Morocco to its south'.[7] The coastline bordering all these different areas had also gradually transformed into a bustling seaside from the mid-1940s. Here, interesting modern structures had cropped up, such as the delightful little café-restaurant La Réserve, which was an annex of the hotel Marhaba.[8]

During the earthquake, the various urban areas of Agadir were either completely destroyed or gravely damaged. This meant that after 1960, the city's urban fabric could be completely rethought and restructured. The reconstruction plan that was drawn up proposed five sectors (or *quartiers*) (Fig. 2). Apart from the Centre Urbain (A), which comprised the key commercial, administrative and recreational facilities for the city as a whole, there was Nouveau Talborjt (B) to the north-east of the new Centre Urbain; the Secteur Touristique et Balnéaire (C), along the coast; the secteur résidentiel (D), where the Ville Nouvelle had been previously; and the Quartier Industriel Sud (E), covering the same area as the former industrial zone. Each of these sectors had its own set of social, cultural, commercial and educational facilities, the architecture of which continued the

conversation between modern and traditional forms that had commenced a few decades earlier. This chapter examines the architectural design of a selection of public buildings and facilities that were realised in Agadir's new urban sectors following the earthquake. First, however, the overall structure that it was given following the disaster of 1960 is discussed in order to understand which paradigms and precedents might have influenced the city's urban (re-)organisation and to probe to what extent Agadir's urban structure was rethought post-1960.

RE-ORGANISING AGADIR: PARADIGMS AND PRECEDENTS

Initially, Agadir's reconstruction was a battlefield for foreign powers to demonstrate their capacity to serve as Morocco's main technical provider and benefactor. France, for instance, invited Le Corbusier to visit Agadir. The Swiss-French architect left quickly, however, when he discovered that he would not be given carte blanche to realise the modern city of his liking in Morocco. The Americans, in turn, proposed Harland Bartholomew, a civil engineer by training, who had taught civic design at the University of Illinois and who also wrote extensively on the subject of city planning. After a year of work, Bartholomew's masterplan was rejected. It was considered too vast, too expensive and not offering an appropriate response to the need for quick implementation. Finally, the Service de l'Urbanisme along with several local architects took it upon themselves to jointly develop a new masterplan for Agadir under the direction of French urban-planner Pierre Mas, who had trained under French urban-planner Michel Écochard.[9]

A source of inspiration for the masterplan that the Service de l'Urbanisme prepared for Agadir in the early 1960s was undoubtedly the dozens of new towns that had been realised across the globe from the mid-twentieth century. The paradigm of the neighbourhood unit in particular, which was adopted in many new towns, seems to have been of import for the organisation of the city's *quartiers* (sectors). This concept had originally been devised in the 1920s by the American social reformer Clarence Perry, who identified the neighbourhood as the fundamental social cell of the city and proposed that the neighbourhood unit 'bring within walking distance all the facilities needed daily by the home and the school'. Perry stipulated that 'no playground for school children should be more than a quarter of a mile from the houses it served; and the same principle applied with the variations to the distance of the primary school and the local marketing area'.[10] Proposing that cities could be segmented into smaller entities featuring all the virtues of village life, Perry's neighbourhood unit became one of the most powerful tools in twentieth-century urban planning and ostensibly had a major influence on the urban (re-) organisation of Agadir post-1960. As specified in the 1966 issue of the *Revue Africaine d'Architecture et d'Urbanisme*, devoted entirely to the reconstruction of Agadir, each new sector of the city contained its own neighbourhood functions. The Centre Urbain housed the key commercial, administrative and recreational facilities for the city as a whole; Nouveau Talborjt had a market, two schools, a day-care centre, a youth club, sporting grounds, two public gardens, a cinema, two mosques and a dispensary; the Secteur Résidentiel had a school, a mosque and a small commercial centre; and the Quartier Industriel Sud had two mosques, a dispensary, a cinema, two child-care centres, three schools, a youth club, sporting grounds, a public garden and a so-called *foyer d'éducation feminine* (women's education centre). In this area, in comparison with other sectors of the city, many buildings had well withstood the earthquake, which is why it was earmarked to house an additional 20,000 inhabitants and required a plethora of new community facilities – contrary to the Secteur Touristique et Balnéaire, which was predominantly aimed at (international) tourism and therefore offered

few functions for local residents. For the most part, it housed new hotels and leisure facilities.[11]

By the time that the reconstruction of Agadir began, Perry's concept of the neighbourhood unit had already been around for several decades and had been widely adopted – and also adapted. Michel Écochard played an important role in its introduction to and adaptation in Morocco, where he had been active since the 1940s when he was appointed Director of the Moroccan Service de l'Urbanisme.[12] One of the most important instruments that he developed was the eight-metre by eight-metre grid for housing, which came to be known as *Trame Écochard* (Écochard Grid).[13] Building on Perry's scheme, Écochard proposed that each neighbourhood realised following his grid should consist of five 'neighbourhood units', which would each accommodate 1,800 inhabitants and would provide everyday collective services such as a mill, an oven, shops and a playground (Fig. 3). Five of these neighbourhood units combined constituted a 'full' neighbourhood (of 9,000 people), and would offer a complete set of commercial, religious, administrative, social, cultural, recreational and educational facilities. Écochard proposed that the hierarchy of the neighbourhood be physically articulated through an intricate network of public spaces. Small *placettes*, with minimum dimensions of twenty-four metres by sixteen metres, for instance, were to accommodate collective life with immediate neighbours, while large commercial squares with communal ovens, hammams and shops were to unite the entire neighbourhood.[14] In Agadir, Écochard's adapted neighbourhood unit was of greatest influence within sectors B and E, Nouveau Talborjt and the Quartier Industriel Sud, where his eight-metre by eight-metre urban grid was adopted most extensively.

Apart from the neighbourhood unit, two other urban design precedents appear to have played a major role in Agadir's urban (re-)

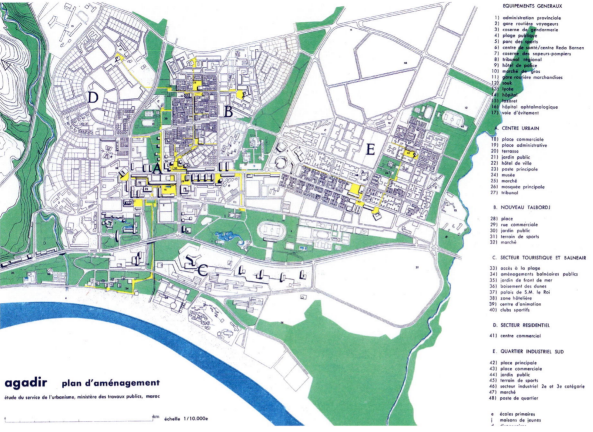

EQUIPEMENTS GENERAUX

1) administration provinciale
2) gare routière voyageurs
3) caserne de gendarmerie
4) plage publique
5) parc des sports
6) centre de santé/centre Reda Barnen
7) caserne des sapeurs-pompiers
8) tribunal régional
9) hôtel de police
10) marché de gros
11) gare routière marchandises
12) souk
13) lycée
14) hôpital
15) lazaret
16) hôpital ophtalmologique
17) voie d'évitement

A. CENTRE URBAIN

18) place commerciale
19) place administrative
20) terrasse
21) jardin public
22) hôtel de ville
23) poste principale
24) musée
25) marché
26) mosquée principale
27) tribunal

B. NOUVEAU TALBORDJ

28) place
29) rue commerciale
30) jardin public
311) terrain de sports
321) marché

C. SECTEUR TOURISTIQUE ET BALNEAIR

33) accès à la plage
34) aménagements balnéaires publics
35) jardin de front de mer
36) boisement des dunes
37) palais de S.M. le Roi
38) zone hôtelière
39) centre d'animation
40) clubs sportifs

D. SECTEUR RESIDENTIEL

41) centre commercial

E. QUARTIER INDUSTRIEL SUD

42) place principale
43) place commerciale
44) jardin public
45) terrain de sports
46) secteur industriel 2e et 3e catégorie
47) marché
48) poste de quartier

e   écoles primaires
j   maisons de jeunes

Fig. 2
Plan for the urban reconstruction of Agadir after the 1960 earthquake.
Fig. 3
Écochard's scheme for the organisation of urban neighbourhoods.

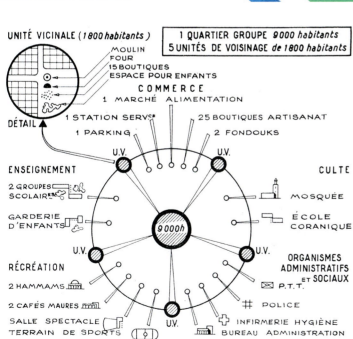

Principe d'organisation d'un quartier marocain.

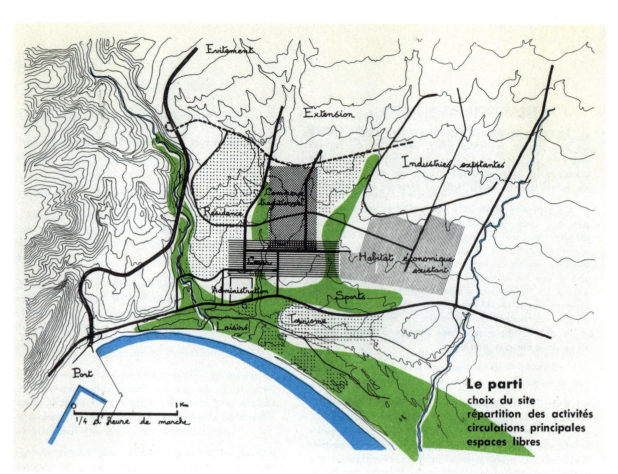

Fig. 4
Schematic drawing
of Agadir's urban
reorganisation.

Le parti
choix du site
répartition des activités
circulations principales
espaces libres

organisation: Le Corbusier's 1924 plan for a Ville Radieuse and Constantinos Doxiadis's Dynapolis model. In his scheme for a Ville Radieuse, Le Corbusier proposed a linear urban layout that could extend towards the east and west. The city itself was organised into distinct functional zones along a north–south axis – from a business centre in the north down to a zone with hotels and embassies, then to a residential zone in the centre and further down to an area with factories and warehouses to, finally, a zone for heavy industry in the south. Proposing a linear urban expansion, the Ville Radieuse presaged Greek architect and urban planner Constantinos Doxiadis's ideas. Doxiadis believed that the city should not and could not be a static entity but was to be planned for growth. In 1960, he published a book entitled *Dynapolis: The City of the Future*, which set out a model for the dynamic expansion of the city. The building blocks for this dynamic urban expansion Doxiadis named 'sectors'. Each sector in his Dynapolis measured two by two kilometres, housed 20,000 to 40,000 people and had its own set of communal functions organised throughout its area in a hierarchical pattern. As the city grew, new sectors could be added – and thus linear bands of urbanity would emerge that were separated from each other by green fingers comprising public parks and recreational facilities for residents.[15] It is important to note that, for Doxiadis, the dynamic character of the city was a matter not only of urban growth but also of evolving family compositions. He believed that the city should be able to adapt to changing social groups and practices and, accordingly, proposed including a variety of dwelling types within each sector so that citizens could move from one type of house to another as their family expanded or shrank, or as their economic circumstances evolved. Le Corbusier's Ville Radieuse project equally proposed mixing socioeconomic groups. In this scheme, he deliberately placed the residential zone between the one with offices to the north and the zone with factories to the south, so that blue- and white-collar workers would mingle and socio economic differences would be mitigated.

A schematic drawing included in the 1966 issue on Agadir of the *Revue Africaine d'Architecture et d'Urbanisme* reveals the mental imprint of Le Corbusier's and Doxiadis's schemes on the urban (re-)organisation of the north African city, post-1960 (Fig. 4). First, it shows a tendency towards functional zoning. Even if every one of Agadir's six sectors offered housing as well as a variety of communal facilities, each was also clearly expected to have a particular functional emphasis – much like the different areas in Le Corbusier's Ville Radieuse. The Centre Urbain (sector A) was the administrative centre of Agadir; Nouveau Talborjt (sector B) was labelled 'commerce', suggesting that the small trades and shops that had existed in this area before were expected to return; the Secteur Touristique et Balnéaire (sector C), along the coast, was to offer spaces for tourism, sports and recreation; the Secteur Résidentiel (sector D) was to become a predominantly residential area (as its name suggests); and sector E, the Quartier Industriel Sud, was to offer *habitat économique* (affordable housing) in close proximity to the existing industry. Second, the drawing also reveals the planners' belief in the need to accommodate Agadir's future urban growth. From the touristic and recreational area along the coast, three green fingers are drawn that extend inland. These are paralleled by major roads that were to structure the urban 'extension' (clearly labelled on the plan), which was expected to occur in the north-eastern direction.[16] Finally, the scale bar included at the bottom of this drawing indicates that the length that it sets out (one kilometre) equates a '1/4 d'heure de marche' (a fifteen-minute walk) – once again, affirming the importance of the neighbourhood unit concept on the urban planning of Agadir. Although the desire to mix different socio economic groups is less evident in the urban reorganisation of post-earthquake Agadir than it is in Le Corbusier's and Doxiadis's plans, the proposed scheme

architect Pierre Coldefy, the Petit Marché de Talborjt was rectangular in plan and modest in size. However, the plinth on which it sat augmented the building's height and emphasised its sculptural roof, which consisted of an array of nine concrete elements that spanned the width of the structure and formed a canopy at either end, protecting the entrances to the shops below (Fig. 6).

The neighbourhood centre of the Quartier Industriel Sud (sector E) was less 'focal' than that of Nouveau Talborjt. Here, a neighbourhood axis emerged instead – along Avenue El Mouqwama, which traversed the sector from the west, near sector C, to the east, where the industrial area of the sector proper is located. This neighbourhood axis gathered some of sector E's main commercial, cultural, recreational and religious facilities along its path. At its westernmost end, near the junction with Avenue Hassan II, was Cinema Salam. This building was realised in the 1950s following the design of Moroccan-born French architect Georges Appéré, who gave it a beautiful ribbed-vault structure that withstood the 1960 earthquake (Fig. 7). On the adjacent urban block along this neighbourhood axis was the Ottoman Mosque Ibno Offane, which overlooked a large square. The next urban block along this axis housed a *hôpital ophtamologique*. Interestingly, this building was rotated vis-à-vis the surrounding urban grid by 45 degrees. One block further, on the other side of Avenue El Mouqwama, was the public garden Le Jardin Lalla Meryem, which was designed by French landscape architects Jean Challet and Jean Daney (Fig. 8). Challet and Daney opted for a strict geometrical layout, with straight paths and rectangular lawns. At the centre of the garden, they placed a paved square with simple stone benches; a small square pond; and a slender pergola structure to provide the necessary shade.

The next two urban blocks, further east along Avenue El Mouqwama, in the Quartier Industriel Sud covered part of the area where the Cité d'Urgence (Emergency City) was built immediately following the earthquake. Of all Agadir's old neighbourhoods, the industrial zone best survived the disaster and was thus best suited to start rebuilding. When the first stage of the reconstruction commenced in the summer of 1960, it included 500 housing units to be constructed in this area by the Housing Department. Accordingly, it was also here that the first new post-1960 mosque was erected. This was the Mosquée Sénégal. On 30 June 1960, King Mohammed V laid its foundation stone, and the building was completed in 1964 (Fig. 9). Adjacent to the mosque was a small market with stalls for fresh produce as well as hairdressers, shops for men's and women's clothing, jewellers, etc. Designed by architects Faraoui and de Mazières – a partnership between Moroccan architect Abdeslem Faraoui and Moroccan-born French architect Patrice de Mazières – this little neighbourhood market was organised around two main shopping streets that ran in parallel, from the north-west to the south-east, and that were connected through secondary pathways that ran perpendicular to them. The whole circulation network of the market, which is only accessible to pedestrians, is covered; its corridors are defined by sequences of concrete portal frames that also delineate the edges of two lush, green courtyards that the market circumscribes.

A final stop along the neighbourhood axis in the Quartier Industriel Sud was the triangular urban plot defined by Rue des Souks (which forms the boundary between the more residential part of the sector in the west and the more industrial part in the east), Avenue El Mouqwama (which sets out the east–west spine around which many of the sector's collective facilities are clustered) and a street called 'Oued Ziz'. This triangular plot is occupied by two remarkable structures: the Halle aux Grains (Grain Hall) and the adjacent Marché de Gros (Wholesale Market), which will be used as music conservatory (Figs. 10 & 11). The Halle aux Grains was designed in the

Fig. 6
The Petit Marché de
Talborjt.

Fig. 7
Cinema Salam, which withstood the 1960 earthquake.
Fig. 8
Le Jardin Lalla Meryem in the Quartier Industriel Sud.
Fig. 9
Mosquée Sénégal with adjacent market in the Cité d'Urgence.

Figs. 10 & 11
The Halle aux Grains
in the Quartier Industriel
Sud.
Fig. 12
The Marché de Gros
in the Quartier Industriel
Sud.

289   REORGANISING AGADIR, RECONSTRUCTING THE NEIGHBOURHOOD

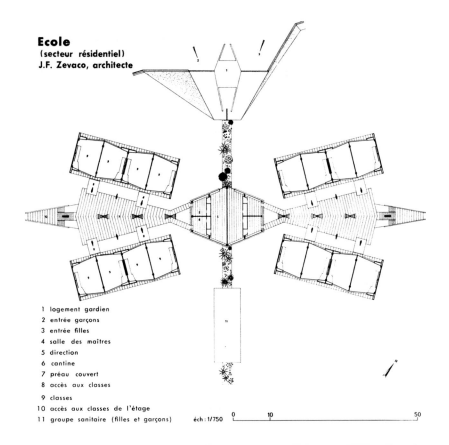

Ecole
(secteur résidentiel)
J.F. Zevaco, architecte

1 logement gardien
2 entrée garçons
3 entrée filles
4 salle des maîtres
5 direction
6 cantine
7 préau couvert
8 accès aux classes
9 classes
10 accès aux classes de l'étage
11 groupe sanitaire (filles et garçons)

éch : 1/750

```
0          10                              50
```

Fig. 13
Plan of the Souss Al
Alima school.
Fig. 14
The Souss Al Alima
school in the Secteur
Résidentiel.

mid-1960s by architects Pierre Coldefy and Claude Verdugo in collaboration with Polish-French engineer Stéphane du Château. It has a large paraboloid roof that touches the ground at only three points. This roof has a space-frame structure composed of tubular members welded together, which was originally covered with polyester. The lightness of this roof contrasts sharply with the thick concrete and pebble-stone walls that surround the various spaces of the Halle aux Grains, which are (partially) sunk into the ground (see Fig. 11). A covered pathway connected the Halle aux Grains to the adjacent (former) Marché de Gros. This building also has a strong geometric shape. It is composed of ten 'slices', each of which follows one of two patterns: five slices have a roof rising up towards the north while the other five, with which they alternate, have a roof rising up towards the south. The result is a building with an undulating, saw-toothed outline. Climatic requirements were considered as well: the top halves of the five tallest slices, on both the northern and southern sides of the Marché de Gros, were louvred to stimulate cross ventilation (Fig. 12).

The Secteur Résidentiel (sector D) in the north-western part of Agadir consists of two lobes, separated from each other by the Avenue Président Kennedy and from the natural hinterland to the north-west by the Rue Mokhtar Soussi. The southern lobe, closest to the waterfront, was to establish a relationship with the Centre Urbain (A) while the northern lobe was destined to connect with sector B, Nouveau Talborjt. Accordingly, the neighbourhood centre of the Secteur Résidentiel was also bipolar – subdivided into two (small) clusters of communal facilities, one for each lobe. The northern lobe was to have a commercial centre, directly connected to Place Tamri de Talborjt via Rue Mehdi Ben Toumert. Today, however, no such commercial centre exists in this area – which also has no tangible connection with Nouveau Talborjt, contrary to what was planned. Instead, the northern lobe of the Secteur Résidentiel is

separated from sector B by Avenue des Forces Armées Royales. In addition to the boundary created by this urban highway – this was one of the thoroughfares accompanying the green fingers that were to structure Agadir's urban growth – socioeconomic differences probably also influenced the estrangement between the northern lobe of the Secteur Résidentiel, which houses large villas with swimming pools, and sector B, where Écochard's eight-metre by eight-metre grid reigns supreme.

The relationship that the new masterplan for Agadir sought to establish between the southern lobe of the Secteur Résidentiel and the Centre Urbain has been more successful. Along this section of the Secteur Résidentiel, the Avenue des Forces Armées Royales was downgraded from a multi lane highway to a regular street, allowing residents to cut across more easily from the Centre Urbain to the Secteur Résidentiel. The Loubnan Mosque, which is the largest mosque in Agadir, plays a pivotal role in extending the collective realm from the Centre Urbain into the Secteur Résidentiel. Rotated by 45 degrees vis-à-vis the surrounding streets, it links the city's central shopping centre and market hall with the Souss Al Alima school, originally called Groupe Scolaire du Centre Urbain (school group of the Centre Urbain) and, together with this educational facility, forms the neighbourhood centre of the southern lobe of the Secteur Résidentiel. Designed by Moroccan-born French architect Jean-François Zevaco, the Souss Al Alima school is one of the architectural highlights of Agadir. The plan of the building was laid out in the shape of a butterfly (see Figs 13 & 14). Its head formed the entrance to the complex (which included a booth for the caretaker) while its tail (quite fittingly) housed the school's sanitary facilities. The body of the butterfly was designed to accommodate the canteen and office spaces, and its wings contained the classrooms – boys in the western wing, girls in the eastern wing. These wings have a tripartite structure: lining their edges are two-storey buildings with four classrooms on either level, and between these classroom buildings are triangular, communal spaces are almost entirely covered by elevated decks. Triangular staircases placed at the far end of each of these decks offer access to the upper levels, from where the upper classrooms can be reached via small bridges (Figs. 15 & 16).

The whole school complex – constructed in concrete, plaster, wood and terrazzo – was finely detailed. The sculptural spirit that informed its design was visible not only in its plan but also in its elevations.[20] For instance, the triangular staircases defining the extremities of the butterfly's wings were given treads that were triangular in section (Fig. 17). Other beautiful detailing is visible in the facades of the classroom buildings. These were slanted in such a way that in plan they outlined various triangular forms. This facade detail assisted in shading the outer walls and windows: as the floor plates and roofs of these classroom buildings retained their rectangular shape, this device formed small canopies for the walls and windows below (Fig. 18). Of the whole complex, only the western half was ever completed. The school is thus a beautiful butterfly with a broken wing, which is perhaps a fitting analogy for post-earthquake Agadir as a whole.

A NEW MONUMENTALITY FOR A NEW CITY?

Hot on the heels of Morocco's independence, the reconstruction of Agadir unfolded in a field of tension between a country seeking to assert its newly won freedom and a desire for foreign powers to gain influence. Concepts of the functional city, the growing city (or Dynapolis) and the neighbourhood unit were adopted in this North African city, and underpinned its urban reorganisation. Surprisingly, the adoption of these international models and paradigms did not fundamentally change Agadir's demographic organisation. The socio-economic 'zoning' that had manifested

itself there before the earthquake was largely replicated after it. Wealthier citizens were housed in the north-western part of the city – in the Secteur Résidentiel, where the Ville Nouvelle had stood before it – and less-affluent citizens were housed in the south-eastern part of the city – in the Quartier Industriel Sud, where the industrial zone and affordable housing for the native population had formerly been situated. Furthermore, in the city's new urban layout, these areas were also neatly separated from each other by a buffer zone formed by fragmentary green spaces (segments of the planned green fingers that were to guide the city's urban growth), the commercial area that is Nouveau Talborjt and the new Centre Urbain. This is quite ironic given that the latter, the Centre Urbain, was intended as a unifying space for the whole city. Furthermore, in Agadir's new urban organisation, the different sectors for local residents are also neatly separated from the Secteur Touristique et Balnéaire for (foreign) visitors by a large sports area that runs parallel to the coast (see Fig. 4). The careful zoning that was part of the city's urban reorganisation has thus ostensibly strengthened its urban segregation.

More than in its urban structure, the desire to turn over a new leaf can be read in the new communal facilities that were constructed in Agadir's novel urban sectors. All sectors were considered entities in their own right, and thus endowed with new sets of communal facilities and squares. Sturdy in materiality and expressive in form, these new complexes and squares continued the experimentation with architectural modernity that the GAMMA group had engaged in from the early 1950s. Accordingly, all the different neighbourhood centres that were realised in Agadir's urban sectors following the earthquake express a new monumentality and a desire to shed the trauma of the past and to shape a new urban future.

Fig. 15
Triangular staircase
at the Souss Al Alima
school.
Fig. 16
Small bridges to
classrooms at the Souss
Al Alima school.

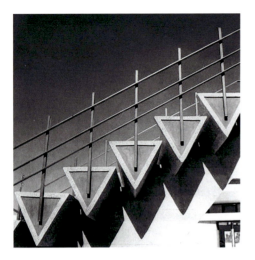

Fig. 17
Triangular steps at the
Souss Al Alima school.
Fig. 18
Sculptural shading
at the Souss Al Alima
school.

1

Roussafi, Lahsen, Yazza Jafri and Abdallah Kiker, *Mémoires d'Agadir au XXᵉ Siècle, Tome I, 1901–1945*, translated by Ali Ahlalay, Rabat: s.n., 2013, p. 60.

2

Original quote: 'les Nouvelles constructions remplacent peu à peu les anciennes et modestes maisons . . . Founti semble poursuivre son ascension vers la modernité. Des constructions de plusieurs étage bâties suivant le style modern avec un cachet marocain.' Caïs-Terrier, Régine (ed.), *Mémoires d'Agadir au XXᵉ Siècle, Tome 2, 1945–1960*, s.n., n.d., pp. 21–2.

3

Ibid., p. 5.

4

Following Écochard, Abdeslem Faraoui became head of the Service de l'Urbanisme (from 1959 to 1961), and then Mourad Ben Embarek (after 1961). See Chaouni, Aziza, 'Depoliticizing Group GAMMA: Contesting Modernism in Morocco', in Lu, Duanfang (ed), *Third World Modernism: Architecture, Development and Identity*, London: Routledge, 2010, pp. 57–84.

5

Initial plans proposed that the Ville Nouvelle would accommodate the European population while Talborjt would be a 'Cité Indigène' (Indigenous City). The administrative quarter, which was situated between the two areas, was expected to function as a buffer. See Dartois, Marie-France, Régine Caïs-Terrier, Lahsen Roussafi and Dominque Bloch-Mazet, 'Agadir: Ville Nouvelle 1930–1960', mfd.agadir.free.fr/vilnouv/index.html (accessed 21 July 2021).

6

Caïs-Terrier, *Mémoires d'Agadir au XXᵉ Siècle, Tome 2*, p. 39.

7

Original quote: 'une des avenues les plus prestigieuses de la ville d'autant plus qu'elle était la seule voie qui reliat le nord du Maroc à son sud'. Ibid., p. 46.

8

Ibid., p. 52.

9

Chaouni, Aziza, 'Agadir: The Coming of Age of Morocco's Post-Independence Modernism', in Elser, Olivier, Philip Kurz, Peter Cachola Schmal, Felix Torkar and Maximilian Liesner (eds), *SOS Brutalism: A Global Survey*, Zurich: Park Books, 2017, pp. 52–7. David Hicks writes, 'The new plan for Agadir was worked out at Rabat in the Bureau Central des Etudes, a permanent department of the Moroccan Ministry of Works. Among its staff were Pierre Mas, town-planner, Mourad Ben Embarek, Claude Beurret, and Jean-Paul Ichter, architects, and Jean Challet, landscape architect. They had already contributed substantially to planning and reconstruction throughout Morocco, and were well acquainted with Agadir's problems.' David T. Hicks, 'Rebuilt Agadir', *Architectural Review* 142 (1967), pp. 293–300 (p. 295).

10

Mumford, Lewis, *The City in History: Its Origins, Its Transformations, and Its Prospects*, San Diego, CA: A Harvest Book, Harcourt, 1961, p. 501.

11

Mas, Pierre, 'Plan Directeur et Plans d'Amenagement', *A+U: Revue Africaine d'Architecture et d'Urbanisme*, 4 (1966), pp. 6–17.

12

Avermaete, Tom, 'Framing the Afropolis: Michel Ecochard and the African City for the Greatest Number', in Avermaete, Tom and Johan Lagae (eds), 'L'Afrique, c'est chic: Architecture and Plannning in Africa 1950-1970', special issue of *OASE: Journal for Architecture*, 82 (2010), pp. 77–100 (pp. 77–9).

13

Ibid., p. 83.

14

Ibid., pp. 77–100.

15

Mahsud, Ahmed Z. Khan, 'Constantinos A. Doxiadis's Plan for Islamabad: The Making of a City of the Future, 1959–1963', unpublished PhD thesis, Department of Architecture, Katholieke Universiteit Leuven, 2008.

16

These green fingers were never fully realised, although some green patches do exist. Along the path of the middle green finger extending from the coast towards the north-east are a few parks, including Agadir's Bird Valley and the Jardin d'Olhao, which mark its general direction, and the trajectory of the southernmost green finger is defined by the Jardin Ibn Zaidoun and the adjacent eucalypt forest.

17

GAMMA meeting minute notes, Élie Azagury private archive, Cité de l'Architecture et du Patrimoine in Paris, cited in Chaouni, 'Agadir: The Coming of Age of Morocco's Post-Independence Modernism', pp. 52–7 (p. 53). For more information about the contested nature of modernism in Morocco, see Chaouni, 'Depoliticizing Group GAMMA', pp. 57–84.

18

Giedion, Siegfried, 'The Need for a New Monumentality', in Zucker, Paul (ed), *New Architecture and City Planning*, New York: Philosophical Library, 1944, pp. 549–68 (p. 550).

19

Ibid., p. 552.

20

Beurret, Claude, 'Architecture et Aménagement Publics', *A+U: Revue Africaine d'Architecture et d'Urbanisme*, 4 (1966), pp. 34–57 (p. 51).

HOUSING FIGURES: SOCIAL AND SPATIAL A-SYNCHRONICITIES

Irina Davidovici

HOUSING
AND URBAN DESIGN

The 1960 earthquake provided the apocryphal modernist tabula rasa for reconstruction. In terms of housing, however, the architects of the new Agadir did not operate in a void – either urbanistically or theoretically. Firstly, by then the city had already been subject to colonial planning experiments. While the old 'Ville Européenne' (European City, also known as the Ville Nouvelle) had been erased, its memory remained in the idiosyncratic curvature of new streets in the city's more prosperous residential district of villas. In contrast, the democratising device of the grid was applied in the more working-class quarters – pointing to a different, subtler form of segregation on socio-economic grounds. Secondly, the architects were contributing to the already rich modern architectural culture in Morocco, which had proven highly experimental in terms of housing.[1] In this context, the common stylistic range generated by the Normes Agadir 1960 was characterised by rectangularity, linear white surfaces and exposed concrete structures – often revealing the dark underbelly of buildings in the manner of Corbusian *pilotis* (stilts). These modernist tropes were at the same time mediated by a sense of cultural adaptation, perceptible in the reduced height of multistorey ensembles, the permeable boundaries articulated by perforated concrete screens and the exploration of individual family dwellings loosely reminiscent of indigenous types.

In its massing and typological heterogeneity, Agadir's new housing closely reflected the principles employed in the overall city planning of the reconstruction. The modernist slabs at the heart of the Centre Urbain, the upmarket villas and more modest patio houses in the Secteur Résidentiel, the anonymous flats above the commercial streets of Nouveau Talborjt and the accommodation for working officials hidden behind or above public institutions around the Cité Administrative (Administrative Centre) correspond quite rigidly to the zoning strategy employed in the Plan Directeur (masterplan) of 1960 (Fig. 1). The resulting housing reflected a zoning that extended from the urban to the social realm: from the relationship between morphology and programme to the distribution of certain groups of citizens to certain neighbourhoods. By assigning particular dwelling typologies to each district, and by matching the different types to specific social and ethnic groups, designers and administrators inadvertently propagated the practices of colonial planning. The result was the continued heterogeneity of urban realm and public sphere alike. At the same time, separately and in ensemble, the housing projects implemented as part of this urban strategy demonstrated architectural ambition, social idealism and sensitivity towards their cultural situation.

Thus, the dependence of Agadir's residential stock on the city's urban planning also masked the tension between a desire for radical change and a deeper cultural conditioning. In ascribing to a shared modernist idiom, the designs of housing and of city districts displayed a persistent ambiguity towards precedent. While the earthquake destruction provided a rare, literal interpretation of the apocryphal tabula rasa, a diverse set of continuities – local cultural and administrative patterns; the professional network of the designers; even, to a lesser extent, the desires and wishes of the local population – continued to exercise a palpable claim. Therefore, the housing strategies employed in the reconstruction of Agadir require contextualisation, in relation to both the city's overall planning and the professional formation of the network of architects involved. The current chapter examines the ambivalence inherent in the modernist principles at work in Agadir's housing projects – arguing that rather than representing a radically new departure, it prolonged the ambiguity of the modernist agenda in relation to the colonial project (Fig. 2).

CONTEXT:
THE CITY BEFORE 1960

Before the earthquake, Agadir gave the impression of an overly ambitious oeuvre impossible to achieve. Next to unpretentious, yet dense and animated districts, traces of monumental routes defined numerous terrains vagues, with a few scattered buildings and some villas. Inorganic, spineless, the city lacked both a centre and overall coherence.[2]
Pierre Mas

The 1960 earthquake occurred, almost to the day, four years after a politically seismic event: the French–Moroccan independence agreement of 2 March 1956. In Agadir's reconstruction, this historical proximity led to an overlapping of related agendas. Looking beyond the tragedy of the natural catastrophe, the authorities and planners seized the chance for a radical rethinking of the city in what they perceived as independent, post-colonial terms. The French urbanist Pierre Mas's description of Agadir before the earthquake criticised its nature as an incomplete, conceptually flawed colonial project. Mas, one of the authors of the urban reconstruction plan, was referring to the inherited, by then erased, dichotomy between the indigenous districts of the city and the elaborately planned yet partly unbuilt colonial European City. The segregated plan for the Ville Nouvelle (New City), drawn up in 1932, showed two elaborately composed nuclei – a smaller administrative centre and a larger residential district, known as the 'horseshoe'. In the pattern and detail of their street planning, these were clearly separated from the traditional kasbah district, Oufella, on the hill above; the fishing village Founti on the beach below; and, to the south, the territory set aside for industry and the new 'Ville Indigène' (Indigenous Town, also known as Talborjt). In that respect, the plan seemed a straightforward prolongation of the French Protectorate's urban planning strategies, as implemented by planner Henri Prost according to the

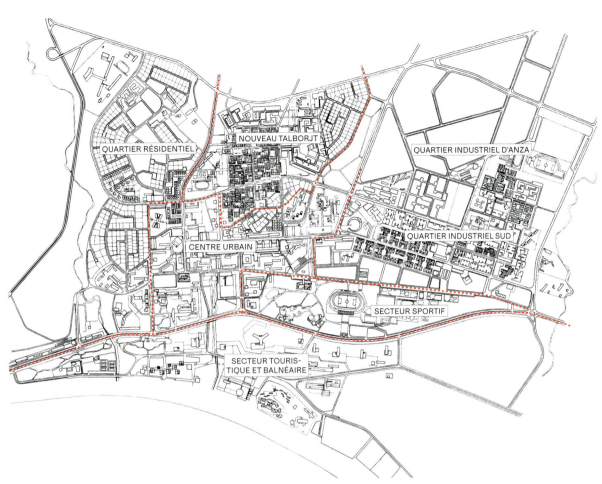

Fig. 1
Agadir's zoning plan creates associations between housing types and social classes.
Fig. 2
Immeuble D today: the loggias are now mostly closed.

QUARTIER RÉSIDENTIEL

NOUVEAU TALBORJT

QUARTIER INDUSTRIEL D'ANZA

QUARTIER INDUSTRIEL SUD

CENTRE URBAIN

SECTEUR SPORTIF

SECTEUR TOURIS-TIQUE ET BALNÉAIRE

preservationist vision of General Hubert Lyautey (both had already left Morocco – in 1923 and 1925, respectively).

However, there were telling differences. During the Protectorate, Agadir's population had risen from a few hundred to 2,000 Moroccan and 1,650 European inhabitants by 1930.[3] Its remoteness and modest size had meant that the delimitation of native and colonial zones was not implemented as strictly as in the larger centres of Casablanca or Rabat. Rather, the 1932 plan was more of an attempt to bring under control the city's accelerated growth, which had been accompanied by rampant speculative development. Instead of sanitary corridors distancing the European and indigenous cities, their separation was achieved by the natural topography. Overlooked by the Oufella kasbah, the city below was divided by two riverbeds flowing into the sea, Waddi Tidli and Waddi Tanaout, which formed three distinct plateaus. Claiming a central role, the horseshoe-shaped Ville Européenne occupied the middle ground. On the northern plateau, a small administrative area was adjacent to the indigenous commercial district of Talborjt, set up as the town's new medina (a traditional, walled town). The southernmost area was reserved for industrial development and workers' housing. In other words, the urban segregation was built into the topographical situation, which cut off the city districts, port and railway station from each other.

Within this scheme, during the three decades before the earthquake, the city had grown in unexpected ways. Despite its central location, the European district, a garden city-like settlement of curved streets and expensive villas, never properly took root. In contrast, the commercial quarter, Talborjt, attracted a rich mix of local and European traders and became a densely populated medina – the uncontested heart of the city. After 1945, its economy buoyed by the booming fishing industry and citrus farming, Agadir continued to grow – reaching a population of almost 40,000, of which 15,000 were Europeans, in the early 1950s.[4] A fledgeling tourist industry led to the building of new hotels along the beach. Nevertheless, the fault lines in the urban design were openly acknowledged in 1952, when French urban-planner Michel Écochard drew up plans for a new working-class district in the south-east, next to the industrial area. Planned as the characteristically low-height, eight-by-eight-metre *Trame Écochard* (Écochard Grid), situated furthest away from the epicentre, this area was able to largely survive the earthquake. In the late 1950s, as the confluence of political and economic crises resulted in a mass exodus of Europeans, the city's population shrank once again. Two-thirds of the European community left after 1956, with fewer than 5,000 still in the city in 1959. Due to these fluctuations, by the time of the earthquake Agadir was unevenly occupied – Talborjt, still dense and lively; the industrial zone, coming along; yet with a dwindling European district in the middle.

RECONSTRUCTION: HOUSING TYPES BY URBAN DISTRICT

The reconstruction masterplan envisaged a new city for 50,000 inhabitants erected on the ruins of the old town. Three general principles underlined the planning: the priority accorded to pedestrian access, needed to nourish 'the social life of the city'; the hierarchisation of autoroutes and their separation from pedestrian ones; and, finally, the creation of distinct city districts, whose own characters would be defined by the main occupations and needs of their inhabitants.[5] Based on assessments of seismic risk, the rebuilt conurbation shifted slightly to the south and east of its earlier location.[6] The large quantities of available debris made it possible to build over Waddi Tanaout, which was partly filled in, facilitating the connection between the new districts. And yet, while the extent of the destruction gave freedom of scope to reconstruction, the planners' closeness to the modernist strategy of zoning only partially allayed Agadir's previous decentralisation. The districts' distinct street patterns, varying building types and functions, and overall densities were in themselves no proof of complementarity and variation. Interstitial spaces, envisaged as green areas, remained empty and often devoid of shade, discouraging pedestrian use. With the increase of coastal motorway traffic, the uniform distribution of recreational and tourist facilities along the beach further separated locals from visitors – cutting off the seaside city from the sea.

The upside was that each of the city's six new districts acquired a distinct sense of cohesion, with characteristic fabrics and atmospheres (Fig. 1). In hindsight, Thierry Nadau saw this decentralisation as an intentional strategy to retain the social status quo: 'each new district has its own small centre – a fragmentation encouraged by the authorities, which are eager, for security reasons, to keep everyone in their place.'[7] Moreover, the planning principle of semi-autonomous, interconnected districts strongly resonated with the contemporaneous notion of the neighbourhood unit. This topic, highly relevant on account of its principles of decentralisation, was widely circulated in the context of postcolonial transnational planning.[8] In Agadir, it lent itself quite by default to its application, albeit implicit, to the city's respective districts. However, in contrast to the prototypical nature of repeated neighbourhood units as applied in Western contexts, in the context of Agadir each such 'unit' claimed its own texture and facilities as dictated by the overall programme.

These overall circumstances delineate the strong correlation between planning principles and housing typologies in the new city of Agadir. The individuality of each urban quarter was largely informed by its predominant forms of housing – often designed as series of semi-standard modules laid out, with small variations, on the available plots. As a result, the residential fabric acts almost as an orientation device, articulating the intended role of each city district. In the Centre Urbain, conceived as a circulation spine connecting the different parts of the city, most housing is massed in modernist slabs with powerful ground connections, often placed atop commercial units at street level. The Secteur Résidentiel was laid out as a garden city of individual plots along curvilinear streets, with villas and single-family houses for middle-class inhabitants. Nouveau Talborjt revived the commercial streets, lined with porticoes, of the destroyed medina. The least damaged of all, the Quartier Industriel Sud, based on Écochard's 1952 plan, continued to develop largely as anticipated by the built *Trame Écochard* of carpet housing. To the north of these blocks were laid out other small family houses over one or two floors, interspersed with small courtyards, gardens and businesses. The gradual transformation of these housing types, whether built into the plan or unforeseen, led to the more familiar, relaxed atmosphere of a low-cost residential district.

CENTRE URBAIN: COLLECTIVE MULTISTOREY HOUSING

Agadir's centre was planned as a typically modernist proposition of neat, rectilinear volumes with landscaped areas in between. A wide range of connecting elements – galleries, covered open spaces, undercrofts and ramps – offers shade and a mix of programmes, and thus greater than usual potential for social interaction. Intended to connect the different parts of the city growing north and south off it, the Centre Urbain operates as an axial spine, defined as much by administrative, commercial and cultural institutions as it is by the parks and plazas in which they are placed. In this sense, housing takes a subservient position – a suitably modern background to complement the monumentality of institutional buildings and public spaces. If, as an urban ensemble, at the time of its planning the Centre Urbain aimed to project the image of a progressive, modern city, this image in many ways continued the colonial tradition of earlier Moroccan postwar architecture.[9]

An intriguing note in the contemporary journal *A + U* described three of the central housing blocks as being 'inscribed within the volumes imposed by the plan so-called of "architectural services"'.[10] In other words, the blocks were predetermined by the masterplan and relegated to a supporting role. This strategy suggests that in this administrative and official part of town, housing was given the role of a connective tissue intended to reinforce the unity of the urban ensemble:

> The town planners did not offer much maneuvering space to the builders. Each sector was assigned to one of the architects of the group, who had to coordinate all buildings with the town planners. The rigorous general urban plans defined even the volumetric relationships. This discipline provided a unity of tone that resulted in a strong sense of urban cohesion.[11]

In this shared condition, the modernist slabs that comprise most of the housing in the Centre Urbain can be read as the vertical and horizontal repetition of largely the same module, whose length and height varies according to parameters levied by the overall urban composition. This reading is reinforced by the way in which they are related through their adherence to a common material palette and tectonic language, and by the adoption of standardised dwelling plans. Most of the blocks are long low slabs, two or three storeys high, seldom going up to five storeys. The relationship between blocks was similarly typified, creating a modernist massing that is not only held in common but also somehow peculiar to Agadir. The low-height, ground-hugging figures reflected the population's reluctance to live far above ground, a combined consequence of traditional dwelling patterns and collective post-seismic trauma.

At the same time, the privilege of the central location imparts to some of these blocks an almost public character. This ran counter not only to their private ownership but, more generally, to the traditional privacy of the Muslim domestic realm. The most important blocks in the Centre Urbain were given letter-long names – A, D, O, etc. This would suggest the intention to denominate general block types rather than individual buildings – modular elements whose relations articulate the urban realm, like letters in the alphabet of the city. And yet, these letter-names also set them apart from the more anonymous residential stock, conferring an identity almost as recognisable as the neighbouring institutional buildings. The letters render explicit a hierarchy that is already established in the blocks' sizes, location and adjacencies to cultural and administrative landmarks.

Thus, Immeuble A (Building A), designed by the French architects Louis Riou and Henri Tastemain and completed in 1966, is undoubtedly the city's most representational, and architecturally ambitious, block (Fig. 3). At almost 200 metres in length, this mixed-use slab combining residential and commercial functions occupies a prominent location across from the Hôtel de Ville (Town Hall) and Poste Principale (Main Post Office). While its metropolitan scale easily dominates in this city of modest size, its form and siting are also significant. The building marks the site of the filled-in ravine Waddi Tanaout, which formerly separated the European City from Ancien Talborjt. Thus, its length is not only functional but also symbolic, underlining the new urban connections achieved along the avenues of the Centre Urbain. Raised on *pilotis*, the slab acknowledges the distant sea front, dramatising the drop from the inland plateau to the north to the beach to the south. The urban topography is negotiated by the angled ramp that runs along the length of the building, leading down to a popular commercial area to the south. Towards the north, a lower block (half Building A's length) is aligned with the

Fig. 3
Immeuble A and the
ramp connecting
it to the commercial
plaza.
Fig. 4
Facade detail of
Immeuble A.
Fig. 5
Immeuble A: external
gallery, with the oppo-
site building mirroring
the closed-up facade.

Fig. 6
Immeuble A living room
interior: European-style
furnishing.
Fig. 7
Immeuble A living room
interior: Moroccan-style
furnishing.
Fig. 8
External gallery circula-
tion gives access to
Immeuble A apartments.

main street. Between the two slabs is enclosed a small, partially covered market that reaches under Immeuble A's cavernous underside. The open spaces below the building take up two levels, both with commercial uses: the market stalls on the raised terrace below the flats and, beneath, shop units opening to the square on the other side. In summary, Immeuble A acts as a monumental stitch – a symbolic connective gesture celebrating the repaired urban fabric. It marks a focal point between Agadir's north–south and east–west axes. From its strategic location between the city's residential and industrial areas, it mediates the change in level from the mountains towards the sea.

Although its multiple ground levels make Immeuble A seem larger than it is, the raised residential slab is only three levels high. It consists of seven segments, marked by expansion joints sandwiched between double pillars. The gridded concrete structure sticks out on the main elevation in the shape of concrete mullions spanning across two storeys, alternatively connected to or aligned with the protruding concrete beams (Fig. 4). A similar visual game ensues on the northern facade, where the openings, overlooking the small market and the lower block, are narrower and placed at eye level (Fig. 5). Although both facades are open, the corresponding balconies are clearly shown to fulfil different functions on each side. The modular concrete grid structures the residential interiors. On the first floor, smaller flats are accessed by a *rue intérieure* (internal street) in the middle of the plan, with balconies towards the south and filigree-screened openings towards the north. On the top two levels there are larger, double-aspect apartments with south-facing balconies overlooking the main square. The modernist layouts, with built-in chimneys in living rooms, lend themselves more easily to Western interior decoration (Figs. 6 & 7). The apartments are accessed through continuous galleries on the north side, widened in places to accommodate the vertical circulation (Fig. 8). Both types

of covered external space are edged by parapets in white concrete, which emphasise the building's horizontality. At the same time, some parapets are open in a staggered manner corresponding with the visual expression of vertical structural elements, so as to counteract the impression of monotony on the facade. The continuity of the volume is likewise attenuated by its nuanced relationship with the ground. As Nadau observes,

> Tastemain and Riou's work here consists of attenuating the effect of the length by carefully working with the vertical building elements that disappear towards the top. The treatment of the floor of the square, the ramp and the porticoed gallery attempts to break the monotony of these overly large spaces.[12]

Overall, Immeuble A manifests the tension between a monumental gesture imposed by the urban masterplan and the architects' efforts to scale down its impact through the detailing of the facade and landscaping of the ground levels.

To the north-east, across the street from Immeuble A, lies a residential ensemble of three blocks designed by the Moroccan architect Abdeslem Faraoui and Moroccan-born French architect Patrice de Mazières. It consists of a long, two-storey slab parallel to the street (Immeuble D) and two shorter, five-storey blocks perpendicular to it (Immeubles O1 and O2), enclosing between them a landscaped garden. While Immeuble D is roughly the same length as A, it shares none of its grandeur – partly because of its broken-up alignment to the street, partly because of the reduced height of the floors and guarded relationship with the public pavement. Its tectonic expression is reprised, with few variations, in the facades of Immeubles O1 and O2 tnearby, hinting at the shared modular system that underlines both types.

This common code appears as a consequence of the buildings' plans (Fig. 9). The floor types comprise a central circulation core, with two apartments per floor served by a staircase in the middle. The double-aspect flats span the width of the building. They are similarly organised with service rooms, kitchen and small balconies gathered around the staircase at the rear, and larger living spaces and bedrooms opening towards continuous, deep loggias at the front. Based on the available floor plans, flats vary in size between one and three bedrooms. Their layouts are distinctly European, with separate living rooms, kitchen, vestibule, bathroom and WC. As signalled on the outside by the open loggias, they cater to a mostly Western lifestyle – unquestioningly reprising the imported model as an expression of progressive, reformed city dwellers.

Immeuble D comprises nine modular 'houses', each with its own staircase serving two apartments per floor. The long building is divided into three segments of varying length (three, two and four modules long), stepping in and away from the street so as to initiate different relationships with the public sphere. Towards the east, two recessed segments are separated from the public pavement by low-walled courtyards: ambiguous filters between the public and private domestic realms. The segment closest to the pavement is raised on *pilotis*, with the resulting undercroft used for parking. Set back from the street and perpendicular to it, Immeubles O1 and O2 are unequivocally residential. Each is formed of three aligned, modular 'houses': the central one shorter with one-bedroom flats, and the lateral ones with two-bedroom flats. Similarly to the vocabulary employed by Immeuble A and much of the Centre Urbain, the grid structure of the housing blocks is expressed on their facades in the form of protruding concrete beams, staggered to counteract the emphatic horizontality of the continuous balconies (Fig. 10). By contrast, the rear elevations, largely corresponding to services and bedrooms, are more closed. Balcony

parapets are raised to become slits. As in Immeuble A, the north-facing rooms of Immeuble D have small ribbon windows.

While adhering, in layout and appearance, to the tropes of Western modernism, overall the housing ensemble signals a different relationship with the public domain in the filtered and guarded way that all three buildings meet the ground. In contrast to the play of shadows and smooth white planes on the upper floors, at entrance level the *béton brut* is exposed – with massive, rusticated stone layers interposed between pedestrian and resident groups. The resulting rampart-like foundations partially acknowledge the privacy required by Muslim customs. The ground level offers the possibility of small external spaces being opened for the lower apartments, in an approximation of the traditional patio. For such spaces to work accordingly, however, they require a level of seclusion that is incompatible with their central location.

There are numerous, less-singular residential blocks throughout the Centre Urbain, whose elevations demonstrate a similar acculturation of the typical modernist prefabricated block. In this category fall, to give only a few examples, the four-storey Immeuble K (Building K) by French Architect Émile-Jean Duhon and the Immeubles H1, H2 and H3 (Buildings H1, H2 and H3) by Abdeslem Faraoui and Patrice de Mazières, manifestly in the same tectonic family as Immeubles O1 and O2 but two floors lower. Without making evident concessions to the local dwellings' patterns and types, they are, however, related through the visibility of their concrete structure on the elevations in the form of protruding beams and staggered mullions. In their massing and appearance, most of these blocks convey the sense of a residential programme subsumed under the urban design schema of a progressive, forward-looking city. The claims of the host culture are only present in the diverse relationships with the ground level, negotiated

Fig. 9
Immeuble D: a typical
plan, with two flats
opening off each stair-
case.
Fig. 10
Facade of Immeuble D.

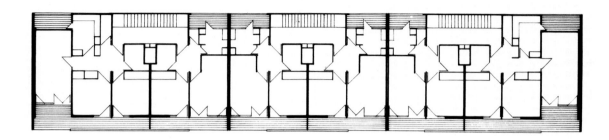

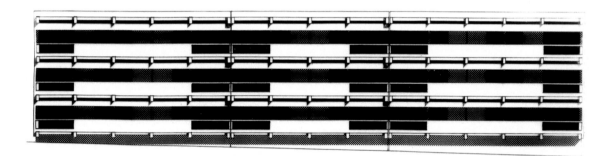

Fig. 11
Immeuble T1 living room
interior: Moroccan-style
furnishing.
Fig. 12
Immeuble T1 today:
the screens to loggias
have been partially
filled in to create more
private spaces.
Fig. 13
Immeuble T2.

through the solid masonry of the various boundaries with the public realm. Nevertheless, the paradox of ascribing to this city the same modernist image as the prior colonial regime is never acknowledged.

It is left to the housing blocks in another part of the centre, close to the Secteur Résidentiel, to show more inflections towards the local culture and climate. At the interface between the city centre and this quieter neighbourhood lies a mixed-height development designed by Moroccan-born French architect Jean-François Zevaco, with two residential slabs arranged perpendicular to each other around the grounds of a school and surrounded by single-storey courtyard housing (see below). With the Immeubles T1 and T2 (Buildings T1 and T2), Zevaco brings into question some of the Western housing tropes that dominate in the city centre. The two slabs are split into modules of different lengths, separated by the recessed slots of the open-air staircases. As well as articulating these external volumes, the architectural expression of the facades creates a staggered chequerboard pattern that emphasises the different dwellings. The resulting shadows and visual rhythms avoid the monotony usually ascribed to this type of housing. The standardised apartment layouts are organised along Western lines, with grouped services and rooms opening off a central hallway, yet the living rooms anticipate Moroccan furnishings (Fig. 11). The most characteristic are the loggias, which, in contrast to the open balconies of Immeubles A and D, here are concealed behind full-height screens that allow the living room and bedrooms a similar amount of exposure to light and air. With their vibrating texture, these elements represent an interpretation of the traditional *mashrabiya* perforated screens that allow women to partake of the life of the neighbourhood while themselves remaining out of sight (Fig. 12). While meant to conceal the domestic lives going on behind them, the screens originally allowed glimpses of the residents' lives: people looking out, laundry put out

to dry. Deferent, yet ambiguous, they have been deemed too revealing, and have in the meantime been partially filled in (Fig. 13).

CENTRE URBAIN AND SECTEUR RÉSIDENTIEL: COURTYARD HOUSING

The Secteur Résidentiel was conceived as a semi-independent garden city neighbourhood for well-to-do officials and entrepreneurs.[13] Surrounded by gardens and provided with garages, the terraced villas and courtyard houses that constitute the bulk of its built fabric represent an advanced stage of the discussions about the 'Habitat Musulman' (Muslim housing) that dominated Moroccan modern urbanism in the 1950s.[14] Unlike the eight-by-eight-metre *Trame Écochard* in the Quartier Industriel Sud, however, they represent less of an integrated system of individual modular plots defining the urban fabric and regulating the formation of streets and squares. They operate more conventionally as modular buildings – built in short, staggered terraces aligned with predetermined streets. Their ingenuity unfolds within the plot, as each house is configured through a composition of built and landscaped spaces. The resulting version of carpet housing valorises the patio as central element of traditional architecture, with an equally valid application to working-class and middle-class residences.

Best known among these are the award-winning courtyard houses designed by Jean-François Zevaco on the municipal land at the border between the Secteur Résidentiel and the Centre Urbain, north of the Cité Administrative. Seventeen units intended for middle-class functionaries and civil servants were built as part of a mixed-height residential ensemble constructed around a school. As the low-rise counterpart to Immeubles T1 and T2, described above, these courtyard houses are grouped into two 'islands' of varying proportions. One island of ten units is accessed from three sides; the other, with seven units, from two. There are two types of dwellings, with three and four rooms respectively in addition to a separate kitchen and bathroom. In the layout of both types, living spaces are interlocked with five patios of varying proportions and characters – as well as a service court (Figs. 14 & 15). All gardens are walled – ensuring, despite their proximity, the privacy of each family. The houses are accessed alongside long planted gardens, which ventilate the deep plan of the plots. The units consist of two L-shaped volumes, one with bedrooms and bathroom, the other with the kitchen and a two-part living room, which can be partitioned in the Muslim manner (Fig. 16). Most rooms have a double orientation, and their opening towards the adjacent patios ensures cooling cross ventilation. The basic but robust construction of reinforced concrete with blockwork infill is supplemented by simple finishes, white-painted walls and locally sourced terrazzo floors (Fig. 17).[15]

On an elevated site with views of the sea, the Secteur Résidentiel, known as 'La Colline', occupies 45 hectares to the west of the city. The neighbourhood announces itself to the rest of the city through two types of *villas en bande* (terraced villas) designed by Abdeslem Faraoui and Patrice de Mazières. One type is single-storey; the other double-height, with the higher volume topped by a double barrel-vaulted roof (Fig. 18). Like the courtyard houses, the *villas en bande* are set back from the street front and accessed via a narrow path along their individual parking space. Two interlocking squares form the L-shape of the built volumes (Fig. 19). The single- and double-storey villas contain two or four bedrooms respectively as well as living room, bathroom and parking spaces – all articulated around three patios and gardens.

Not all villas in the Secteur Résidentiel were so upmarket. Deeper inside the neighbourhood, Moroccan-born architect Armand Amzallag produced a low-budget villa type for 60,000 francs: a simple cube with white-painted walls and exposed concrete parapets, an upstairs loggia and individual garages (Fig. 20).[16] Other villa types, on one or two floors, were structured by the same principles of L-shaped volumes on rectangular plots built in short, staggered terraces. The ground-floor *villas en bande* by French architect Pierre Coldefy and Moroccan-born Spanish architect Claude Verdugo retain a similar organisation of rooms around an internal patio, separated from the living room by means of a screened partition.

With their elevated positions above and recessed from the street, the various villa types of the Secteur Résidentiel hold in common a quasi-Western openness towards the public domain. White and simple, they ambiguously evoke a Mediterranean vernacular mixed with modernist motifs: narrow apertures, horizontal windows. However, both in materiality and elevations, they indicate the influence of a colonial vernacular – apparent in their timber-shuttered windows and exposed masonry walls. The upmarket residential architecture offers a reliable indicator of the cultural outlook of the architects and presumed middle-class inhabitants. And yet, subsequent modifications infer that openness and transparency were not appreciated in the longer term. The characteristic retaining walls of roughly sawn stone blocks, a throwback to the rubble of the earthquake, were originally topped with lightweight wire fences. In time, visibility barriers were added. The initial wire fences were replaced by opaque screens, and railings were backed up with painted tin sheeting on the inside, suggesting that the higher degree of privacy was imposed by the inhabitants themselves at their own cost. Similarly, some loggias were closed and window sills raised. These modifications recall friction between the architects' ambition and the residents' wishes. Nadau records that this cultural clash of Eastern and local values, postcolonial and traditionalist, were already present at the time of design:

Fig. 14
The patio house: entrance at the end of a narrow planted courtyard that ventilates the depth of the plot.
Fig. 15
Patio house entrance.
Fig. 16
The patio house: living room interior with Moroccan-style furnishing.
Fig. 17
The patio house: service yard with drying lines.
Fig. 18
Villas en bande in the Secteur Résidentiel: originally, the garden terraces raised above the street levels were enclosed with wire fences.
Fig. 19
Villas en bande in the Secteur Résidentiel: terraces of different villa types, arranged in parallel with and perpendicular to the street.

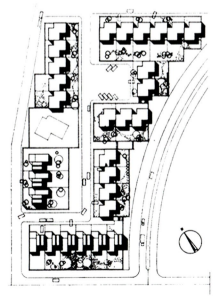

Fig. 20
Low-budget villa in the
Secteur Résidentiel.
Fig. 21
Working-class housing
in Nouveau Talborjt.
Fig. 22
Patio houses with com-
merce at street level in
Nouveau Talborjt.
Fig. 23
Two-storey house type
in Nouveau Talborjt.

This architecture was intended to be pedagogical at a time when these artists still believed they could educate taste. Amzallag recalls the bitter negotiations to save a tree in a patio, to respect volumes and the coherence of the urban block confronted with the inhabitants' desire to exploit the surface area that they had purchased fully.[17]

NOUVEAU TALBORJT AND LE QUARTIER INDUSTRIEL SUD: HOUSING FOR WORKERS

Often overlooked in contemporaneous records of Agadir's landmark modernist architecture, Nouveau Talborjt is nevertheless one of the most animated parts of the new town. The quarter retains closer relationships with both the fabric of the traditional medina and the 'culture-specific' low-cost housing that emerged in Morocco during the later decades of the Protectorate.[18] Built in a manner closest to vernacular urban patterns, it was more familiar and arguably more accommodating towards the locals' needs than the prevailing modernist idiom. The housing in this part of town, designed by less-prominent architects and undistinguished by individual names (even letters), combines commercial functions along the main streets with heavily residential areas to the rear. It is difficult not to associate the popularity of this architecture, sparse and modern whilst making visible concessions towards traditional ways of life, with a case for casual anonymity.

Nouveau Talborjt was planned as one ensemble of mostly two-storey row buildings, many with shops on the ground floor, organised in blocks forming an orthogonal grid (Fig. 21). Within the block, narrow pedestrian alleyways led to small collective spaces – recalling the traditional medina fabric.[19] Commercial streets along the main axes were lined with porticoes. Patio dwellings were placed above the shops in a housing type developed by the German

Hans-Joachim Lenz, Moroccan-born Armand Amzallag and French architect Alain Le Goaster, built with few variations across many blocks. Low-tech details, such as inscribing the small windows into bands of render and the patios' patterned screens, brought a level of finesse to the otherwise basic architecture (Fig. 22).

The two-storey housing types with walled backyards, designed by Amzallag and Le Goaster respectively, are nearest to popular notions of the indigenous urban dwelling (Fig. 23). The white facades, now peeling, are more closed than the modernist blocks in the city centre, with narrow horizontal apertures and solitary French windows stamped into otherwise opaque elevations. The compactness of this traditional-looking housing is countered by the cross ventilation provided by the axial planning. Whilst the low budgets resulted in a certain austerity, this sits well with the sensitive interpretation of traditional forms. The decorated entrances and inscriptions bring an indispensable patina, without breaking the unity of the ensemble.[20]

A similar logic, albeit yet more basic, was applied to the so-called Cité d'Urgence (Emergency City) planned by French architects Jean-Paul Ichter and Éliane Castelnau at the forefront of the post-earthquake reconstruction in the Quartier Industriel Sud. Originally a sparsely built-up area, this district was less damaged than others in the earthquake and it became one of the first to house the resulting refugees.[21] Much like the housing of Nouveau Talborjt, this 'first stage of reconstruction' was built with modest means, reflected in the smaller size and the higher density of its dwellings. This part of town, in proximity to Agadir's fisheries and canning factories, housed 4,000 people. It comprised 500 dwellings realised by the national Service de l'Habitat (Ministry of Housing), with an additional 350 dwellings later built on state-owned grounds, grouped around a small civic centre with a market designed by Abdeslem

Faraoui and Patrice de Mazières, a mosque, hammam and public garden (Fig. 24). The housing is systematically grouped in a rectangular grid, positioned in the tradition of the eight-by-eight-metre *Trame Écochard* and related to the varieties of grid housing proposed by Jean-François Zevaco at the other end of town. Most of the family dwellings were built at ground-floor level, with a patio at the centre and two or three rooms, kitchen and bathroom around it. Ninety-two units were built as larger, two-storey houses with a courtyard (Fig. 25). Despite the evident repetition of the modular housing, monotony was deliberately avoided through the different dispositions of various broken alignments in relation to the street. The introduction of small planted openings in the dense residential fabric proved salutary as modest expressions of a modern outlook.

WORKPLACE HOUSING

One less-visible housing type particular to Agadir's reconstruction are the flats integrated at the rear, above or behind public buildings and intended for the employees working in them. The dwellings that result from this strategy of coupling the workplace with residential functions reflect the character and use of these public buildings. They can be generous apartments above the more prestigious administrative buildings, or dingy flats above the modest public schools on the city outskirts.

The expressive *béton brut* facade of the Poste Principale, the compact but undisputed landmark of the new city of Agadir designed by Jean-François Zevaco, hides two substantial apartments for the families of higher-ranking officials. Both are placed on top of the post office, in a roof pavilion set back from the facade and invisible from the main square. Each of the apartments has three bedrooms, living room, kitchen and laundry room, with terraces at the sides and narrow loggias at the rear (Fig. 26). Their windows are ingeniously

masked or set back from the facades, opening towards the roof terrace. It is only at the rear, where the rooms open towards two separate loggias, that the residential function of this part of the building becomes apparent.

More visible, yet nonetheless at odds with its surrounds, is the small residential block attached to the Bâtiment de l'Économie (Economy Building) in the Cité Administrative, designed by Élie Azagury. Stepping back from the covered walkway that structures the entire site, this square block applies the same language of exposed concrete structure with infills on its facade. The pronounced grid gives the impression that the interior spaces are hung from this strong outer structure. The ground floor is partly occupied by an open undercroft hall with planted patios around the staircase, with a smaller flat oriented away towards the landscaped areas. Each of the three floors above ground is taken up by one generous three-bedroom apartment with a large balcony.

In the Centre Urbain, several blocks have flats above commercial ground floors – Immeuble J2 (Building J2) by Swiss architect Albert Froelich being one of them – but none of them nearly as unexpected as finding a fully residential block in the Cité Administrative and flats above the Poste Principale. Whilst the decision to house functionaries near their workplace seems pragmatic, it brings the private residential domain into the heart of administrative, and essentially public, functions.

CONCLUSION: EXPERIMENTATION WITH RESTRICTED MEANS

As in any city, the housing of the new Agadir takes up most of its built fabric, offering a societal cross-section. In this ready-made city, the systematic way in which the housing realm has been tackled renders a comprehensive review of all its residential types almost

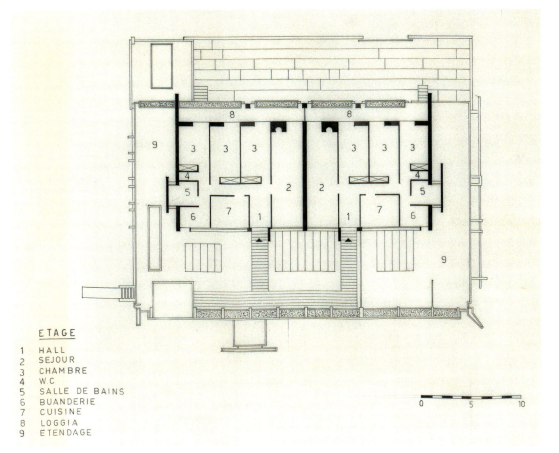

ETAGE

1 HALL
2 SEJOUR
3 CHAMBRE
4 W.C
5 SALLE DE BAINS
6 BUANDERIE
7 CUISINE
8 LOGGIA
9 ETENDAGE

0   5   10

Fig. 24
The Cité d'Urgence in
the Quartier Industriel.
Fig. 25
Two-storey houses in
the Quartier Industriel.
Fig. 26
Apartments for
high-ranking employees
above the Poste
Principale.

feasible. As a consequence of the centralised rules established by the Normes Agadir 1960, the housing types that dominate in each part of the city have much in common – even when emerging from the offices of individual architects. What is most remarkable is the close association between housing types and zoning, both determined within the rigid order of a hierarchical society. The Western-style apartment housing in the Centre Urbain, the upmarket patio housing and *villas en bande* of the Secteur Résidentiel, and the modest medina-style house types of the working-class neighbourhoods find their place in the city as neatly and unquestioningly as their inhabitants do in society.

The overarching theme of this collective oeuvre is experimentation – at a variety of scales, pertaining both to architectural and urban design. In the development of representational housing types for the various city districts, architects experimented with nuanced means best suited to each. Thus, the modernist slabs that project the image of progressive reform appropriate for a civic urban centre played with bold volumes and experimental tectonic elevations. These physiognomies counteracted the monotony of modernist mass housing, at the same time binding the different blocks in the coordinated aesthetic of a cohesive urbanism. As suggested by the daring monumentality of Immeuble A, the expression of these blocks has been carefully calibrated to work in relation to nearby public buildings and civic spaces. In most instances, it is therefore toned down, working as a connective tissue correlated to the landscaped and public functions. In contrast, the pragmatic anonymity of the commercial and working-class districts forms a more pliable backdrop to everyday life, and has consequently been embraced, modified and adapted by the local population in ways more closely described in the chapter Architecture of Resilience: Privacy and Privatisation in Agadir Housing later in this volume.

Some of the most ingenious innovations are apparent in the housing types inwardly structured by the vernacular device of the patio. Their close knitting of private, social and service extensions of the domestic realm is centred around walled gardens. This is particularly true of Jean-François Zevaco's courtyard houses, but also in the nearby *villas en bande* that combine Moroccan and European-style living spaces. Here, interiors and exteriors are interlocked, flowing in and around each other. Such attempts at a synthesis of traditional and modernist motifs contrast with the standard dwelling types deployed in the city's multistorey apartment buildings, in which interior and exterior spaces are clearly separated. Here, the energy of experimentation seems mostly placed into the adoption of conventionally Western configurations, rather than their adaptation. The hybrid spaces and heavy socles at the ground level of many of these blocks suggest a subliminal need for further grounding in the local ways. The ambiguous balance thus achieved between modernism and the vernacular reflects the challenge faced by postcolonial Morocco in articulating a vision of progress intimately connected with, and instilled by, its previous colonisers.

Another experimental aspect, in contrast to much of the often monofunctional European planning of postwar decades, arises in the frequent combination of Agadir housing with collective functions. The pervasive adjacency of living and working quarters has led to experimental types such as the camouflaged residential function above the Poste Principale, one of the city's most representative public buildings. Moreover, as shown, this combination of programmes occurs transversally across city districts and social classes. In opposition to the Taylorist duality of private family dwelling and public workplace, the combination of live–work programmes is both atavistic and, speaking with the benefit of hindsight, forward-looking. In the end, its residential architecture articulates a nuanced range of relationships between the city's private and public domains. The principle that unites the varied and sometimes contradictory types, devices and strategies deployed in this articulation is one of invisible proximity. The close adjacency of different functions separated by visual barriers seems to best fit in with local expectations. It achieves high density without inevitable contact – an apparently ahistorical feature, equally suited to traditional living patterns and modern economic logics. This results in the synthesis of cultural outlooks that is perhaps the most experimental feature of Agadir housing.

The investigations of the relationship between housing types and urban zones conducted in the context of Agadir's reconstruction resonated internationally, receiving significant coverage amongst professionals. One reason for this attention was the image quality of this architecture: its capacity to be projected, and received, as an architecture of the times. The buildings' unquestionable photogenic qualities hit a very contemporary nerve, initiating a warm stylistic reception. At the same time, however, their local, everyday acceptance was more muted – indicating that, here, they played a more ambivalent role. The misalignment of professional projection and everyday, direct, involved experience is almost palpable. One cannot quite shake the feeling that the progressive residential models, designed for a most modern class of citizens, were out of step with the existing social structures on the (earthquake-stricken) ground. This was not merely a question of architecture being ahead of the times. As is often the case in the history of housing, the new models carried within their configurations an implicit social-engineering agenda. The aims of projecting outwards an image of modernity while creating a stable, pliable citizenry at home were only partly successful. Architecture operated at a different temporal scale from society – as demonstrated by the tensions between the private interior and shared territories, whether collective or public. Even in the case of the

educated middle classes, visual transparency and free flows of access proved too much of a contrast with the inherited and established ways of life. In a culture that traditionally traded visibility for dense proximity, Agadir's housing experimentation demonstrates the asynchronous temporalities created by modernisation across all scales, from the dwelling to the city.

1
See the chapter 'Brutalism: "The Gem of Morocco's Contribution to World Culture"' in this publication.

2
'Avant le séisme, Agadir donnait l'impression d'une oeuvre trop ambitieuse, impossible à achever. A côté de quartiers modestes (mais denses et animés), s'étalaient des tracés de voies somptuaires délimitant de nombreux terrains vagues, où se dispersaient un petit nombre d'immeubles et quelques villas. Inorganique, lâche, la ville n'avait ni centre, ni unité.' Mas, Pierre, 'Plan Directeur et Plans d'aménagement', A + U: Architecture + Urbanisme, 4 (1966), pp. 6–18 (p. 7). [Translation by the current author.]

3
Segalla, Spencer D., 'The Soul of a City', in Empire and Catastrophe: Decolonization and Environmental Disaster in North Africa and Mediterranean France Since 1954, Lincoln, NE: University of Nebraska Press, 2020, pp. 141–64 (p. 151) / JSTOR, www.jstor.org/stable/j.ctv10crdt6.9 (accessed 11 July 2021).

4
Ibid., p. 151.

5
Mas, 'Plan Directeur et Plans d'aménagement', p. 13.

6
Furnished by foreign experts, the geological reports providing this assessment were in themselves not free from sociopolitical implications. See Daniel Williford, 'Seismic Politics: Risk and Reconstruction after the 1960 Earthquake in Agadir, Morocco', Technology and Culture, 58.4 (2017), pp. 982–1016, dx.doi.org/10.1353/tech.2017.0111 (accessed 11 July 2021).

7
'Chaque nouveau quartier sécrète son petit centre, éclatement souhaité per les autorités, soucieuse pour des raisons de sécurité de tenir chaqun à sa place'. Nadau, Thierry, 'La Reconstruction d'Agadir, Ou Le Destin de l'architecture Moderne Au Maroc', in Culot, Maurice and Jean-Marie Thiveaud (eds), Architectures Françaises Outre-Mer: Abidjan, Agadir, Alep, Alger, Bangui, Beyrouth, Brazzaville, Cansado, Casablanca, Conakry, Dakar, Damas, Hanoi, Libreville, Niamey, Orléansville, Ouagadougou, Riyadh, Tananarive, Tunis, Yaoundé, Collection Villes, Liège: Mardaga, 1992, pp. 146–67 (p. 159).

8
For the transnational flows of planning discourse, see Ward, Stephen V., 'Transnational Planners in a Postcolonial World', in Upton, Robert and Patsy Healey (eds), Crossing Borders, London: Routledge, 2010, pp. 47–72, doi.org/10.4324/9780203857083-12 (accessed 11 July 2021). For the participation of Moroccan architects in transfers of professional knowledge – notably, in the framework of postwar CIAM activities – see Chaouni, Aziza, 'Depoliticizing Group GAMMA: Contesting Modernism in Morocco', in Lu, Duanfang (ed) Third World Modernism: Architecture, Development and Identity, London: Routledge, 2011, pp. 57–84.

9
Moroccan (as well as Algerian) architecture in the late 1940s and early 1950s had provided the context for modernist architectural and urban experimentation that would have important reverberations not only in post-independence Morocco but also in postwar France.
See Tom Avermaete, '"Une Architecture Autre": Brutalism, Decolonization, and Mass Consumption in Postwar France', in Deschermeier, Dorothea (ed) SOS Brutalism. Brutalism: Contributions to the International Symposium in Berlin 2012, presented at the symposium 'Brutalism'. Architecture of Everyday Culture, Poetry and Theory', Zurich: Park Books, 2017, pp. 95–104 (p. 97). See also the chapter 'Brutalism: "The Gem of Morocco's Contribution to World Culture"' in this publication.

10
'Immeubles D, O1 et O2', A + U Architecture + urbanisme, 4 (1966), p. 46.

11
'Car les urbanistes n'ont guère laissé de marge de manoeuvre aux bâtisseurs. Chaque secteur était confié à un des architectes du groupe qui devait coordonner l'ensemble des constructions en concertation avec les urbanistes. Les plans masse très stricts définissent jusqu'aux rapports de volumétrie. Cette discipline donne une unité de ton qui procure un fort sentiment de cohésion urbaine.' Nadau, 'La Reconstruction d'Agadir', p. 160. [Translation by the editors.]

12
'Le travail de Tastemain et Riou consiste ici à atténuer l'effet de longueur par un travail soigné des verticales qui vont en se divisant vers le haut. Le traitement du sol de la place, de la rampe et de la galerie en portique tente de rompre la monotonie de ces espaces trop grands.' Nadau, 'La Reconstruction d'Agadir', p. 160. [Translation by the editors.]

13
mfd.agadir.free.fr/Agadir-reconstruction/index.html (accessed 11 July 2021).

14
See Monique Eleb, 'The Concept of Habitat: Écochard in Morocco', in Avermaete, Tom, Serhat Karakayali and Marion von Osten (eds), Colonial Modern: Aesthetics of the Past – Rebellions for the Future, London: Black Dog, 2010, pp. 152–61. Cohen, Jean-Louis and Monique Eleb, Casablanca: Colonial Myths and Architectural Ventures, New York: Monacelli Press, 2002, pp. 325–45.

15
Holod, Renata and the Aga Khan Award for Architecture, Architecture and Community: Building in the Islamic World Today, New York: Aperture, 1983, pp. 94–5.

16
Nadau, 'La Reconstruction d'Agadir', p. 162. 'Lorsqu'Armand Amzallag doit pour 60000 F réaliser un modèle de villa, il s'efforce avec un minimum de moyens de préserver des espaces intermédiaires comme la véranda, le seuil de la porte, ménager l'intimité familiale et satisfaire un certain désir d'ostentation tout en exprimant les recherches formelles qui lui sont chères. (Modèle de villa à budget minimal, A. Amzallag, 1965)'.

17
'Cette architecture se veut pédagogique à une époque où ces artistes croient encore pouvoir éduquer le goût. Amzallag se rappelle les âpres négociations menées pour sauver un arbre dans un patio, imposer ses volumes et respecter la coherence de l'îlot face aux désirs des habitants d'exploiter à outrance la surface achetée.' in ibid., p. 162. [Translation by the editors.]

18
See Cohen and Eleb, Casablanca, pp. 235–46.

19
mfd.agadir.free.fr/Agadir-reconstruction/index.html (accessed 11 July 2021).

20
'Le style très sobre choisi par les architectes – notamment Armand Amzallag – s'accorde aux budgets réduits mais constitue aussi une réinterprétation sensible des formes traditionnelles. Les portes décorées , les inscriptions apportent la patine indispensable sans altérer la cohésion de l'ensemble.' Nadau, 'La Reconstruction d'Agadir', p. 156.

21
mfd.agadir.free.fr/Agadir-reconstruction/index.html (accessed 11 July 2021).

INHABITING AGADIR

Michael Blaser, Maxime Zaugg

After its swift reconstruction during the 1960s, the city of Agadir has undergone a significant transformation – with public spaces and reconstructed buildings being adapted, appropriated and expanded. Two main drivers were essential for the city's transformation by its inhabitants: first, the generous and thoroughly planned public spaces in Agadir and, second, the rationalised, outspoken and robust architecture.

The city of Agadir has a considerable amount of open public space for a Moroccan city. For each project designed for its reconstruction, special care was taken to provide sufficient public space and to have this public space connect the buildings within the city. The sequence of open public spaces in Agadir is associated with architectural elements such as covered pergolas, ramps, stairs and covered public spaces – creating a network of threshold and transition spaces. During the city's development over the last sixty years, it has become apparent that the large and open public areas, such as Place Hassan II (Hassan II Square), are little frequented as it is climatically and socially unusual to use such exposed spaces. On the other hand, the continuity of transitional spaces, the threshold spaces between the buildings, and the smaller, open, public spaces have been appropriated and inhabited by the citizens of Agadir.

A second driver that enabled the transformation and appropriation of the built fabric in Agadir was the sturdy Brutalist architecture of the reconstruction. To give the architecture an impression of solidity and strength after the devastating earthquake, the decision was taken to construct the buildings with ample sand-coloured *béton brut* (raw concrete). In the case of the many single-storey houses in Nouveau Talborjt and the villas in the Secteur Résidentiel, the solid architecture allowed citizens to expand their living space with a two- to three-storey extension. Furthermore, many buildings were adapted by their inhabitants to the climatic conditions of Agadir – for example, by converting the spacious outdoor spaces of the apartments, such as balconies or loggias, to indoor spaces. As a result, Agadir's citizens have appropriated the built structures and the surrounding public spaces – thereby significantly transforming the city's appearance.

This chapter introduces axonometric drawings of Agadir's current state, focusing on the mutual relationship between its public space and its built architecture. At the Chair of the History and Theory of Urban Design at the ETH in Zurich, we used axonometrics to document the transformation of the city. In a first step, in preparation for the seminar week with students from ETH Zurich, the original state of the reconstruction of Agadir was factually redrawn using original plans and historical photographs. The resulting axonometric representations of the 'planned city' were assembled in a so-called *Carnet de Voyage* (Travel Diary). These were offered to the students during the seminar week and served as a basis for recording the 'transformed city' in drawings, notes and observations. The students used a variety of tools for this purpose. The drawings provided received an additional layer of precision by measuring with laser devices or scales, or simply walking through the public spaces and buildings. Students could also insert the changes into the axonometric drawings by interviewing the inhabitants or by attentively observing Agadir's daily life. During the trip, their fieldwork was continuously recorded in the *Carnet de Voyage* and, in a final step, translated back into a new set of axonometrics. Using a neutral axonometric drawing as a point of departure, the students' observations were translated into these axonometrics, providing a powerful modus operandi to record the transformation and adaptation of the city of Agadir by its inhabitants.

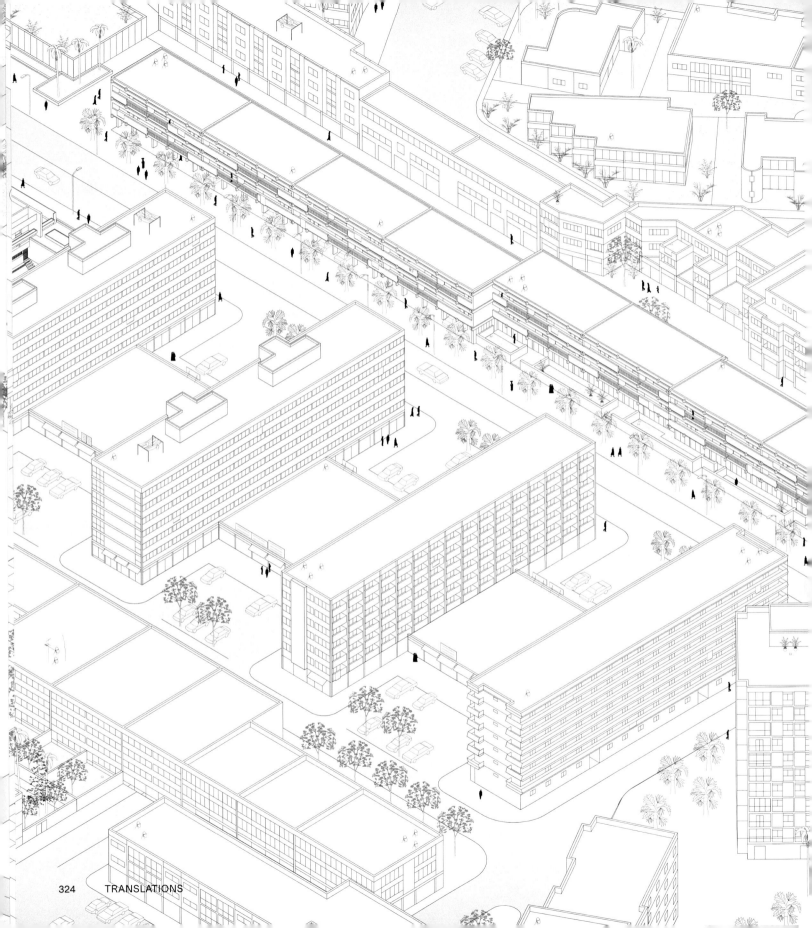

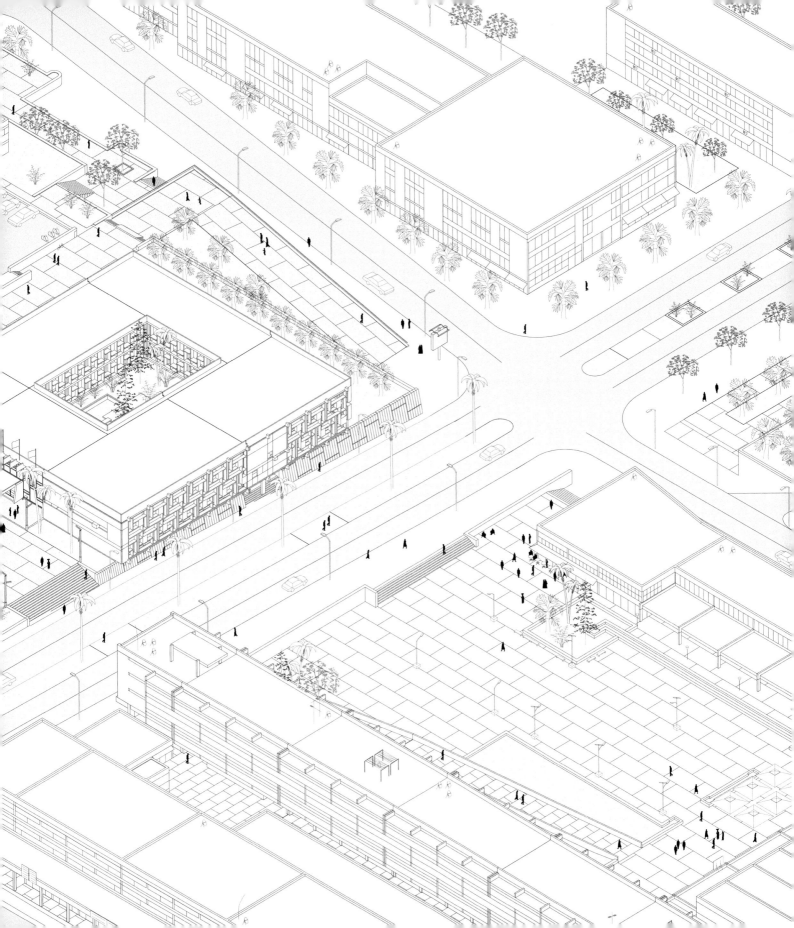

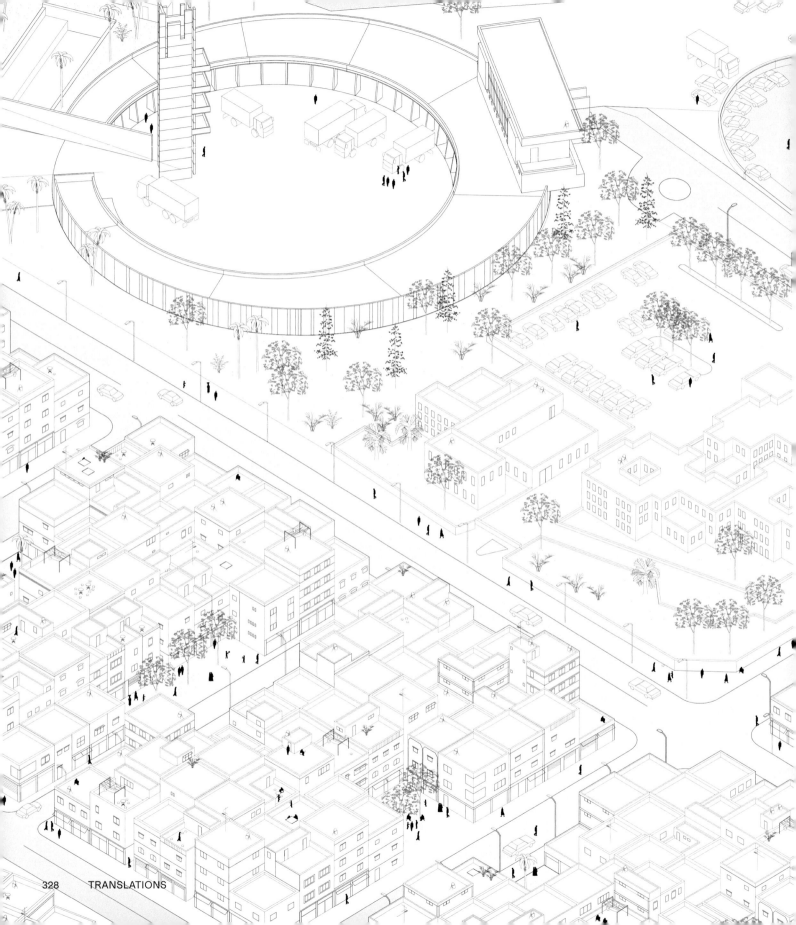

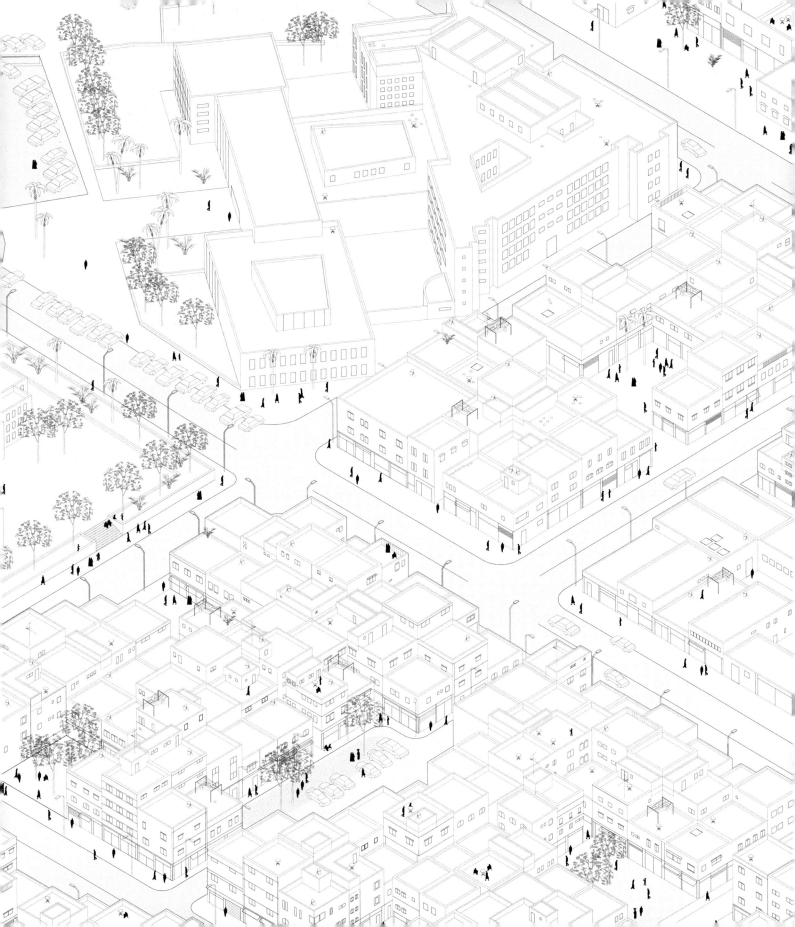

TRANSFORMATIONS

THE EVOLUTION OF THE CITY

Lahsen Roussafi

The centre of Agadir, with its large spaces and public buildings which had been at the centre of the reconstruction, appears almost empty today. There aren't many people in the streets and in the public spaces. What happened to bring this about after 1960?

In the beginning there were 16,000 residents and today there are many more. For the original 16,000 inhabitants, the city centre was adequate, but that would change.

One important moment was the Green March [in 1975] of Moroccan King Hassan II. To retake the Saharan territories that had been occupied by Spain under [Spanish dictator Francisco] Franco, King Hassan II asked the people (each city had its quota of men and women) to march on the Sahara and settle there. It was called the Green March because it was completely peaceful. There were no armaments; everyone carried just a Moroccan flag and the Qur'an. After the conclusion of international negotiations, people were free to go home but most stayed in and around Agadir. Life was good there: you could find everything.

Why did people choose to stay in Agadir after the Green March?

Agadir's Hôtel de Ville (Town Hall) was considered a sacred place because it was the point of departure for the Green March. It was where the king made his speech.

The result was the retreat of Franco. At the frontier, it had been possible to turn back this dictator. As a result, negotiations were held at the Hague in the Netherlands where King Hassan II explained the ties between Morocco and the Sahara. The result of these negotiations was that Morocco acquired a large territory with a lot of natural resources, like open-pit phosphate mines.

From the beginning of the negotiations, the king allowed people to return to Agadir – but no farther. Only when the negotiations were over did he allow them to go home. But many stayed in the city. This surplus population led to the construction of large tenements. Before, they were three or four storeys tall, but now, large housing complexes were being built to a height of ten storeys.

How did the city evolve afterwards?

After 1975, there was a demographic explosion. The peripheral neighbourhoods mushroomed. The administrators in the Hôtel de Ville couldn't keep up with them. It seemed impossible to catch up with this rapid growth.

The enormous population growth was connected to the emergence of new housing styles and new styles of living. Younger generations were earning more money, buying cars and preferring to live on the periphery of town. The Centre Urbain had been developed as a walking city, which didn't correspond with the ways in which the younger inhabitants of Agadir were locating themselves in the city. The city grew southwards.

This new idea of mobility is a real problem for the Centre Urbain. Families have on average one or two cars. When they need to go to the Cité Administrative (Administrative Centre) of the city, they don't find parking places. They can't move about freely. Everyone gets annoyed.

Concrete plans already exist for moving administrative offices to the city's periphery. People are thinking about leaving. Every five or six years, there is a turnover of administrative staff and changes take place. It is very rare that high officials stay in Agadir for the rest of their lives. After a few years, they leave for home or elsewhere. The result is that the Centre Urbain is being emptied: the movie theatres no longer function and the number of small traders is in decline.

The biggest change came with the souk, which isn't like what came before. Today, the inhabitants of Agadir do their shopping in department stores. You find everything there: ranging from costumes costing two to three thousand DM (Moroccan Dirhams) and other, even less expensive, ones from overseas, to ones selling for ten DM. Fish, poultry, pigeons . . . everything! So, you don't go any longer to the smaller merchants. They have been broken by the department stores.

For me it's simple. The Centre Urbain has evolved to become a big museum that one can visit on foot from the hotels. This is perhaps the future of the Centre Urbain: a museum-like zone where you can learn about the impressive project of the reconstruction.

How do outsiders regard the city?

It doesn't interest the general public. People outside of Agadir, other Moroccans, those with money, like to come to Agadir to go to the beach. The beaches where they arrive with their families are magnificent. It's a case of domestic tourism. Some families come to enjoy the holidays. They come in the thousands to stay in hotels that were built for Europeans.

How do you think we should consider the architectural and urban experience of Agadir? Are there any lessons to be learnt?

I'm going to respond as an old inhabitant of Agadir, someone who has known the city since 1960. We must give value to and protect its buildings so they can show people what Agadir was before and after the earthquake. The Centre Urbain is a big part of the story. Will it continue to exist after us? I hope so. Along with other people, a friend and I have created an association to protect the memory of Agadir. With this association, we aim to make a large model of the Centre Urbain in miniature so that people can understand the city's fascinating history.

We hope that the authorities will support our initiative. It would be good for outsiders, but also for locals, to know about the development of the city so they don't forget its important history. The people of my generation think that what the Haut Commissariat à la Reconstruction d'Agadir (High Committee for the Reconstruction of Agadir) did is something important and precious. We are fighting to ensure that what remains is protected and, above all, is developed for future use.

ARCHITECTURE OF RESILIENCE: PRIVACY AND PRIVATISATION IN AGADIR HOUSING

Tom Avermaete, Irina Davidovici

The project for the urban design of Agadir started under the most ambitious of circumstances. In his famous speech following the earthquake, the Moroccan King Mohammed V envisioned the reconstruction of Agadir as not only an act of its recovery from the rubble but also as part of a larger project of building the country anew as a modern society of forward-looking citizens. This vast political ambition would be echoed in the proposals and projects of architects and urban designers for the reconstructed city. Many of them conceived of Agadir as an innovative urban environment, a true modern Afropolis for the modern citizenry of a nation state that had claimed its independence only a few years earlier. Its destruction offered them a blank sheet on which to visualise urban forms and atmospheres that would live up to these enormous spatial and social aspirations.

Today, Agadir's buildings and urban fabric testify to the reconstruction as an ambitious architectural and social enterprise. Urban designers and architects envisaged the most radically modern environments possible for the city's 'new citizens'. They delivered a novel urban model with a vast administrative and commercial pole at the Centre Urbain, combined with smaller, well-equipped neighbourhood centres such as the district of Nouveau Talborjt. The planners were dedicated to offering the new citizens a variety of public spaces, multi level plazas, new streets and parks, with innovative combinations of buildings and public spaces. Interesting examples of the latter are the Cité Administrative (Administrative Centre), combining a megastructure of office buildings with a park, and Immeuble A (Building A), which hybridised housing with interior shopping streets and a souk. At the level of commercial spaces, Agadir did not temper its ambitions. The multi-level interior market and the large supermarket in the Centre Urbain, the monumental local commercial centre in Nouveau Talborjt and the Marché en Gros (Wholesale Market) are but a few examples of the way in which the new Afropolis was planned as a modern centre for trade. The new Moroccan citizens were not only imagined as milling around these state-of-the-art public and commercial spaces but also as dwelling in a manner both rooted and progressive. In the hands of international and Moroccan architects, the city of Agadir became a veritable laboratory for housing. Generous outdoor spaces, seen to resonate with the vernacular dwelling patterns of the inhabitants, were combined with innovative apartment layouts in unprecedented collective-housing typologies. Experimental single-family houses were designed to offer new ways of living whilst recalling – albeit relatively lightly – more traditional patterns of living organised around cooling, shaded courtyards.

Sixty years after the reconstruction of the earthquake-hit city, it is clear that the enormous expectations regarding the public, collective and private life of the citizens of Agadir were not met. To phrase it differently, the reality of the people's lives seems to have been out of step with the progressive and reforming ambitions of politicians, urban planners and architects. The unrealistic hope that the people of Agadir would, in the short

and challenging moment of the reconstruction, transform into the most modern citizens possible never materialised. Moreover, this asynchronicity between social ambitions and social lives had unanticipated effects. The inhabitants resolved the deviating relationship between their conventional social practices and the avant-garde urban and architectural environments that they were given to inhabit by developing a set of tactics. These devices ranged from a radical decoupling of spatial configuration and social use – resulting, for instance, in the displacement of shopping practices from the Centre Urbain to peripheral local centres and to a more intrusive transformation of the materiality and spatiality of the public and private spaces of the city, so as to align them with the reality of the everyday practices. In other words, the citizens claimed their places of residence through a set of techniques and practices of appropriation that highlights their informal agency. Retrospectively, it seems that the city of Agadir silently accommodated all these different tactics – incorporating their traces in the weathering, adaptations and transformations of its modern fabric.

CENTRE URBAIN: RECALIBRATIONS AND REINTERPRETATIONS

The expression of the rebuilt city as new and progressive, in a definitive break from the past, was achieved through adherence to modernist aesthetics. As one contemporary commentary suggested, in the projects, 'the staging of materials is accompanied by interesting plays of volumes and light – with the help of loggias, principally'.[1] Through their visibility and openness, these loggias remained symbolic of a greater ambiguity at play. The multistorey collective buildings, as well as the modernist elements that helped to ratify the architecture as a symbol of progress and independence (loggias, horizontal windows, *pilotis* [stilts], etc.), were, at the same time, elements alien to the local culture. As scholars Monique Eleb and Jean-Louis Cohen observed of slightly earlier modernist housing in Casablanca, 'the inversion of accepted notions of private and public space in slab buildings (had caused) great confusion, for here corridors are often used for tasks that are usually confined to private courtyards in true Moroccan dwellings'.[2]

Indeed, the tension between traditional ways of living and the notion of progress associated with European modernism is most evident in the current state of the residential blocks in the city centre. Their usage and adaptation indicate a breakdown of the social mobility envisaged by the urban planners in the early 1960s. Immeuble A is a poignant testimony to the strategies adopted by the people of Agadir in adapting to their new, perplexingly modern, life settings. More than fifty years after its completion, it is still the imposing heart of the Centre Urbain – clearly a place of recognition in the city. And yet, despite its prominence, the building does not seem a residential address of much prestige. The small flats, inhabited mainly by single people, do not lend themselves to making long-term, carefully maintained homes. Neither residents nor the building administration seem willing to claim responsibility for the shared areas, which are relegated to the status of a no man's land. The square at the front, never exactly a bustling place, seems at present nearly deserted. Few people hang around, and the building's other public areas – including the undercroft and market – look abandoned and shabby. However, on closer inspection, pockets of intense everyday life can be encountered within this large and silent urban formation: exceptions animated by an uncontrolled vitality. Most of these are spaces have proved capable of accommodating micro-transformations, appropriations, re-materialisations: small shops, restaurant terraces, the customised entrances to some apartments.

These uncontrolled, unanticipated episodes reveal a specific aptitude of the Brutalist modern architecture of central Agadir: its ability to function as a long-lasting infrastructure that can accommodate recalibrations and reinterpretations. Indeed, in many instances, its inhabitants have been adding elements to the architecture of Immeuble A with entirely different expressions to its original concrete and infill. Moreover, their materiality explicitly contrasts with the materials planned by the architects and the urban designers, with the effect of taming the building's imposing scale and systematic physiognomy. In contrast to prefabricated and in-situ concrete surfaces, the residents have added a local dialect of vernacular elements: richly patterned and colourful tiles, decorative timber screens, coloured glass doors and metal gates forged in traditional Moroccan patterns. Taken together, these elements carve niches in the vast and sturdy urban architecture of Immeuble A. More importantly, by doing so, they provide a setting sympathetic to the small-scale practices of everyday life. Time and time again, the perennial concrete architecture of Agadir has provided its inhabitants with the possibility of constructing their own narratives – of personalisation, of memory, of private interest – within the collective and public spaces of their Centre Urbain. As such, these small-scale interventions can be read as the expression of an architecture of resilience.

In contrast to Immeuble A, with its predetermined mixture of residential and commercial premises, Immeuble D (Building D) was planned as exclusively residential. Despite this intention, the central location and, perhaps, something in its long, low massing parallel to the street have caused the building's inhabitants to use it in a more public way. Notwithstanding the lack of shopfronts, many units in Immeuble D are used for small businesses and service companies – notaries, lawyers, dentists, etc. – which are accessed through decidedly residential entrances. As so often in modernist buildings raised above ground, the resulting undercroft is used by residents for parking their cars. These informal changes of use can be understood in two ways. On the one hand, the commercialisation of private space may be seen as a pragmatic, opportune way of taking advantage of the privileged address and direct connection to the street. Moreover, as a lucrative and partly public transformation, it could have only occurred through the indifference of the municipal authorities, or even with their tacit approval. On the other hand, the building might have been seen as insufficiently private to provide good homes, in the socially and culturally

accepted sense. While the small private businesses might have been able to claim additional legitimacy from the privileged address, the case could always be that the dwellings were, simply, too much spaces of appearance for the private lives of Muslim families.

Another detail favouring this second reading is the pervasive closing off of loggias, not only in Immeuble D or A but also in the majority of residential blocks. It is remarkable how balconies and galleries, particularly on lower floors, have been filled in by residents with partitions: glazing, walls, curtains, even arches. These offer a clearer separation from the public domain than that originally offered, and visually interrupt the intended horizontality by emphasising individual gestures of ownership and appropriation. At Immeuble A, while many loggias have also been enclosed with glass panes, the building fabric has suffered more from the abnegation of responsibility regarding the maintenance of common areas: entrances, access galleries and sections of the undercroft. Rooted in the tension between the individual ownership of flats and the official management of collective, shared spaces, this issue is once again quite pervasive in Modernist housing – particularly, low-cost housing lacking an explicit infrastructure of administrative care. The resulting decay has affected the quality of life and thus the affective value of the flats. The emptiness suggests that many residents have moved out to peripheral suburbs, found to be more amenable to a traditional way of life. The residential landmarks of the modernist Centre Urbain show, in consistent and multiple ways, an awkward and thinned out urbanity, which can be understood as a misinterpretation of 'centrality'.

NOUVEAU TALBORJT: SLOWLY FORGETTING THE MEDINA

The architects who planned the commercial and residential quartier of Nouveau Talborjt held the traditional medina and the destroyed Talborjt foremost in their minds. Before the earthquake, Talborjt had been the multicultural, heterogeneous, dense heart of the city. Its dynamic development, rather than that of the Ville Nouvelle (New City), had obfuscated the initial expectations of the protectorate authorities. Indeed, Talborjt's interwar popularity was partly accountable for the extent of its destruction, as many of the speculative street-front buildings had been overloaded, on the cheap, with additional storeys. Rising from the ruins of the old Talborjt, the renewed district had high expectations to live up to.

It was hoped that not only would the built fabric be replaced but that this would also result in the same thriving sense of community as hitherto. On the one hand, the planners of the new Talborjt approached this task by leaning upon tropes of modernist planning: standardised building types; a wide, axial main street; and the zoning of predominantly commercial and exclusively residential areas. On the other hand, the building and block typologies that they adopted stayed close to traditional medina types. Low-rise buildings, mostly two floors and with terraces on the roof, are densely packed in blocks separated by narrow alleyways, which occasionally open into a communal square. While normative porticoes and shops line the commercial streets, developments in the residential areas are more heterogeneous. Typologies vary from rows of modular houses to detached villas and the occasional multi family block. In the intervening decades, these typological and programmatic (functional) distinctions have been greatly attenuated by a shared patina of wear and tear.

Today, this working-class residential and commercial district exudes a resigned lassitude. Most of its mixed commercial and residential buildings, with arcades lining the main streets and with shuttered shops on the ground floors, were modest to start with. While well-weathered, they have not changed beyond recognition. Governed by a mixture of interests, the residential and commercial buildings along the main streets have been changed the least. Centralised maintenance means that the original (white or off-white) colour scheme, two-storey height and modernist aesthetic are still clearly identifiable. On the residential streets and squares, however, the initial heterogeneity has been accentuated in relation to the degrees of ownership. Some private houses have gained a storey or two, and the height variations are complemented by a wider range of different colours. This gentle contrast (since they are all, more or less, equally in need of restoration) lends credence to the hypothesis that, where private homes are concerned, the residents will assert their possession through more visible customisation. People demonstrate a sense of ownership through the addition of layers: layers of screens and window grilles, layers of wall tiles, layers of coloured paint that serve to delineate territories and assert individuality. The same procedure has been extended – albeit for different reasons – to the neighbourhood school, where the classrooms, pavilions, steps and even trees are painted in a rainbow of colours.

These appropriations undercut and humanise the original, modernist language of the buildings as types. Nouveau Talborjt demonstrates how the scope for adaptation increases away from institutional and administrative headquarters, strengthening the resilience of the district even when its fabric suffers through lack of regular maintenance. As a result, the neighbourhood feels more informal and more animated than the city centre.

SECTEUR RÉSIDENTIEL: THE RAISING OF THE WALLS

Intended for professional, middle-class families, the Secteur Résidentiel remains relatively unchanged in terms of its original scale and density. The privileged status of its inhabitants has prevented the kind of speculative densification that is the mark of other, more popular, districts. However, the mostly aesthetic changes speak of a different kind of misalignment between the expectations of the original architect/planners and the ambitions of the predominant demographic group. Here, the divergence is less typological and speaks more of a cultural, rather than an economic, shift.

To be sure, the combination of social privilege and private ownership has had an impact on the built fabric. *The villas en bande* (terraced villas) along Avenue Président Kennedy and Avenue des Forces Armées Royales no longer stand in their neatly spaced original rows. Their protruding and retreating contours, planned into Z-shapes to create shelter and shade, have now melted into amorphous volumes in which the original and additional fabric blend together. Some have been extended and now cover their front garden, while others have been conserved within their initial footprint. Some of the signature vaulted roofs are still visible, helping with the identification of the villas, while others have been obliterated by the addition of extra floors, which change their proportion and shape beyond recognition.

However, the most telling, even if unintrusive, change has been that of the relationship between the villas and the street. An original masonry wall mediated the changes in level between the public pavement and the private front lawns (in themselves, a European or Western concept with no direct equivalent in the traditional architecture). In a great majority of cases in the intervening time, the masonry wall has been extended upwards – most often with solid fences that screen the gardens and ground floors of the villas from the domain of the street. For cultural, and possibly security,

reasons, the original transparent relationship with the street has become opaque.

The least affected have been the single-storey courtyard houses designed by the Mococcan-born French architect Jean-François Zevaco at the boundary between the Centre Urbain and the Secteur Résidentiel. As the dwellings that made the most concessions to the traditional patio types, these have remained almost unchanged – with the exception of air-conditioning units, antennae and satellite dishes added over time. Originally as high as the houses, the patio walls served to render the family enclosures virtually invisible from the street and there was no obvious reason for their modification. By contrast the original gates, made of metal railing, have been backed up with tin sheets, obstructing the view inside, and crowned with decorative spikes as an additional security measure. This suggests that the success of the attempts to adapt the vernacular type of patio housing to a modernist, progressive outlook has depended upon their adherence to the traditional definition of the public and private domains.

The consistently increased heights of walls and opacity of fences indicates the existence of cultural resistance to the porosity of boundaries between public and private domains – visual or actual. This suggests that the progressive attitudes held by the architects, and their expectation that Europeanised dwelling models might take hold among the educated middle classes, have gone largely unfulfilled. The resulting misalignment invites the conclusion that progress is not linear. While technological developments and the consequent increase in comfort were enthusiastically embraced, the cultural and religious values imposing strict borders between public and family life proved less negotiable than perhaps the architects had envisaged. Comparing the original and current state of the architecture is, nevertheless, inconclusive. It is not clear if the new opacity stems from a pervasive conservatism (in the Muslim world, but also in general as a way of capitalising on privacy) or is the result of a generational shift. In any case, the raising of walls signals the inhabitants' resistance to a Western-dominated model of living based on porous boundaries between the public and the private domains.

TRAME ÉCOCHARD (ÉCOCHARD GRID): WORKING WITH AND AGAINST THE SYSTEM

A specific instance of the resilience of Agadir is provided by the Quartier Industriel Sud, which

was developed – before and after the earthquake – according to principles that were initially defined by French urban-planner Michel Écochard, the director of the national Service de l'Urbanisme (the Town Planning Department of the French Protectorate in Morrocco) during the last decade of the Protectorate. In the course of his tenure in Morocco, he developed a particular urban design instrument – the so-called Écochard Grid – based on a module of eight by eight metres and used for the development of new urban neighbourhoods.

For Écochard, this grid encompassed various elements of urbanisation: it provided an allotment system; a clear logic for effectively constructing the city; and a rational canvas for the distribution of technical equipment such as water supplies, electricity and sewage. Above all, the Écochard Grid functioned as an integrator of single-family houses into a dense, regulated, low-rise urban pattern.[3] Indeed, it was primarily a way of combining the typology of courtyard houses, considered to be the expression of rural patterns of living, into an urban morphology. However, Écochard maintained that the built environment is subject to constant redefinition due to changing economic conditions and modernisation – thus altering dwelling aspirations, needs and forms. Therefore, he paralleled an evolutionary vision of social dwelling patterns with an evolutionary perspective on the physical characteristics of the built environment. From a typical colonial perspective, he looked upon the inhabitants of his projects as *'evolués'*, citizens whose lifestyle was situated somewhere between a rural and an urban way of living. The built environment in which the *evolué* lives was thought of in an analogous, intermediate fashion – as something that starts from a rural formation and gradually acculturates more urban patterns. Within this entire urban transformation process, the grid acted as a stable basis. The *Trame Écochard* thus offered the spatial framework within which the different physical and social transformations could occur. From this viewpoint, Écochard made a clear distinction between the temporalities of architecture and urbanism – the first standing for the short-term and the latter for the long-term parts of the built environment: 'Put the factors into order: Urbanism (permanent) in the first place, Construction (transitory) afterwards.'[4] The grid belonged to the perennial realm of urbanism while 'construction', or architecture, was considered part of a process of continuous change: 'Moroccan Habitation, like any object of mass consumption, follows the cycle: conception, production, distribution, utilisation, elimination. One must take this fact into consideration, and one must be far-seeing.'[5]

Écochard's interpretation of the 'Habitat Musulman' (Muslim housing) in Agadir withstood reasonably well not only the earthquake but also the test of time. The particular importance that he accorded to the different temporalities of architecture and urbanism seems to have been prophetic. Écochard's urban grid is omnipresent in the Quartier Industriel Sud of Agadir, but the architecture of the courtyard houses that he designed has almost entirely disappeared behind additions and alterations. Instead, the grid has meanwhile functioned as the basis for hypertrophied vertical urban growth – fuelled by changing family compositions, altered dwelling needs and speculation. Indeed, nowadays, the single-level courtyard functions as the base for a three- to five-level terraced house. All over the Quartier Industriel Sud of Agadir, people have been adding concrete constructions that recall the Corbusian Dom-Ino system to their courtyard dwellings, thereby creating the opportunity to drastically intensify and extend their houses in a vertical fashion. Within this common constructive system, a variety of infills have come to determine not only the interior composition of the houses but also their facades.

Ignoring the numerical purism of the grid, two adjacent parcels of land on Rue D'Oujda are now split between five garage units – maybe to cater equally for five children of one family, or simply the expression of entrepreneurial acumen. A few doors up, somebody has built two extra floors on a quarter of the original parcel – resulting in a thin, tower-like building with a deep recess to one side. Elsewhere, owners embellish their homes with coloured tiling, improvised fencing, solid gates and stone frames for the windows. Some plant a small garden in front of their homes where the pavement should be. The result is a very diverse and vivid urban fabric, subject to continuous change and adaptation to incessant building and rebuilding.

Surprisingly, Écochard's urban system has maintained a recognisable quality of public space within this hypertrophied condition of change and densification. While streets and alleys that were initially proportioned to be aligned with single-level houses are now bordered by buildings of four storeys and more, they stand – as variations on the theme of the medina – as a qualitative system of urban spaces. Écochard's horizontal grid, originally designed to respond to the so-called unhygienic conditions of *bidonville* (slum) and medina, has returned after several decades of urban development to a condition that is very similar to its counter model. With its tall, narrow streets, the resulting system –

punctuated by inner-block open squares surrounded by collective functions, such as shops and ovens – seems to comply with contemporary ways of dwelling in Agadir.

The same can be said of the vertical extensions of the grid. Here also, the initial aims of bringing sun and light into every room of the dwelling have been entirely discarded by the contemporary typology of terraced houses. Nevertheless, the figure of the vertically extendable terraced house seems to live up to the current needs, aspirations and realities of the Agadir citizens. Indeed, many dwellings have been vertically extended due to changing family compositions or altered dwelling expectations. It is not abnormal that with each new adult generation in a family, a floor is added. Moreover, additional storeys have also offered the opportunity for rental activities – securing a financial basis for many of these extended families.

TRANSVERSAL CONCLUSIONS

Since the 1960s, the many recalibrations and reinterpretations to which the architecture of Agadir has been subjected stand witnesses to the radicality of this modern project. On the one hand, its militant progressiveness has elicited various degrees of mediation in order to suit the demands of everyday life. On the other hand, the alterations and adaptations that resulted from the many processes of intermediation can also be seen as proof of a double resilience. They speak both of the capacity of architecture to incorporate change and of that of users to recalibrate the configurations of space, form and material to suit their own needs. In other words, the resilience of the residential architectures of Agadir stands for two complementary phenomena. Firstly, the post-earthquake housing production, as governed by the Normes Agadir 1960, can be understood as a modernist, Western imposition upon native ways of life. It represents an attempt to render them more efficient, clearcut and transparent to reason. In that respect, this modern architecture can be seen as an expression of over-rationalisation: an appeal to reason that is misjudged inasmuch as it assumes (wrongly, it turns out) that it can control and fulfil people's needs and aspirations. Secondly, a direct correlation can be observed between transformation and ownership, between the degrees of freedom to change and adapt and the extent of actual appropriation. Privately owned buildings, or private dwellings in a multi-occupancy situation, bear the brunt of the changes, sometimes beyond recognition, to the original modernist fabric. The

architectural expressions of appropriation occur in relation both to large-scale collective and public areas and to micro-adjustments to the private realm. The aim of these transformations is to find a mid-way compromise between the modernist vision of architects and the more conservative expectations of the citizens of Agadir in relation to their own habitat.

The two-way resilience of design and use manifests itself architecturally in a variety of ways and at a range of scales. The most pervasive are the micro-transformations that can be identified at points of access to, and encounter between, public and private areas: doors, fences, the external surfaces of private properties. With the addition of screens, railings, colours, tiles, etc., the originally radical, perhaps harsh, modernism of the various buildings is adjusted into a neo-vernacular hybrid style. Such micro-transformations can be identified across the new city: in the ostensibly modernist dwellings in the city centre, in the upmarket villas of the Secteur Résidentiel, and the working-class dwellings of Nouveau Talborjt and the Quartier Industriel Sud. At mid-scale, the transformations contaminate entire buildings. This is very much the case for the Grid Écochard, wherein the anticipated built-in capacity to accommodate

changes is challenged by the creativity of pragmatic improvisation. Finally, a macro-level of resilience can also be identified at the scale of the entire city. In time, following their culturally instilled aspirations, people moved from the 1960s modern centre to newer peripheries where they felt enabled to cultivate traditional ways of dwelling and land-ownership patterns. The widespread aspiration to move out of modernist central apartments and into suburban houses with a patio has changed the character of all affected neighbourhoods, and has created new geographies of urbanity across the Agadir municipal territory. Urban liveliness has followed domestic liveability.

1
Faraoui, Abdeslam and Patrice de
Mazières, 'Immeubles D, O1 et O2',
*A + U: Revue Africaine d'Architecture
et d'Urbanisme*, no. 4 (1966), p. 46.
2
Cohen, Jean-Louis and Monique Eleb,
*Casablanca: Colonial Myths and
Architectural Ventures*, New York:
Monacelli Press, 2002, p. 355.
3
For a more elaborated introduction
to Écochard's approach, see Avermaete,
Tom, 'Framing the Afropolis: Michel
Ecochard and the African City for the
Greatest Number', in *OASE. Architectural
Journal*, no. 83 (2010), pp. 77–101.
4
Habitat for the Greatest Number Grid,
Panel series: 'The Problem', Archives
Service de L'Urbanisme, ENAC Rabat.
5
Ibid.

AGADIR'S SHIFTED CENTRALITIES

Janina Gosseye, Hans Teerds

THE EMPTY HEART

Even though it today houses the most important public, commercial and religious buildings of the city and region – from the town hall and central post office to the covered market and main mosque – Agadir's Centre Urbain has lost its central position in the daily lives of its inhabitants. Many of its shops, terraces and restaurants are empty, its buildings are deserted and most of its streets are quiet. In downtown Agadir, there is barely any sign of the vibrant urban life that is so prominent in many other Moroccan cities. Now, in 2021, urban life has moved elsewhere. Agadir's heart is empty.

In a recent publication entitled *Empire and Catastrophe*, American historian Spencer Segalla suggests that this is perhaps not so surprising as many people, both Moroccans and foreigners, believe that Agadir has no soul. According to Segalla, this belief stems from the particular way in which the seismic event of 1960 reshaped the built environment in Agadir: atomising its urban fabric into different disconnected sections.[1] As early as 1970, Belgian architect Jean Dethier suggested that 'this fragmentation [*éclatement*] of the modern city – established in all good faith in the name of hygiene, space and circulation – annihilates in large measure the sentiment of the city, of community and animation'.[2] Phrased differently, Dethier believed that Agadir was too spread out and insufficiently dense to accommodate and engender the vibrant urban life that is characteristic of so many other Moroccan cities.[3]

Yet when the 1959 plan of Agadir, which shows the city's urban fabric before the earthquake, is compared with the reconstruction plan as it was published in the 1966 issue of *A+U: Revue Africaine d'Architecture et d'Urbanisme*, the reconstructed city seems to cover about the same area as pre-earthquake Agadir. What's more, the new areas of the city have ostensibly been given a greater density than those that existed prior to the quake and, inspired by the concept of the neighbourhood unit,[4] each of Agadir's new urban sectors was also provided with its own set of local communal and public facilities. So, why is downtown Agadir today largely abandoned?

When the Service de l'Urbanisme (Department of Urbanism) drew up the reconstruction plan for Agadir in the early 1960s, it proposed that the city would (in time) grow inland, in a north-easterly direction. Accordingly, the various sectors constituting the reconstructed city were aligned with a set of growth corridors, separated from each other by urban highways and green strips.[5] But the growth of the city did not occur as planned. Instead of expanding towards the north-east, Agadir grew towards the south-east, parallel to the coastline, as a result of booming beach tourism and the development of new commercial complexes along Avenue Mohammed V, which connects the city to the airport and, beyond, to the village of Sidi Mimoun. As Segalla rightly notes,

> [t]he growth of the tourist sector engulfed what the planners had envisioned as the commercial center of the city, which became an area of hotels, restaurants, and shops for tourists. Moroccans shopped elsewhere, and increasingly lived elsewhere, too. State control of construction prevented an increase in population density in the planned city, and the new seismic codes made officially sanctioned housing more expensive. Consequently, non-tourist commerce shifted to the southeast, pulled by the growth of residential construction beyond what had been originally conceived as the industrial zone.[6]

This chapter examines the character of the new urbanity that sprang up along this new growth corridor and also casts an eye over the scattered fragments of urbanity that have emerged on the other side of the N1 motorway – in Agadir's dry hinterland, which was once earmarked for the city's planned expansion.

THE TOURISTIC CITY: BOOMING BEACH TOURISM

In the 1966 issue of *A+U: Revue Africaine d'Architecture et d'Urbanisme* devoted entirely to the reconstruction of Agadir, Moroccan architect Mourad Ben Embarek, who was affiliated with the Moroccan Service de l'Urbanisme, urged the government to pay special attention to the development of the city's coastal zone.[7] While he thought that 'user comfort' should be paramount, Embarek also warned that Agadir's redevelopment needed to avoid overly dense construction as this could ruin the city's aesthetic appeal. He stressed that, in the reconstructed city, views of the sky and the sea had to be preserved, and that 'commercial and speculative considerations [could] not and should not affect this concept'.[8] Embarek was convinced that in a tourist city, urban design and state control needed to go hand in hand.[9]

In the 1960s reconstruction plan for Agadir, the coastline was reserved exclusively for two related functions: *loisir* (leisure) and *tourisme* (tourism). In the northern part, where the coastal zone touched the administrative sector of the city (particularly, the Cité Administrative), public bathing facilities, sports clubs, an animation centre and several other leisure attractions intended for the inhabitants of the town were planned. The remainder of the coastal zone – this was the majority of the coastline – was reserved for international tourism, and was divided into two parallel areas on the basis of the site's topography. The low area of wooded dunes, which was more natural and sandier, and which stood in direct contact with the beach, was reserved for low and scattered constructions, while the higher

ridge beyond, separating (and sheltering) this lower area from the city, was destined to accommodate hotels with views over the beach and sea. Many of these hotels included a slew of ancillary facilities such as lush gardens, swimming pools, tennis courts and golf courses. These two parallel areas were separated from each other by Boulevard du 20 Août and, further south, by Boulevard Oued Sud.

The Secteur Touristique et Balnéaire was envisaged as part of the green structure of the city: the 1960 reconstruction plan for Agadir proposed direct, physical connections between the coastal zone and the city's mountainous hinterland by means of green fingers situated on either side of the Centre Urbain. The main connection between the beach and Centre Urbain was via the former valley, which was filled in with rubble from the collapsed buildings. This green corridor ran from Place Prince Héritier Agadir, via a passage underneath the busy Avenue Mohammed V, to Boulevard du 20 Août, where it provided access to the beach and sea by means of a large square. The idea was that the city and coastal zone would be developed in a certain balance, whereby the city could benefit from its location between the mountains and the beach – not only through the revenue generated by tourism but also geographically: with views of the Atlas Mountains and the ocean.

Nevertheless, notwithstanding these good intentions, the purposeful functional zoning of the city and the zoning within the Secteur Touristique et Balnéaire itself – with only a small portion for the local population and a much larger area for international tourism – has meant, as Segalla points out, that 'a disproportionate share of the city's natural assets, like access to the beach [and] views of the mountains, were "monopolized" by the tourist district'.[10] Embarek's concerns were thus soon proven justified: propelled by the demands of international tourism, and with Moroccan and foreign commercial and speculative investment, the coastal zone developed rapidly

and beyond its intended boundaries. Soon, the city itself followed the shifting centre of gravity that this investment-driven coastal urbanisation had brought about.

Today, Agadir's tourist zone stretches from the city's commercial port and marina in the north to the Sofitel hotel and spa in the south. Here, it reaches a natural boundary formed by the Palais Royal, with its Royal Gardens and private beach, and the estuary of the River Souss beyond. The whole territory between the seafront to the west and Avenue Mohammed V to the east is now occupied by large hotels, apartment buildings, holiday homes and other commercial and touristic ventures. Especially at the southern end, little remains of the envisaged distinction between a beach area with small-scale tourist attractions and a more urban hotel area: large hotel complexes are situated directly on the seafront, sometimes locked behind a perimeter wall or fence.

Avenue Mohammed V forms a strong border between this Secteur Touristique et Balnéaire and the urban territory of the city proper. For tourists, there is little incentive to cross this border – especially not on foot. The larger leisure attractions in the hinterland – like the crocodile farm, Adrar Stadium, Karting Agadir and the 'Xtreme Park' – can all only be reached by car, while the 'everyday' tourist destinations – from bars to bakeries, restaurants and shops – can be found within the tourist city that has taken shape between Avenue Mohammed V and the beach. Accordingly, only a few physical connections have been provided to cross this urban highway – most of them, pedestrian crossings. An exception is the aforementioned former valley. This park-like zone, which today houses the 'Agadir Birds Valley', connects the city's seaside to the Centre Urbain by means of a tunnel underneath Avenue Mohammed V, as originally planned. Surrounded by bars, restaurants, clubs, souvenir shops, a large car park and a mini mosque, this junction is a central point on the esplanade. Here, all kinds of activities take

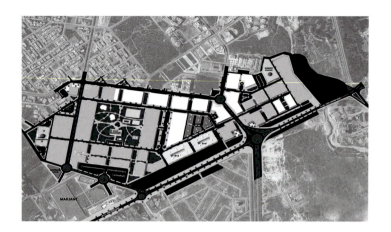

Fig. 1
The project Agadir City
Center, currently under
construction at the
intersection of Avenue
Mohammed V and
Avenue Abderrahman
Bouabid.

Fig. 2

1 Boulevard
2 Mosque
3 Avenue Casablanca
4 Motorway N1
5 towards Danialand
6 towards Centre Urbain
7 Adrar Stadium/
   Xtreme Park/Karting

place: children can drive electric karts; visitors can board a tourist train along the esplanade; and, in the evening, luminous pens or large gas-filled balloons are sold by street vendors who spread out carpets on the red-brick pavement that today covers most of the lower, 'natural' area to the west of Boulevard du 20 Août. This pavement has become a distinguishing feature of Agadir's esplanade, whose concrete edge to the beach more or less follows the coastline in an elegant movement while at the same time functioning as boundary, bench, stairs and slope.

AVENUE MOHAMMED V: A NEW URBAN AXIS

Parallel to Agadir's coastal zone, a new urban axis has emerged along Avenue Mohammed V that connects the city with the airport. Gathering residential estates, shopping centres and other commercially oriented, developer-driven projects along its path, this new urban axis – together with the booming tourist zone – has played a major role in directing the urban growth of Agadir (towards the south-east) and evacuating urban life from its Centre Urbain.

A key commercial development along this new urban axis is the project Agadir City Center, currently under construction at the intersection of Avenue Mohammed V and Avenue Abderrahman Bouabid, just south of the city's Quartier Industriel Sud. Covering eight hectares, this project is destined to include a conference centre, a shopping mall, a business district (with office space for 'first-class' companies and small and medium-sized enterprises),[11] a new five-star hotel with approximately 150 rooms, various tourist residences, a cinema complex (called Megarama), a bowling alley and large car parks. Planned to open in 2024, Agadir City Center is to become the 'largest business centre in Morocco' (with a surface area of more than 10,000 square metres) and is expected to 'enable the city to diversify its tourist clientele'.[12]

Backed by the Al Maghribia Lil Istitmar group, the budget for this new multifunctional complex has been announced at 1,475 million DM, or about € 150 million. Renderings that have been prepared for this commercial venture show a strange blend of nondescript, ubiquitous shopping centre architecture alternating with highly specific (although not really place-specific) 'starchitect'-inspired buildings. These include a conference centre that allegedly combines 'Berber inspiration with hi-tech devices', resulting in a design that is somewhat reminiscent of the famous 'Bird's Nest' stadium in Beijing by the Swiss architects Herzog and de Meuron, who worked in collaboration with Chinese artist Ai Weiwei and others (Fig. 1).

Similar, albeit smaller, commercial developments can be found all along Avenue Mohammed V. Around 500 metres south of Agadir City Center (under construction at time of writing) is Marjane Agadir, a shopping centre organised around a vast car park. To one side of the car park is a large, enclosed, 'big box' shopping mall of the kind that Victor Gruen popularised in the US from the 1950s onwards, while the other sides of the complex are lined by a petrol station, a McDonald's restaurant and several large stores – of the 'decorated shed' variety – for sporting goods, white goods, furniture and DIY supplies. In the vicinity of Marjane Agadir, new residential developments have also sprung up. Across Boulevard Mohammed V, for instance, is a large new suburban estate called Haut Founty, which is laid out in a grand semicircular pattern and which consists of medium-sized apartment buildings, all about five storeys high.

Another 500 metres further south, at the junction of Avenue Mohammed V with Avenue Assa, a carefully landscaped green area reveals a different part of the city. Lined with trees on both sides, Avenue Assa leads away from Avenue Mohammed V in the direction of the coast. Along this road, beyond a gentle curve, one finds a grand gate that gives access to the lush gardens surrounding the Royal Palace as well as to some other villas, at the edge of the Palais Royal estate, and to the Ocean Golf Club, which is situated near the estuary of the River Souss. The carefully placed trees along the avenue, together with the deliberately planned and well-maintained park, not only form an 'introduction' to this more exclusive part of the city or simply define the green character of this territory but also make it visible from the busy Avenue Mohammed V. The lush, green, well-maintained park articulates the other-worldliness of this part of the city of Agadir – an aspect that is thrown into even sharper relief when compared with the urban development that has occurred at this spot along Avenue Mohammed V but on the other side of the road. There, squeezed between the perimeter of the airport and this major traffic artery, an entirely different 'suburban development' to the one seen 500 metres further north can be found, called Ben Sergao. With low (one- to three-storey) houses and an organic street pattern, this neighbourhood, which is littered with small shops, brings to mind the hustle and bustle of Agadir's old kasbah as well as the urban life that once thrived in the rebuilt city's Centre Urbain.

JUNKSPACE BEYOND THE N1

Apart from the growth of the city towards the south-east along Avenue Mohammed V, scattered, nucleated urban development has also occurred (and continues to occur) to the north and north-east of Agadir on the other side of the N1 highway. There, large dormitory estates such as Cité al Mohammadi and Cité Iligh have been laid out in carefully considered geometries amid the dry hinterland. Reminiscent of Agadir's former Ville Nouvelle, which was originally designed by the Service de l'Urbanisme from the 1920s onwards and was almost completely destroyed in the 1960 earthquake, Cité al Mohammadi is composed

of grand urban boulevards – some straight, some curving – that are joined together by a set of monumental roundabouts (Fig. 2). Its plan brings to mind the Beaux-Arts/City Beautiful urban planning of the turn of the twentieth century – an impression that is reinforced by the presence of a central mall consisting of a sequence of gardens, which is the focal point of the western part of the estate. On either side of this grand, green mall are multistorey apartment buildings five to ten storeys high, which display some variation in plan: some take the form of perimeter blocks with shared internal courtyards, while others break open the urban block, much like the blocks à redents (with set-backs) that Le Corbusier proposed for his Ville Contemporaine in 1922.

Notwithstanding their plan variation, the architectural manifestation of these multistorey housing blocks is rather limited. Here, a twenty-first-century iteration of the Normes Agadir has emerged which, contrary to its 1960s predecessor, has much less to do with architectural inventiveness and establishing a common code for the architecture of the city than it does with monetising (and standardising) urban housing.

Contrary to its western part, the eastern section of Cité al Mohammadi has a more fine-grained urban structure. It consists of smaller apartment buildings, which are three to five storeys tall. Along with this reduction in the height and footprint of the buildings, the width of the central mall that traverses this part of the development has also been reduced significantly by comparison with its western counterpart. It is less grand and less green: more motorway than public park. The downscaling of the mall in this eastern section of Cité al Mohammadi is accompanied by a change in its orientation. A massive roundabout at the heart of the settlement facilitates this shift and also creates a large – albeit infrastructural – forecourt to the Mokhtar Essossi Essaada Mosque, which is the communal heart of the entire Cité al Mohammadi.

Like Cité al Mohammadi, Cité Iligh displays a somewhat unusual penchant for the forms and elements of colonial urban planning such as axiality, symmetry and monumentality – even if it is significantly smaller in size. Situated to the west of Cité al Mohammadi and to the north of the city itself, the focal point of this settlement is an elongated semicircular space that houses an open, partially paved central square as well as a few commercial establishments, a polyclinic and a mosque (the Mosquée Aicha Oum Mouminine). From this central area, gently curved streets extend to the east and the west in a mirrored urban layout. Large villas with lush green gardens, swimming pools and tall perimeter walls line these streets – as do numerous empty plots, pegged for future residential development. If Cité al Mohammadi is designed to cater to the middle classes, then Cité Iligh is home to those with greater purchasing power.

Places to spend money are never far away. Apart from these residential cités, Agadir's urban hinterland is also home to several large commercial leisure facilities. To the east of Cité al Mohammadi are the Adrar Stadium, which was inaugurated in 2013; Karting Agadir; and the 'Xtreme Park', a sports and amusement park that on its Facebook page proudly proclaims itself to be '100 % ITALIAN in its construction and management'.[13] However, the most sensational of these new, private-investment-driven recreational developments is yet to be constructed: Agadirland, also known as Danialand. Located in the foothills of the Atlas Mountains to the north of the city and west of Cité Iligh, Agadirland, as planned, consists of two related entities: Agaland, an amusement park; and Souss Camp, a holiday park with small chalets.[14] When first announced in 2016, the whole complex was expected to cover an area of about twenty hectares, cost over 330 million DM (approximately € 30 million) and create more than 1,000 jobs. Agaland would feature a water park with a dolphinarium; a so-called 'Ladies Club'; a playground with a merry-go-round, Ferris wheel and roller coaster; a panoramic esplanade; mini-karting; sports fields; 'Miniature Morocco'; restaurants and cafés; and a solar-power-driven cable-car system more than 1.5 kilometres long, along with several other recreational attractions.[15] Souss Camp is to offer accommodation for Agaland's revellers: 1,900 beds and 624 caravan pitches. Backed by Abdelaziz Houays, a developer, Agadirland was touted as the tourist attraction of the century for the whole region of southern Morocco. However, soon after the project was announced, concerns were voiced about the seismological safety of the complex's location – allegedly in a *non-aedificandi* ('not constructible') zone that the Schéma Directeur de l'Aménagement Urbain (the Urban Development Masterplan), prepared by the Agence Urbaine d'Agadir (Agadir Urban Agency), had reserved for forestry. After several years of delay, and a slight relokation of the project, construction has resumed at time of writing. Ground levelling for Souss Camp has commenced, and the cable car – which links the Tildi Bridge to the kasbah (Agadir Oufella) in a first phase, and from there to the Souss Camp in a second stage – gained approval in October 2020.[16] The realisation of Agadirland thus seems to be firmly on the horizon.

Apart from residential compounds and large leisure landscapes, other, heterotopian urban elements have also found a place in Agadir's hinterland – including cemeteries, an impound site and a 'waste management service'. A smorgasbord of functions and forms, it is difficult to call what has occurred beyond the N1 'urban development' – 'urban entropy' seems a more accurate term. Either absolutely chaotic or frighteningly aseptic; overdetermined and indeterminate at the same time, Agadir's hinterland has become an eclectic space that bears all the hallmarks of what architect and architectural theorist Rem Koolhaas has called 'Junkspace'.[17]

EPILOGUE:
INVESTMENT-DRIVEN URBANISM
AND AN EMPTY HEART

While Jean Dethier's 1970 premonition
has proven correct, one could ask if what has
occurred in Agadir was indeed its fate from
the very beginning. After all, the city did not
grow as planned. Instead of expanding
towards the north-east, into the mountainous
hinterland, urban development followed
the path of least resistance: towards the south-
east, along the coast and around Avenue
Mohammed V. Since the city's reconstruction,
government seems to have largely withdrawn
from the process of urban development.
Instead, tourism and commercial investment
have driven Agadir's growth. This has had
a major impact on the city's urban, and also its
social, fabric: the racial segregation that in
Agadir (as in many other African cities) was
strongly expressed in the city's urban layout in
colonial times has today been replaced by
economic segregation. Along the coastline,
massive investments have been made in
plush hotels and resorts, while on either side
of Avenue Mohammed V shopping centres
and 'cookie-cutter' housing estates have
cropped up – the former designed to cater to
(mostly international) tourists, the latter to
serve local inhabitants. Meanwhile, the city's
hinterland, beyond the N1, has become a
free-for-all. In this area, which was initially earmarked for urban expansion, only a few
residential estates (with a strange penchant
for Beaux Arts, colonial urban design) can
be found – along with large leisure functions,
such as stadia and amusements parks, and
other non-conformist elements. The resulting
amorphous urban form makes it difficult to
locate the heart of the city. Agadir's Centre
Urbain is empty. But the city is not without
a soul, or beyond salvation. The strong Normes
Agadir 1960 that once guided the city's reconstruction could, once again, be activated
to guide its redevelopment.

1
Segalla, Spencer D., *Empire and Catastrophe: Decolonization and Environmental Disaster in North Africa and Mediterranean France Since 1954*, Lincoln, NE: University of Nebraska Press, 2020, p.142.

2
Dethier, Jean, 'Soixante Ans d'Urbanisme au Maroc', *Bulletin Economique et Social du Maroc*, nos.118–19 (1970).

3
Dethier's critique is symptomatic of that which is commonly levelled against modernist urban planning. For a reflection on such criticism in relation to public space in Agadir, see Hans Teerds' chapter 'On Squares, Stairs, Paths, Plinths, Trees and Shade in Agadir's Reconstructed Centre' in this volume.

4
For more information about the application of the neighbourhood-unit concept in Agadir, see Janina Gosseye's chapter 'Reorganising Agadir, Reconstructing the Neighbourhood' in this volume.

5
For an account on the urban structure that was proposed for Agadir post-1960, see ibid.

6
Segalla, *Empire and Catastrophe*, p.159.

7
Embarek, Mourad Ben, 'Tourisme et Urbanisme', *A+U: Revue Africaine d'Architecture et d'Urbanisme*, 4 (1966), pp.64–5.

8
Embarek, cited in Segalla, *Empire and Catastrophe*, p.155.

9
Segalla, *Empire and Catastrophe*, p.155.

10
Ibid., p.147.

11
'Palais des Congrès d'Agadir: ambitieux projet avec la capacité d'accueillir 5,000 personnes', www.lejardinauxetoiles.net/post/palais-des-congr%C3%A8s-d-agadir-ambitieux-projet-avec-capacit%C3%A9-d-accueillir-5-000-personnes (accessed 29 July 2021).

12
'Agadir City Center (liste des magasins)', mall-center.shopping/2021/06/01/agadir-city-center-liste-des-magasins (accessed 29 July 2021).

13
'Xtreme Park', Facebook, www.facebook.com/xtremeparkviviani/about/?ref=page_internal (accessed 29 July 2021).

14
'Agadir Land', YouTube, www.youtube.com/watch?v=8b6LIY9tdp8; www.youtube.com/watch?v=qTKK7J_ufOU (accessed 29 July 2021).

15
Y. J., 'Agadir: le projet controversé de téléphérique refait surface', Medias 24: La Référence de l'Information Économique, 12 October 2020, modified 11 April 2021, www.medias24.com/2020/10/12/agadir-le-projet-controverse-de-telepherique-refait-surface (accessed 29 July 2021).

16
Ibid.; Vautravers, Jean-Luc, 'Le Parc d'Attraction Agadirland se Transforme en Souss Camp et Dania Land et Génère des Craintes', Le Jardin aux Etoiles, modified on 5 April 2020, www.lejardinauxetoiles.net/post/le-parc-d-attraction-agadirland-se-transforme-en-souss-camp-et-dania-land (accessed 29 July 2021). Work on Agadirland has resumed, as shown in this video, which was shot in November 2019: 'Avancement du projet "Souss Camp Agadir"', YouTube, www.youtube.com/watch?v=SRovIAGqvZE (accessed 29 July 2021).

17
Koolhaas, Rem, 'Junkspace', *October 100* (Spring 2002), pp.175–90.

CODA

Cathelijne Nuijsink, Maxime Zaugg

The book *Agadir: Building the Modern Afropolis* follows the idea of an *inventaire raisonné*, a reasoned inventory of involved actors, events and buildings of the reconstruction of Agadir after the great earthquake in 1960. This study aims to explore, from different perspectives, the urban experiment of rebuilding the city. Hence, *Agadir: Building the Modern Afropolis* does not claim to document the reconstruction of the city of Agadir conclusively and completely. Instead, this book offers a set of hitherto untold testimonies by witnesses and survivors of the earthquake, reveals previously unexamined archival and photographic documentation, and discloses unwritten histories composed by researchers from within and beyond the city.

The research for *Agadir: Building the Modern Afropolis* started with a profound interest in the exchange of architectural ideas between local and foreign architects and urban planners, postcolonial cooperation and a contemporary engagement with local actors and citizens in Morocco that dates back to the late 1990s. Those early investigations of postcolonial urban developments in Morocco have resulted in the books *Colonial Modern: Aesthetics of the Past, Rebellions of the Future* (Avermaete, Karakayali and Von Osten, 2010) and *Casablanca Chandigarh: A Report on Modernization* (Avermaete and Casciato, 2014). These books, and the accompanying exhibitions, constituted an attempt to tell different stories of urban design that had emerged in decolonising and postcolonial conditions. Their pages speak about the charged political, cultural and economic regimes in which urban design comes into being. They address actors and realities that had been excluded from the canonical histories, and position the architecture and urbanism of the non-Western world as realities in their own right. Having extensively explored and documented the city of Casablanca, it became all the more evident that the Moroccan city of Agadir was an equally interesting yet much overlooked 'Afropolis' from which much could be learnt.

As a point of departure, the Chair of the History and Theory of Urban Design at ETH Zurich organised, in the spring of 2019, a week-long study trip to Agadir, taking twenty-two students from ETH's Department of Architecture as well as London-based photographer David Grandorge. During this seminar week, it soon became clear that the reconstruction of Agadir had all the potential to become a much larger research project in collaboration with a variety of actors and researchers working on urban planning in Morocco generally, and those working on the reconstruction of the city of Agadir in particular. As a result, an interdisciplinary research team was formed consisting of researchers and students from ETH Zurich, researchers from Casablanca and Agadir, international and local photographers, and interested people whom we met in Agadir – such as architects and historians.

This combination of different actors made it possible to look at the reconstruction of the city of Agadir from multiple angles. The historian Lahsen Roussafi, himself a survivor of the Agadir earthquake and passionate about the history of the city, vividly shared his memories and vast knowledge of the various neighbourhoods and buildings during the seminar week and subsequent trips to Agadir. His captivating stories about the history of Agadir before and directly after the earthquake, as well as his expertise on the different steps taken during the reconstruction of the city, crystallised our initial ideas for a book project. Casablanca-based French architect Laure Augereau was our indispensable guide during the seminar week. Thanks to her negotiation skills with local authorities, we were able to visit many of the buildings discussed in this book. Moroccan architects and scholars Lahbib El Moumni and Imad Dahmani shared, in a lecture at the campus of the École National d'Architecture de Casablanca, their views on the development of Brutalist architecture in Morocco. The local architects Yasser Hachim, Oudad Abdeslam and Bougarba Azzouz provided critical feedback during the final presentations in Agadir, in which the students shared the observations and ethnographic drawings that they had made of a selection of buildings from the reconstruction. As Chair of the History and Theory of Urban Design, we contributed our interest in how the city of Agadir was rebuilt from a historical perspective. This resulted in an approach that posed queries such as 'Is there an archive, and where is it?'. By asking such straightforward questions, in the case of the city of Agadir, we made a rare and valuable discovery of almost all the plans of the reconstruction. Unlocking this historical material and cooperating with researchers on the ground sparked a chain of research questions, probing into the attitudes of the inhabitants of Agadir towards the modern architecture that was imposed on them and the meaning of this built heritage on subsequent generations of architects and urban planners. The Chair of the History and Theory of Urban Design's interest in finding original archival materials, and in activating historical documents concerning the reconstruction of Agadir, in turn exposed researchers working in Morocco, already familiar with the history of the city, to new sources.

The research for this book was thus based as heavily on the contributions and expertise of all the actors involved as on the sources and archival documents found and accessed in the months following the seminar week. Throughout the research process, the extensive website developed by Lahsen Roussafi and his colleagues Marie-France Dartois and Régine Caïs-Terrier was of inestimable value.[1] This website documents, in detail, the reconstruction process of the city, cataloguing a large number of reconstruction projects and the town's historical development before the earthquake of 1960. Lahsen Roussafi's books, such as *Memoires d'Agadir* (2013) and *Agadir 1960: Mémoires d'un Séisme* (2002), were essential literature sources for understanding the culture of Agadir before the earthquake, as well as the way in which eyewitnesses experienced the city immediately after the earthquake. Additional important written sources on the reconstruction projects included the magazines *Revue Africaine d'Architecture et d'Urbanisme (A+U)* and *L'Architecture d'Aujourd'hui*. Furthermore, the extensive image collection of Agadir-based architect Omar Ech-Chafadi, Vice President of the Municipality of Agadir, and photographer Hassan Bouziane reveal a never-before-published visual documentation of the city's reconstruction. A collaborative trip to Agadir with all Chair members during the summer of 2019 allowed us access to local archives and the discovery of a catalogue documenting their content. During a follow-up trip to Agadir, we discovered 'hidden archives' – unknown even to our local experts – full of floor plans, sections and facade drawings of most of the buildings built during the reconstruction. Additional sources were retrieved from the International Federation of Red Cross and Red Crescent Societies (IFRC) archives in Geneva, the Swiss Red Cross archives in Wabern and newspaper articles documenting the immediate and longer-term help with the reconstruction. In short, this book project is the product of a collaboration of people interested in the reconstruction of Agadir and brings together many different sources and fields of expertise.

Agadir: Building the Modern Afropolis aspires to present an outlook on the urban experiment of Agadir's reconstruction based on the collaboration of researchers and on the vast body of historical sources without claiming to be complete and final. The city has been rebuilt since 1960 at an incredible speed, with a limited budget but with an astonishing level of care for details and diversity in programmes. This swift reconstruction and the strong transformation in the following decades raised questions about the necessity of processing this rapid history and the vulnerability of archives. Without Lahsen Roussafi's tireless

efforts over decades to preserve historical documents relating to the reconstruction of Agadir in all possible forms, and without the somewhat accidental discovery of the planning documentation in the municipal archives of the Hôtel de Ville (Town Hall) in Agadir, it would not have been possible to produce this publication. In addition to the historical research of plan and photographic documentation, this project has revealed the necessity of an oral history of the city. The three in-depth interviews with Lahsen Roussafi have activated a part of the history of Agadir that probably could not have been told otherwise. The detailed description of the earthquake and the following events that led to the reconstruction gives this story an otherwise unattainable profundity.

While our collaborative research project has revealed a rich compilation of information and documentation about the reconstruction of Agadir, open questions and unexamined topics remain – requiring further research. This book has not yet explored, for example, the influence of large-scale developments such as industry and mass tourism on the city of Agadir. Since the early 1950s, an inexplicable asynchronicity seems to exist between the form and life of the Centre Urbain and that of the tourist areas with their hotels devoted to mass tourism. In addition, particular groups of actors remain under-represented in this book. Though we have made attempts, we were only able to identify a single female architect who contributed to the reconstruction of Agadir. The names of other female actors remain unknown today: those who – as commissioners, administrators or designers – played critical roles in the reconstruction of the city. There is also little information or knowledge available on the actual construction workers of Agadir. Where did such an enormous building capacity suddenly come from, and where did they learn their skills? Some parts of the built environment of the reconstructed Agadir remain difficult to comprehend. For example, there is little (visual) documentation of the interior spaces of the new housing estates that were built. Hence, it is difficult to generate knowledge on the ways in which residents appropriated the radical new buildings that were designed for them.

Neither the archives of architects, politicians and the urban planning department nor the visual collections of Lahsen Roussafi, Marie-France Dartois and Régine Caïs-Terrier; Omar Ech-Chafadi; and Hassan Bouziane could offer us satisfactory answers to such questions. To give an indication of the 'volatile' character of our archives, by chance we found a digitalised map of the Hôtel de Ville on a USB stick but we are still searching for floor plans of buildings as crucial as Immeuble A (Building A). This coincidental discovery emphasises, once again, the vital role of documentation and the careful preservation of historical documents for the history of a city. Safeguarding these archives and making them easily accessible to national and international researchers will open up new perspectives and conclusions. Therefore, this *inventaire raisonné* has the modest aim of giving future researchers and interested readers an introduction to the reconstruction of the city of Agadir and making them aware that many documents remain unexplored in the local archives. The vast knowledge that survivors of the earthquake and active contributors to the reconstruction of the city still carry with them urgently requires an additional oral-history project.

1
http://mfd.agadir.free.fr

REGARDING AGADIR

David Grandorge
Introduction by Irina Davidovici

The following sequence of cityscapes was commissioned from London-based photographer David Grandorge. A close observer of built and natural environments, as well as a charismatic teacher of architecture, Grandorge played an essential role during the student trip that initiated the current research. His photography workshop inspired students to frame and to shoot with the care instilled, in older generations, by the preciousness of analogue film. He taught them to press the shutter only when they could both visualise and, at the same time, conceptualise the reason for doing so. The lessons resulted in students volunteering to assist the photographer and lug the heavy equipment on day-long walks through the city. On the final day, one last trip resulted in an overzealous policeman taking Grandorge and the on-duty student to the local police station, provoked by their suspicious interest in the city's water-storage infrastructure. While the two figures in the back of the patrol car cut a rather unforgettable image, they made it to the airport just in time for the flight home.

David Grandorge's visual essay presents a languishing, deserted Agadir, its progressive modernism overcome by fine dust, sun and administrative indifference. Some of the initial optimism still shines through, as does the subdued vitality of the locals. Traditional motifs and modernist figures intertwine, and their juxtaposition – within one frame or, in dialogue, across double spreads – is the source of multiple tensions.

The graphic formatting of the pictures reflects the morphology of the architectures depicted. Double-spread layouts are reserved for two landmark horizontal structures: Immeuble A and Cinema Salam. Only partially framed in the photographs, both act as idealised backdrops – contrasting with the signs of appropriation related to their current use. Thus, French architects Louis Riou and Henri Tastemain's 1963 residential and commercial block is read as a layering of horizontal bands of light and shadow, rendered even more abstract by the absence of people. On closer scrutiny, this canvas is brought into scale by the gentle disorder of shop signs, restaurant umbrellas, air-conditioning units and improvised glazed screens – as so many small, rebellious scars of inhabitation and defacement. The ramp, itself marked by timid graffiti, cuts across the composition as the negation of architectural intent. From the other side of the earthquake caesura, the side elevation of Cinema Salam by Moroccan-born French architect Georges Appéré (1946) appears like the ribbed torso of a gigantic sleeping animal, its skin caked with fine cracks. It is the backdrop for signs of actual life: people wait at a bus stop – some placed with unerring accuracy in the meagre shadow of the palm trees that dot the pavement, others using the reclining wall of the building as improvised seating.

Apart from the two aforementioned double-page spreads, David Grandorge has arranged his images in thematic pairs facing across pages, which invite various interpretations. Across the divide of the book's spine, these pairings initiate open-ended games of 'spot the difference', 'find the connection': readings of commerce versus religion, traditional versus modern, renovation versus decay, open versus closed, colour versus black and white. In one such paired spread, two images of multistorey modernist blocks – tower versus slabs – are united by common, monochrome obsolescence. To the Western reader, the regime of openings on the facades is a marker of cultural difference. The strips of narrow windows and screened openings signal a different regime of domestic privacy in the public sphere of the Centre Urbain. The gaze of the photographer projects unseen values and regrets onto Agadir's buildings and people. Quiet, empty streets and markets; shuttered shops; and gates left open indicate a city whose life is now elsewhere.

379

BIOGRAPHIES

TOM AVERMAETE is professor for the History and Theory of Urban Design at ETH Zurich. His research focuses on the architecture of the city and the changing roles, approaches and tools of architects and urban designers from a cross-cultural perspective. Recent book publications include *Casablanca – Chandigarh* (with Casciato, 2015), *Shopping Towns Europe* (with Gosseye, 2017), *The New Urban Condition* (with Medrano and Recaman, 2021) and *Urban Design in the 20th Century: A History* (with Gosseye, 2021).

LAURE AUGEREAU is a French architect. She started as the Director of Ardepa, an association for the promotion of architecture that offered educational programmes for schoolchildren, created contemporary architecture tours for the general public and organised study trips for professionals. From 2009 to 2014, she worked as a project coordinator for Casamémoire, an association for the preservation of 20th-century architectural heritage in Morocco. She has been teaching at universities since 2011. In 2015, she founded Made in A. to promote architecture through training, films, educational workshops and publications. She contributed to the *Global Encyclopedia of Women in Architecture* (2022).

IMAD DAHMANI graduated from the School of Architecture in Casablanca in 2015; his first professional experience was in Paris at Architecture Studio in 2016. Upon his return to Morocco, he joined MAG Architecture in Casablanca and opened his office ADA in 2021. He is the cofounder of the association MAMMA and currently teaches at the School of Architecture in Casablanca.

IRINA DAVIDOVICI has been the Director of the gta Archives since 1 January 2022. She is a trained architect and historian, having obtained her doctorate in history and philosophy of architecture at the University of Cambridge in 2008 and her habilitation at ETH Zurich in 2020. Her research straddles housing studies, the history of housing cooperatives, and Swiss architecture. She is the author of *Forms of Practice: German-Swiss Architecture 1980–2000* (2012, second expanded edition 2018) and editor of *Colquhounery: Alan Colquhoun from Bricolage to Myth* (2015). Two more books will be published in 2022: *Common Grounds: A Comparative History of Early Housing Estates in Europe* (Triest Publishers, Zurich) and *The Autonomy of Theory: Ticinese architecture as Tendenzen, 1965–1985* (gta Publishers, Zurich).

LAHBIB EL MOUMNI is an architect and professor at the School of Architecture in Casablanca, Morocco. After a year at OMA-Rotterdam, he launched his own practice in 2016. He cofounded in 2016 the association MAMMA (Mémoire des Architectes Modernes Marocains) to help highlight the postcolonial heritage of Morocco during the period between 1940 and 1980 He is currently a Ph.D. candidate at the Chair of the History and Theory of Urban Design, gta, ETH Zurich under the supervision of Prof. Dr. Tom Avermaete.

JANINA GOSSEYE is Associate Professor of Architecture in the TUDelft Department of Architecture. Her research focuses on 20th-century architectural and urban design history. Her recent books include *Urban Design in the 20th Century: A History* (2021, with Avermaete), and *Speaking of Buildings: Oral History in Architectural Research* (2019, with Stead and van der Plaat). Gosseye is currently series editor of the 'Bloomsbury Studies in Modern Architecture' book series (with Avermaete), International Editor of *The Journal of Architecture,* Honorary Senior Fellow of the University of Queensland (Australia) and Honorary Member of the Australian Institute of Architects (AIA).

DAVID GRANDORGE is a photographer and academic living and working in London. As a photographer he undertakes commissioned work, collaborating with architects, artists and art institutions. He also makes work independently. His work has been shown in numerous exhibitions including the Venice (2008) and Prague (2005) biennales and has been published internationally in magazines, journals and books. He has written several published articles on architecture and photography. Grandorge is also a senior lecturer in structure, construction and materials at The Cass School of Architecture. He has been a visiting lecturer, tutor and/or critic at the University of Bath, Robert Gordon University, Aberdeen, ETH Zurich, Cambridge University and Kingston University.

CATHELIJNE NUIJSINK is a senior lecturer at the Chair of the History and Theory of Urban Design at ETH Zurich. Her research engages with the development of new historiographic methods that enable histories of architecture in the latter half of the 20th century to be written in a way that is more inclusive and polyvocal. Nuijsink obtained a Ph.D. in East Asian Languages and Civilizations from the University of Pennsylvania in 2017 and was a Horizon 2020-funded Marie Sklodowska-Curie postdoctoral research fellow at ETH Zurich during 2018–2021, contributing, besides peer-reviewed papers and book chapters, the exhibition *Call for Lost Entries: The Shinkenchiku Residential Design Competition 1965–2020*, and the online archive www.callforlostentries.com.

LAHSEN ROUSSAFI was born in Agadir in 1942. After obtaining his Certificate of Primary Studies (CEP), he enrolled at the Youssef ben Tachafine high school in Agadir for his secondary studies. However, following the 1960 earthquake, he was forced to move to Rabat, where he completed his secondary education at the Lycée des Orangers. Roussafi began his professional career at the Office Chérifien du Phosphate, first in Khouribga and then in Youssoufia, where he worked until his retirement. Currently Roussafi documents the history of his native city, Agadir, and has set up the website www.agadir1960.com.

HANS TEERDS is architect and urban designer. He is senior lecturer at Chair of the History and Theory of Urban Design at ETH Zurich. He received his Ph.D. from Delft University of Technology on a study of public aspects of architecture, including public space. His research focuses on the intersection between political and urban theory and the built environment. Teerds is a member of the editorial board of the journal *OASE*, and published, amongst others, *Architectural Positions* (2009, with Avermaete and Havik), *Levend landschap, Manifest voor stad en land* (2012, with Van der Zwart) and *At Home in the World* (2017).

MAXIME ZAUGG obtained his master's degree in architecture at ETH Zurich and is currently Ph.D. candidate at the Chair of the History and Theory of Urban Design, gta, ETH Zurich under the supervision of Prof. Dr. Tom Avermaete. His Ph.D. project entitled 'Exploring Urban Scale Models' examines how strong performative and participative capacities have enabled urban scale models to play a key role in urban planning, focusing particularly on the period from the late 1960s to the early 1990s. Zaugg founded the practice STUDIO (2017) and has published his research in journals such as the gta Papers and attended various international conferences.

FURTHER READING

American Iron and Steel Institute. *The Agadir, Morocco Earthquake*. (New York: A.I.S.A, 1962).

Baziz, Orna. *Tremblement de terre d'Agadir : Récits d'une rescapée 1960–2020*. (Paris: La Croisée des Chemins, 2021).

Bensimon, Jacques. *Agadir, un paradis dérobé*. (Paris: Harmattan, 2013).

Beyler, André. "Agadir." *Radar*. no. 11. (1960): 3–17.

Cappe, Willy. *Agadir, 2. février 1960, histoire et leçons d'une catastrophe* (Marseille: 1967).

Chaouini, Aziza. 'Depoliticizing Group GAMMA: Contesting Modernism in Morocco', in Lu, Duanfang (ed), *Third World Modernism: Architecture, Development and Identity*. (London: Routledge, 2011): 57–84.

Culot, Maurice, and Jean-Marie Thiveaud (eds.). *Architectures Françaises Outre-Mer*. (Liège: Mardaga, 1992).

Dartois, Marie-France. *Agadir et le Sud Marocain: A la recherche du temps passé: Des origines au tremblement de terre du 29 Février 1960*. (Paris: Courcelles Publishing, 2008).

Fouad, Val de. *Agadir* (Saint-Cyr-sur-Loire: A. Sutton, 2009).

Hicks, David T. "Rebuilt Agadir." *Architectural Review*. vol. 142. (1967): 292–300.

Khair-Eddine, Mohammed. *Agadir*. (New Orleans: Dialogos Books, 2020).

Le Toullec, Roger. *Agadir 1960: Mémoires d'un séisme*. (Nantes: Marines Editions, 2002).

Mrini, Driss. *Le Triangle du Souss & Agadir*. (Rabat: Editions Intaj.com, 2010).

Oswald, Suzanne. "Fahrt nach Agadir." *Das Schweizerische Rote Kreuz*. vol. 69, no. 4. (1960): 4–8.

Rabinow, Paul. *French Modern: Norms and Forms of the Social Environment*. (Cambridge, Mass.: MIT Press, 1989).

Revue africaine d'architecture et d'urbanisme: A + U. vol. 1–6. (Rabat: 1964–69).

Roussafi, Lahsen et al. *Mémoires d'Agadir au XXe siècle*. (Agadir: 2010–15).

Royer, Jean, Hubert Lyautey, E. du Vivier de Streel and Henri Prost. *L'urbanisme aux colonies et dans le pays tropicaux*. (Paris: Editions d'Urbanisme, 1932).

Schwyter, Annemarie. "Agadir Ist Tot." *Das Schweizerische Rote Kreuz*. vol. 69, no. 3. (1960): 5–9.

[S.N.]. "Bau Eines Schweizer Quartiers in Agadir." *Das Schweizerische Rote Kreuz*. vol. 70, no. 5. (1961): 37–38.

---. "Die Rotkreuzhilfe Für Agadir." *Das Schweizerische Rote Kreuz*. vol. 69, no. 3. (1960): 9–11.

---. "La Catastrophe d'Agadir." *La Croix-Rouge Suisse*. vol. 69, No. 3. (1960): 14–15.

---. "Souvenez-Vous d'Agadir..." *La Croix-Rouge Suisse*. vol. 73, no. 2. (1964): 3.

Segalla, Spencer D. *Empire and Catastrophe: Decolonization and Environmental Disaster in North Africa and Mediterranean France Since 1954*. (Nebraska: University of Nebraska Press, 2021).

Vago, Pierre, Ludovico Barbiano and J.H. Calsat. "Union internationale des architectes: le Colloque d'Agadir." *Habitation : revue trimestrielle de la section romande de l'Association Suisse pour l'Habitat*. vol. 41, no. 11. (1968): 22–39.

Wahbi, Hassan. *Agadir, la ville impassible* (Agadir: Azigzao, 2014).

ACKNOWLEDGEMENTS

This book is the result of intense and, above all, inspiring collaborations between colleagues and friends. We would like to thank our authors Laure Augereau, Imad Dahmani, Irina Davidovici, Lahbib El Moumni, Janina Gosseye, Cathelijne Nuijsink and Hans Teerds for embarking with us on the challenging venture of writing this book and for the stimulating viewpoints that they share in their chapters.

The book could not have been written without the valuable contacts with local partners. We are grateful for the work of Lahsen Roussafi, a passionate Moroccan historian, earthquake witness and project partner, who generously offered his memory of the events that made Agadir during a set of interviews and beyond. Hassan Bouziane, a Moroccan photographer, kindly gave us access to a unique collection of original photographs of the earthquake and reconstruction of the city of Agadir. Lahbib El Moumni, a professor at the Casablanca School of Architecture and cofounder of the MAMMA Group, took the key role of project partner and a friend-on-site, establishing many crucial local human contacts in this time of digital exchange.

We are grateful to the numerous individuals, archives, institutions and architectural offices who have kindly given permission to let us reproduce images in this book. Lahsen Roussafi, Marie-France Dartois and Régine Caïs-Terrier have, with their website, provided an online resource and never-ending source of inspiration on old and new Agadir. The architect Omar Ech-Chafadi, who is vice president to the mayor of Agadir and head of the department of urban planning, generously provided us access to his outstanding private collection of photographs, which we proudly use in this publication. Jama Zahir, archivist of the municipality of Agadir, helped us to get access to the drawings and plans at the municipal archives. We wish to thank other archival collections, including the private collection of the MAMMA Group, and also those of the Aga Khan Trust for Culture, the IFA, the Red Cross, the FRAC and the INA, for offering us access to the most precious and valuable historical material.

This book is not only a collection of written histories, but also a series of precisely constructed visual narratives that are articulated in images and drawings. We would like to thank the following people for their invaluable contributions: David Grandorge, the English artist and photographer, joined our seminar trip to the city of Agadir in spring 2019 and provided us with incisive photographs that not only speak about the qualities of contemporary Agadir but also recalibrate our understanding of the archival material; El Mahdi Meslil, the Moroccan photographer who, together with our colleague Lahbib El Moumni, and despite all the difficulties and barriers of the present time, managed to gain access to a number of private spaces, giving the book a previously unseen and invaluably intimate note; Irina Davidovici, our colleague and project partner, who with a wonderfully modest gaze contributed to the third part of the book with a series of photographs; Luca Can, student assistant, who contributed to the Mapping Agadir chapter with a series of telling and carefully drawn maps; Selin Risi, Frederik Kaufmann, Rico Muth and Chiara De Libero, student assistants, who with great readiness managed to redraw and create revealing drawings that make the complex processes of urban development visible; Michael Blaser, Friederike Merkel and Stefanie Peter, former student assistants, who from the findings of the seminar week created a unique set of axonometries.

The character of this book is largely the achievement of graphic designer Bruno Margreth. We are very grateful for his open and explorative attitude, which we got to know during numerous shared Thursday afternoons over the countless reiterations of our book. We always looked forward to the intriguing discussions with Bruno, which we will not soon forget. We would also like to thank the lithographer Marjeta Morinc for her commitment, especially with regard to her meticulous work on the historical plans and photographs.

We are thankful to Thomas Kramer, director of Park Books, who from the very beginning shared the belief in the relevance of publishing a study on the reconstruction of the city of Agadir. Lisa Schons and Chris Reding, lectors at Park Books, played an important role in the later phases of the book, which they coordinated. Ian McDonald, who copy edited our texts, Diana Wylie, translator of our French texts, and Colette Forder, who acted as a proofreader, were of key importance in the final stages. Agnes Davidovici made an important contribution in providing us with the first French transcription of the interviews.

We are very grateful for the continuing support that our colleagues, student assistants Frederik Kaufmann, Selin Risi and Justinas Zuklys, have provided. They held the reins together at all stages of the book and assisted the whole team individually during its production. Due to their perseverance, patience and excellent overview, the book process developed smoothly. Our gratitude also goes to the other student assistants who have provided valuable support throughout the process: Michael Blaser, Luca Can, Friederike Merkel, Rico Muth, Chiara De Libero, Selin Risi, Maria Lamott and Stefanie Peter.

Colleagues that are not represented in the book have also made important contributions. Our gratitude goes to Hamish Lonergan for the careful and attentive first proofreading and to Luca Thanei for contributing in detailed ways to our conceptual framework. During the process of making this book, colleagues from other institutes and cultures also helped to propel our work. We wish to explicitly thank Patrick Bondallaz of Croix-Rouge Suisse, who as a very dedicated historian took great effort in supporting us with all kinds of archival material. In Morocco, Yasser Hachim, Oudad Abdeslam and Bougarba Azzouz were instrumental in providing us in the early stages of the research with valuable perspectives of local practitioners.

This book was developed within the context of our research and teaching at ETH Zurich. We want to thank the Department of Architecture (D-ARCH) for providing us with this opportunity, but especially our students who have, together with us, explored the saga of the city of Agadir – particularly the participants in the seminar week (Spring Semester 2019) who helped us to understand the past and present of the urban condition in new ways. We wish to wholeheartedly thank Margherita Chiozzi, Siyi Dai, Juliet Ishak, Raphael Freudiger, Leo Galler, Max Grünig, Xingyu He, Anna Hess, Mario Kündig, Antonina Nikolic, Florian Reisner, Nathalie Reiz, Senia Mischler, Timothy Schärer, Marco Steinacher, Lorenz Strologo, Nico Stutz, Hannes Teräsvuori, Daniel Weber, Robin Weber, Julia Werlen and Yves Wäger.

Tom Avermaete, Maxime Zaugg

IMPRINT

Edited by: Tom Avermaete and Maxime Zaugg
Copy editing: Ian McDonald
Proofreading: Colette Forder
Design: Bruno Margreth
Lithography: Marjeta Morinc
Printing and binding: DZA Druckerei zu Altenburg,
Thuringia

© 2022 Tom Avermaete, Maxime Zaugg,
and Park Books AG, Zurich

© for the texts: the authors
© for the images: see image credits, pp. 393–394

Park Books
Niederdorfstrasse 54
8001 Zurich
Switzerland
www.park-books.com

Park Books is being supported by the Federal
Office of Culture with a general subsidy for the
years 2021–2024.

ISBN 978-3-03860-276-7